MOHAMMED & CHARLEMAGNE
REVISITED

D1566129

MOHAMMED & CHARLEMAGNE REVISITED:

THE HISTORY OF A CONTROVERSY

BY EMMET SCOTT

Published by New English Review Press
a subsidiary of World Encounter Institute
PO Box 158397
Nashville, Tennessee 37215

Cover Design by Kendra Adams

Sassanid King Khosrau II submits to Byzantine Emperor Heraclius
from a plaque on a 12th century French cross

ISBN 978-0-578-09418-2

Second Printing

NEW ENGLISH REVIEW PRESS
newenglishreview.org

CONTENTS

INTRODUCTION

The book that follows is not a history in the normal sense, but, as the subtitle explains, the history of a controversy. The controversy in question is the one which has raged for many years around the question: What ended Roman civilization and brought about the Dark Ages?

Theories about the fall of the Roman Empire as a political institution have of course been thick on the ground for centuries; but the present study is not so much concerned with this event as with the fall of the civilization associated with the Roman Empire. That civilization – more properly called "classical civilization" – survived the fall of the Empire and was not, in any case, a creation of the Romans at all, but of the Greeks, which the Romans imbibed wholesale, and which they proceeded, with their conquests, to spread throughout the western Mediterranean and northern Europe. This Graeco-Roman civilization may be described as largely urban, literate, and learned, and characterized by what could be called a rationalist spirit. It was a society which, in theory at least, respected reason and the pursuit of knowledge, and which was not given to religious extremism or fanaticism. We know that this civilization did not come to an end with the fall of the Western Roman Empire. It survived in Constantinople and the Eastern Empire, and it survived too even in the West, a region administered, from 476 onwards, by "barbarian" kings and princes. The rulers of the Franks, Visigoths and Ostrogoths – and even of the Vandals – tried hard to preserve the culture and institutions they found in place when they crossed the Imperial frontiers. Yet, in spite of all this, Graeco-Roman civilization did indeed die in the West, and it died too in the East. In both regions it was replaced, eventually, by a society and civilization that we now call "medieval," a society whose most outstanding characteristics were in many ways the precise opposite of the classical; a society that was overwhelmingly rural, generally illiterate, had a largely barter economy, and tended to be inward-looking rather than open and syncretic. (The latter of course is a clichéd and formulaic view of medieval civilization, but it does contain important elements of the truth).

It is the purpose of the present study to examine the causes of this, or, more precisely, to examine a highly controversial thesis about it which appeared in the early years of the twentieth century. This was the thesis of Henri Pirenne, a Belgian historian whose specialism was the early medieval period. Pirenne maintained that the real destroyers of classical civilization were the Muslims. It was the Arab Invasions, he said, which broke the unity of the Mediterranean world and turned the Middle Sea – previously one of the world's most important trading highways – into a battleground. It was only after the appearance of Islam, claimed Pirenne, that the cities of the West, which depended upon the Mediterranean trade for their survival, began to die. With them went the entire infrastructure of classical culture. Pirenne found that from the mid-seventh century onwards a host of luxury products, which had hitherto been common in Gaul, Italy and Spain, disappeared, and that with them went the prosperity upon which classical culture depended. Towns shrank and society became more rural.

Essentially, what Pirenne was saying was that Islam caused the Dark Age in Europe. This was, even in the 1920s, when the thesis was first published, an extremely controversial idea, and went quite against the grain of contemporary opinion: for the tendency over the previous century had increasingly been to see Islam as the harbinger of medieval Europe's civilization; as the great preserver of classical knowledge and learning; as an enlightened and tolerant influence which reached Europe in the seventh century and which commenced then to raise the continent out of the darkness into which it had sunk. This had been the default mode of thought amongst perhaps the majority of academics for almost half a century before the appearance of Pirenne's thesis, a view of history deeply rooted in contemporary European thinking. And then along came Pirenne to claim the precise opposite!

As might be imagined, such a remarkable counter-thesis generated heated debate; a debate that endures to this day. And to this day, the two camps are divided rather precisely as they were in the time of Pirenne, who died in 1935. There are those who, with varying degrees of passion, maintain that Islam essentially saved the remnants of classical culture and learning, which they transmitted to a benighted Europe; and there are those (a much smaller group) who, with Pirenne, maintain that Islam was the destroyer of that very culture and learning; and that if Europe was benighted after the seventh century, it was benighted precisely because of the actions of the Muslims. How strange is this situation! How is it that one topic can give rise to such radically differing perspectives? We are, we might say, once more in what was known during the Middle Ages as "the world's debate." In those days, during the Crusades, the "debate" was waged by force of arms. The academic and in some respects ideological battle being fought today is waged in newspapers, books, journals, television, radio and the internet; though another "theatre" of the debate is arguably being waged precisely as it was in the time of the Crusades: by force of arms.

Why then is this debate still with us; and why does it elicit such radically opposing responses? What is it about Islam and its history that gives rise to such intense controversy? The answer to these questions shall, I hope, be presented in the pages to follow. And if it is not an answer that everyone can accept, then at least the evidence shall be presented in a way that is accessible to all and that may enable the reader to make up his/her own mind.

* * *

As this is the history of a debate, it is appropriate to begin with a look at how it developed over the centuries; for the story does not begin with Pirenne.

Until the eighteenth century scholars had generally assumed that classical civilization came to an end with the dissolution of the Western Roman Empire in 476. However, as the eighteenth century progressed and the study of history became a proper scholarly discipline rather than a simple chronicling of events, educated Europeans became aware of the fact that the "barbarian" tribes who conquered the Western Empire in the fifth century never intended to destroy Roman society or culture; and as our knowledge of late antiquity improved, the obvious question became progressively more urgent: What then brought classical civilization to an end? If it was not, after all, the "barbarians," who were responsible, who or what was, and when?

Concomitant with research into Roman history, Enlightenment scholars began a detailed examination of early medieval Europe. As they did so, they began to notice how great was the debt owed by medieval Europe to the Islamic world. They read letters, official documents and chronicles, which seemed to point to Islamic Spain and the Islamic Middle East as the source of all real knowledge and learning at the time. They read accounts of how European scholars slipped across the borders of the Islamic world, often in disguise, to learn their secrets. They noticed how European thinkers of the time, from

Abelard to Roger Bacon, couched their debates in the language of Islamic scholars such as Averroes and Avicenna. They noticed that very many of the scientific and scholarly terminologies found in the languages of Europe, were of Arab origin. We used the "Arabic" numeral system, which gave us the concept of zero – a direct borrowing from the Arabic *zirr*, whilst our word "algebra" was directly taken from the Arabic *al-jabr*. They found indeed that numerous technical and scientific terms, such as alcohol, alkali, etc, and many others, were of Arab origin.

Thus by the early nineteenth century scholarly opinion about Islam began to change dramatically. True, even then Muslim pirates were a problem in the Mediterranean, and Muslim societies – most notably the Ottoman Empire – were rather impoverished and often brutal. But these negatives were increasingly viewed as an accident of history, not as something logically deriving from Islam. After all, if slavery was then a problem in the Muslim world, had it not been a problem too in the Christian world? And if the Muslims killed apostates and heretics, did not the Christians do the same until the seventeenth century?

The trend towards a negative view of European civilization accompanied by a positive view of Islamic civilization continued throughout the nineteenth century. Indeed the "talking up" of Islam went rather precisely in tandem with the "talking down" of Christianity. This was particularly the case amongst a certain class of politicized intellectuals, who, as the nineteenth century progressed, adopted an increasingly hostile approach to all things European; and the trend only accelerated with the First World War. Following the cataclysmic events of those years, fewer and fewer of Europe's and America's intellectual class subscribed to the view that European civilization was in any way superior to others. On the contrary, an age of disillusionment dawned. As this view gathered strength, so the criticism of medieval Europe, and medieval Christendom, became more virulent. More and more the medieval world was seen as a "dark age," and any learning that we now possess surely did not originate in it.

Christian writers at the time – there still were many – tried of course to counter this movement; but they were outnumbered and in a sense outgunned. The tide of thought was flowing decidedly against them.

Even as this occurred, the study of late antiquity and the early medieval world in Europe moved on. Archaeology, as well as the discovery and translation into modern languages of more and more texts of the fifth to tenth centuries began to transform our understanding of the period. As we saw, it had been known, since the time of Gibbon at least, that the "Barbarians" had not intended to destroy Roman civilization. The archaeological evidence proved that they did not. On the contrary, it became increasingly clear that classical, or Graeco-Roman, civilization had survived the Barbarian Invasions of the fifth century, and that there had even been, in the sixth century at least, something of a revival of that civilization, at least in places like Gaul and Spain. Yet the world of Rome and her civilization did indeed come to an end, and that event, it was increasingly clear, occurred sometime in the seventh century. After that time, the western world was distinctly medieval in all respects. But why, it was asked, should this have occurred? If the barbarian rulers of the West could manage and cultivate prosperous and largely urban societies for two centuries, especially in places like North Africa and Spain, why did they finally "lose the plot" in the seventh century?

By the early years of the twentieth century this had become a pressing problem, and it was addressed by two outstanding historians of the time: Alfons Dopsch and Henri Pirenne. Both Dopsch and Pirenne devoted considerable effort to an examination of Italian and Gaulish societies during the fifth and sixth centuries, and both became prominent in their rejection of the notion of a barbarian-created Dark Age during that period. Yet Dopsch came to believe that he could detect a general "decline" of Roman culture in the years between 400 and 600, and he eventually threw his weight behind the idea that the Germanic peoples who ruled the West proved in the long run incapable of administering an efficient urban civilization. With time, thought Dopsch, the "barbarian" and uncivilized nature of these peoples prevailed, and, notwithstanding their initial efforts to save Roman culture and institutions, in the end they presided over the collapse of these very things.

Henri Pirenne studied the same epoch and used more or less the same materials as Dopsch. The conclusions he came to, however, were very different. Like Dopsch, he saw that there was no "Dark Age" in the first two centuries after the sack of Rome by Alaric (410), and that Roman culture and institutions survived. He saw too that the demise of this culture could be dated to the first half of the seventh century. Unlike Dopsch, however, he could find no evidence of a gradual decline. For Pirenne, the end of the late classical civilization seemed to come suddenly. What, he thought, could have caused it?

Early in the 1920s, he came to a novel and controversial conclusion: Roman society and the culture we associate with it had been destroyed by the Arab conquests. Saracen pirates and raiders, he claimed, had blockaded the Mediterranean from the 640s onwards, terminating all trade between the Levant and western Europe. The cities of Italy, Gaul and Spain, which depended upon this trade for their prosperity, began to die; and the Germanic kings who controlled these regions, deprived of the taxable wealth generated by the same trade, lost much of their authority and power. Local strongmen asserted control of the provinces. These were the medieval barons. The Middle Ages had begun.

What Pirenne was now saying went completely against the grain of contemporary academic thought about Islam, which had come to see the Arabian faith as a civilizing, rather than a destructive, force. The debate which he ignited then has never really died or been resolved and, on the contrary, has only taken on a new and urgent resonance in the modern world. As we shall see, Pirenne's thesis was accorded, for a while, somewhat grudging acceptance in some areas of academia, though even then he was viewed as the person to argue against. By the 1980s, however, a general consensus had arisen, at least in the English-speaking world, that Pirenne had been effectively debunked; and from that time on more and more books and academic studies of the period failed to mention him or his theory.

The anti-Pirenne consensus was largely, as we shall see, galvanized by archaeological work carried out in Italy during the 1960s and 1970s. There it was found that, whilst classical culture survived during the fifth and sixth centuries, there had nevertheless been a marked decline in all aspects of civilized life from the fifth century onwards. The Italian excavations were to form the basis of the argument presented by the most influential of Pirenne's critics, Richard Hodges and David Whitehouse, who in 1982 published what was advertised as a definitive refutation of Pirenne. The book, *Mohammed, Charlemagne and the Origins of Europe*, proved to mark a watershed in the debate. Using mainly the Italian material, but also some data from North Africa, Hodges and Whitehouse argued the Graeco-Roman civilization was in terminal decline in the years prior to 600. So decrepit were the economies of Italy, Spain, and North Africa after the 550s, they declared, that classical culture did not need to be killed off by the Arabs: it was already effectively dead by the time they arrived.

But there were serious flaws in Hodges' and Whitehouse's thinking, as we shall see. For one thing, the data they presented was extremely limited in its scope, and essentially failed to look beyond central Italy. Claims that the economy and civic life of North Africa had also collapsed before 600 can be shown to be without foundation. In Chapters 6, 7, 8, and 9 we do what Hodges and Whitehouse failed to do and look beyond Italy to Gaul, central Europe, Britain and Spain, where we find apparently thriving and vital late classical cultures during the fifth and (more especially) sixth and early seventh centuries. This in spite of the fact that none of these societies – with the possible exception of Spain – can be described as major centers of classical culture, either in late antiquity or earlier. Indeed, the archaeology of western Europe in general, with the exception of Italy, shows a pronounced expansion of population, culture, and trade during the latter half of the sixth century and the first half of the seventh – precisely those years during which Hodges and Whitehouse claimed Europe and classical civilization was dying a slow and tortuous death. Everywhere we find evidence of expansion of cultivation, of population increase, of the growth of towns and the revival of building in stone, of the adoption and development of new technologies, and of new regions, such as Ireland, northern Britain (Scotland) and eastern and northern Germany, being brought within the orbit of Latin civilization for the first time.

So much for Europe. Yet, in order to get to the bottom of this question, we need to look further afield. For Pirenne, as for most of his critics, the debate about the "Dark Ages" was entirely a debate about what happened in Europe, particularly western Europe, and most especially in Gaul and Italy. But the West, with the exception of Italy herself and perhaps Spain, had never been much more than a backwater even at the height of the Roman Empire. The reality of the situation is described succinctly by Patrick J. Geary:

"During the more than five centuries of Roman presence in the West, the regions of Britain, Gaul, and Germany were marginal to Roman interests. The Empire was essentially Mediterranean and remained so throughout its existence; thus Italy, Spain, and North Africa were the Western areas most vital to it. However, the Empire's cultural, economic, and population centers were the great cities of the East: Alexandria, Antioch, Ephesus, and later Constantinople. The West boasted only one true city ... Rome. In the first centuries of the Empire, Rome could afford the luxury of maintaining the Romanitas [Roman territories] of the West. Still, these regions, which supplying the legions of the limes, or borders, with men and arms and supporting the local senators with the otium, or leisured existence, necessary to lead a civilized life of letters, contributed little to either the cultural or economic life of the Empire." (Patrick J. Geary, *Before France and Germany*, pp. 8-9)

From this, it is clear that if we wish to chart the decline and fall of classical civilization we must not confine our gaze to the West, but must pay close attention to what happened in the East: It was here, and not in the West, that was located the core area of that civilization. Pirenne failed to notice this, perhaps because of the habitually Eurocentric mindset of academic culture in his time. Yet examine the East we must, and this is the task we set ourselves from Chapter 10 onwards.

As we shall see, whatever might be said about the disappearance of classical civilization in the West, in the East there is no question at all that it was terminated in the mid-seventh century, and that it was terminated by the Arabs. On this point Hodges and Whitehouse were strangely ambiguous: on the one hand, they recognized that the Arabs wrought immense destruction in the Levant, and they even admitted to the appearance in North Africa of a "Dark Age" following the Arab conquests; yet on the other hand they strove to suggest that classical civilization in the East was wrecked more by the Persians than by the Arabs, and that, in Asia Minor at least, classical civilization was already terminally damaged by the time the Arabs arrived.

Our own survey of the evidence leads us to a somewhat different conclusion: namely that classical civilization was indeed weakened by Byzantium's destructive war with Persia, which commenced in 612; but that it was still sufficiently powerful and vibrant to recover from that conflict, had not the Arabs arrived immediately afterwards to devastate the region permanently. These are the facts as uncovered by archaeology, yet, as we shall see, they prompt another urgent question: What then was it about the Arabs, or, more accurately, about Islam, that could bring about such universal and complete destruction?

At this point we must pause to take note of the remarkable fact that very few of the historians who have commented upon Pirenne's thesis have paid much attention to the nature of Islam or its beliefs. They have, virtually without exception, assumed that Islam is or was a faith no different from any other. Indeed, almost all of modern academia treat the religious systems of mankind as an amorphous whole, and see no difference between them. If they do pick out one for special criticism it is invariably Christianity that they target. There are, or have been, interesting exceptions to the rule, such as Joseph Campbell, who spoke of "the sleep of Islam" which overtook the Middle East in the seventh century; but in general twentieth century scholarship has been remarkably positive about the Arabian faith. Yet even a cursory examination of the tenets of Islam is enough to convince us that it is not a faith like any other; and that it is, on the contrary, a religio-political ideology whose fundamental principle is aggressive expansionism. In Chapter 13 we find that, through the doctrine of perpetual "holy war," or jihad, plus the notion of entitlement central to sharia law, Islam had a thoroughly and unprecedentedly destabilizing influence upon the Mediterranean world. It was the perpetual raiding of Muslim pirates and slave-traders that brought about the abandonment throughout southern Europe of the scattered settlements of classical times and the retreat to defended hilltop fortifications – the first medieval castles. The same raiding led to the abandonment of the old agricultural systems, with their irrigation dikes and ditches, and caused the formation throughout the Mediterranean coastlands of a layer of silt just about the last of the late classical settlements.

We find then that Islam did indeed cause the end of classical civilization, in its heartland at least, the Middle East. Yet that statement does not exhaust the complexity of this question. For the three centuries which saw the rise of Islam and the Dark Ages in Europe, the seventh to the tenth – the three least known of our entire history – have other mysteries to unravel. And these are mysteries that archaeology has done little to resolve. Indeed, it may even have further deepened them.

Whoever studies early medieval history cannot fail to note the fact that, apart from the economic impact which Pirenne claimed to detect in the seventh century, the real cultural and ideological impact of Islam upon Europe only begins in the late tenth and early eleventh centuries. Documents from that period onwards leave us in no doubt that the world of "the Saracens" was regarded by Europeans as one of fabulous wealth; a region to which they cast envious eyes not only on account of its riches but because of its learning and knowledge. From the late-tenth century onwards educated Europeans made continuous efforts to tap into the learning of the Arabs. And here of course we arrive at the very nexus of the radical disagreement over Islam which has bedeviled the study of early medieval history for two centuries. Here precisely is the reason why, on the one hand, some academics may describe Islam as tolerant and learned, whilst others, with equal conviction, can describe it as violent and intolerant. Whatever damage Islam may have caused Europe in the seventh century, argue the Islamophiles, it was more than compensated for by the knowledge and wisdom bequeathed to Europe in the tenth century by the same faith. For whilst Europe may have lingered for three centuries in a Dark Age limbo of poverty and ignorance, Islam enjoyed three centuries of unparalleled splendor and prosperity, a veritable Golden Age.

That, at least, has been the narrative until now. Yet over the past half century the discoveries of archaeology have undermined this picture, and have revealed facts which may well eventually compel a radical rethink.

Whilst some historians of medieval Europe, relying on the traditional written sources, have consistently argued for the removal of the term "Dark Age" from our historical nomenclature, the archaeological evidence has served only to demonstrate how thoroughly appropriate the term is. For try as they might, excavators have signally failed to discover any civilization worthy of the name in Europe between the late seventh and early tenth centuries. Indeed, the progress of research has repeatedly demonstrated that even the pitifully few monuments and artifacts hitherto assigned the "dark" centuries have, on further investigation, usually been shown not to belong to that epoch at all; but invariably either to the period immediately following the Dark Age, or to the period immediately preceding it.

Surely, archaeologists have said, ample proof that Europe was indeed a dark and barbarous – and largely unpopulated – land during those long years.

But the mystery has deepened further: for we now know that Europe is not the only region devoid of archaeology between the seventh and tenth centuries. The same gap is observed throughout the Islamic world. Here then is a real shock to the collective system! Whilst depopulation and non-culture might just have been expected in Europe, it was certainly not expected in North Africa, Egypt, Syria, and Mesopotamia. These regions, after all, formed the very heart of the Caliphate, the very core of population, commerce, and cultured life during the three centuries of what has been called Islam's Golden Age. At this time excavators had expected to find luxurious mosques, palaces, baths, etc, standing in the midst of truly enormous metropolises. The fabulous Harun al-Rashid in the ninth century, after all, is supposed to have reigned over a city of Baghdad that was home to in excess of a million people. Cordoba, capital of the Spanish Emirate at the same time, is said to have housed half a million souls. Yet of this splendid civilization hardly a brick or inscription has been found! It is true that from the very beginning of the Islamic epoch there is occasionally (although infrequently) found some archaeology. This usually dates to the mid-seventh century. Then, after this, there are three full centuries with virtually nothing. About the middle of the tenth century archaeology resumes, and there is talk of a "revival" of cities in the Muslim world, just as in Europe at the same time. Indeed, the mid-tenth century reveals a flowering and in many ways splendid Islamic civilization, clearly more wealthy and at a higher stage of development than anything in contemporary Europe. Yet this civilization seems to spring out of nowhere: It is without any archaeological antecedents.

These discoveries have served to underline the dichotomy at the heart of all discussion on Islam, and have in fact added another strand to it: On the one hand, as we saw, in the mid-seventh century, there is proof of massive destruction carried out by the Arabs throughout the Near East. So great was the destruction that many of the cities and towns which were thriving under the Byzantines and remained prosperous until the first quarter of the seventh century were then abandoned and deserted, never to be reoccupied. Their gaunt ruins lie everywhere throughout the Middle East and North Africa. Yet on the other hand, immediately after this destruction, the Islamic regions were always believed to have enjoyed a "Golden Age" which lasted into the tenth and eleventh centuries. That, at least, was the narrative and the argument until recently.

We should note that the archaeological appearance of the first rich Islamic culture in the tenth and eleventh centuries coincides with written history which always indicated that the cultural impact of Islam only reached Europe in the tenth and eleventh centuries.

What can all this mean? Is this a conundrum that can be solved, or is it utterly beyond the ingenuity of men to get to the bottom of?

As we shall see in the final chapter of the present study, so great has this problem become that it has prompted some very radical, even outlandish, solutions. One of these, favored by not a few historians and climatologists, is that some form of natural disaster struck Europe and perhaps the entire earth during the seventh century. Several writers, referring mainly to medieval chronicles, speak of a mini-Ice Age or perhaps a period of global warming. Others look to the skies and see cometary or asteroid causes. These writers agree that there was a Dark Age, but that it was caused by nature, rather than man. Another school of thought, most influential in Europe, denies the existence of a Dark Age at all and claims that the three hundred years between the early seventh and early tenth centuries never existed, and were merely a fictional creation of scribes working for the Emperor Otto III at the end of the tenth century. The most important proponents of this theory are German writers Heribert Illig and Gunnar Heinsohn. It would be impossible to do justice to either of these theories or to examine all their implications in a volume, never mind a chapter. We shall look briefly at some towards the end of the present study. Suffice to say that whilst Illig's thesis may be seen as solving several hitherto intractable conundrums (eg why does "Romanesque" art of the tenth and eleventh centuries look so much like Merovingian art of the seventh), it has been almost universally rejected by mainstream academia, and remains a decidedly "fringe" idea.

Leaving such questions aside, the present study concludes by noting that scholarship has now arrived at a several conclusions which are really beyond dispute, and which tend to offer definitive support for Pirenne.

First and foremost, the evidence suggests that classical or Graeco-Roman civilization was alive and well into the late sixth and early seventh centuries. This was particularly the case in the Middle East and North Africa, which were the ancient heartlands of Mediterranean culture, and in which were located by far the greatest centers of population, wealth, and industry. Evidence shows that until the first quarter of the seventh century these regions were flourishing as never before. But classical civilization was also alive and well in Europe, a region which (aside from central and southern Italy), had always been peripheral to Graeco-Roman civilization. And outside of central Italy we find none of the signs of decay that Pirenne's critics claimed to have detected. On the contrary, Gaul and in particular Spain supported a thriving and vigorous late classical culture; and this was a culture that was growing, rather than declining. Indeed, by the latter years of the sixth century classical civilization had begun to spread into regions never reached by the Roman Legions, and Latin, as well as Greek, was now studied along the banks of the Elbe in eastern Germany, and in the Hebrides, off northern Scotland.

Secondly, the evidence shows that this culture went into rapid and terminal decline in the 620s and 630s. The great cities of Asia Minor and Syria everywhere at this time show signs of violent destruction; after which they were never rebuilt. Whatever archaeology appears on top of them is invariably impoverished and small-scale; usually little more than a diminutive fortress. Contemporary with the destruction of the classical cities, we find a universal decay in the countryside: Top-soil is washed away and a layer of subsoil, known as the Younger Fill, covers settlements in river-valleys and blocks harbors. This stratum appears throughout the Mediterranean world, from Syria to Spain, and is the geographical signature of the end of Graeco-Roman civilization. With the appearance of this layer, classical patterns of settlement and land-management are abandoned. This is the pattern too in southern Europe, where we now find a retreat of settlement to defended hill-top sites – the first medieval castles. Both these developments can be explained by the appearance of Muslim raiders and pirates throughout the Mediterranean coastlands from the 630s onwards; and if that is not the accepted solution, then no answer is forthcoming.

Thirdly, from the mid-seventh century onwards there is an almost total disappearance of archaeology in Europe and throughout the Middle East and North Africa for a period of three centuries. This disappearance, it seems, has nothing to do with what has always been called the "Dark Age" of Europe, because it appears also in the Islamic lands. By the mid- to late-tenth century cities and towns revive both in the Islamic and Christian lands, and (though the great cities of classical times are gone forever), the material culture of the new settlements looks strikingly reminiscent in many ways of the material culture of the seventh century.

That, in brief, is what the archaeology says. At the end of the present volume we take a brief look at events subsequent to the rise and spread of Islam. There we find that not only did the Arabs terminate classical civilization in the Levant and North Africa, and therefore cut Europe off from the humanizing and civilizing impulses which had previously emanated from those regions, but they now began, in the tenth century, to exert their own influence upon the West. And that influence was anything but benevolent. It is of course widely accepted that Islam had a profound cultural impact upon early medieval Eu-

rope. Indeed, the all-pervasiveness of that impact has been traditionally seen as underlining the cultural superiority of Islam at that time.
Yet, as we shall see, in addition to some commentaries upon Aristotle,
and a few scientific and technological concepts (which were not "Arab"
inventions at all) Islam was to communicate to Europe a whole host of
ideas and attitudes that were far from being enlightened. Most obviously, the concept of "holy war", which Europe adopted (admittedly
somewhat reluctantly) in the eleventh century, was entirely an Islamic
innovation; as was the tendency towards theocracy (enshrined in the
all-powerful medieval Papacy) and the suppression, by force, of heterodox ideas.

* * *

It goes without saying that a work such as this cannot claim to be
exhaustive, or the last word. Many of the topics covered could profit-
ably have been examined in greater depth; yet so diverse is the range
of evidence and so wide the territories and epochs it covers, that a
detailed examination of everything is a complete impossibility. I have
been compelled to look at written and archaeological evidence for the
fifth to tenth centuries from the western extremities of Europe to the
borders of Persia. And, as might be expected, the literature dealing
with these diverse eras and areas is immense, and growing more so by
the day. So much has been written on the economic and political histories of the Byzantine, Frankish, Visigothic and Early Islamic states
in the English language over the past twenty years that a complete
bibliography might fill an entire volume of its own. But a bulging
bibliography does not necessarily indicate a convincing argument or
even a coherent line of thought. As such, I have endeavored simply to
select some of the most representative material, and to examine the
arguments and evidence found therein in detail. And since this is an
examination of the Pirenne thesis I have concentrated, on the whole,
on those authors who have dealt with his work, or whose own work
has a direct impact upon his.

So the scope of the present work is limited. On the whole, I have
tended to concentrate upon the evidence of archaeology. If we have
learned anything about this epoch, it is that written sources cannot be
taken at face value. They must be supported by archaeology. And the
archaeology of late antiquity and the early Middle Ages has, so far,
produced far more puzzles than answers.

So, much work remains to be done. Having said that however, I am convinced that the evidence now accumulated points decisively to a vindication of Pirenne, if not in exactly the manner he imagined. Islam did indeed terminate classical civilization in its main centers, in the Middle East and North Africa. Its impact upon Europe however was more nuanced, and did not perhaps amount to the economic catastrophe Pirenne believed. Temperate Europe was already economically self-sufficient before the arrival of the Arabs; and their presence in the Mediterranean did little more than block the importation to the West of certain eastern luxuries which were enjoyed by the elites of Gaul, Spain and Italy. Much more serious however was the termination of the papyrus supply, an event which led, inter alia, to the loss of the great bulk of the heritage of classical literature and to the general loss of literacy amongst the population of Europe. This led, very quickly indeed, to the "medieval" mentality with which we are all too familiar.

Henri Pirenne, 1862 - 1935

WHO DESTROYED CLASSICAL CIVILIZATION?

F or centuries scholars assumed that the civilization of ancient
Rome, the civilization we now call "classical," was destroyed by
the barbarian tribes of Germany and central Asia who, during the
fourth and fifth centuries swarmed into the Empire and destroyed the
political power of the Eternal City. The migrations of the Goths, Vandals, and Huns were held responsible for reducing Europe to an economic and cultural wasteland, and initiating the long period of backwardness we now call the "Dark Ages."

This was the view that prevailed till the sixteenth century, at
which point, in the wake of the Reformation, a new suspect was added:
the Christian, or more accurately, the Catholic, Church. According to
this idea (one that remains strikingly popular in the English-speaking
world), Christianity was corrupted beyond recognition after the time
of Constantine and from the fourth century onwards a power-hungry
Church hierarchy, in cahoots with the Imperial authorities, kept the
population of Europe in subservience and ignorance, effectively completing the destructive work of the Barbarians.

With the advent of a more stringent historical method in the
seventeenth and eighteenth centuries cracks began to appear in the
above edifice; and by the mid-eighteenth century Gibbon was ready
to exonerate the "innocent barbarians." He remained however highly
critical of the Church, which he blamed for extinguishing the rational
spirit of the ancients. Even as Gibbon was writing however, scholars'
understanding of the period was evolving; and the nineteenth century
was to bring forth a plethora of new types of evidence. The discovery and translation of more and more medieval documents gradually
revolutionized our understanding of late antiquity, whilst by the mid-
nineteenth century the new science of archaeology was casting its
own fresh and unexpected light on the problem. Thus by the start of
the twentieth century it had become evident that, as an imperial power,
Rome was already in a fairly advanced state of decay by the middle of
the third century – two hundred years before the official "end" of the
Empire in 476. Historians began to speak of the "crisis" at that time.
They noted a contraction of Roman power in the third century: the
loss and abandonment of several provinces, beginning with Dacia and

parts of Germany. They noted too a general shrinking of cities and the cessation of construction on a monumental scale. All the great structures which to this day dot Europe and elicit the admiration and astonishment of the tourist – the aqueducts, the amphitheatres and the city walls – were raised before the beginning of the third century. After that, there was almost nothing. More and more historians began to discern "a fundamental structural change" at the time, "which the great emperors at the end of that century, and Constantine himself at the beginning of the next, did but stabilize."[1] A new consensus developed, according to which there were "two successive Roman Empires. … First, there is the Roman Empire of Augustus and the Antonines, of which we mainly think, the majestic web of planned cities and straight roads, all leading to Rome. … Secondly, after the anarchy of the third century, there is the 'Lower Empire', the rural military empire of Diocletian and Constantine, of Julian the Apostate and Theodosius the Great. This was an empire always on the defensive, whose capital was not Rome, but wherever warring emperors kept their military headquarters: in the Rhineland, behind the Alps or in the East; in Nicomedia or Constantinople, in Trier, Milan or Ravenna."[2]

The Roman Empire, it thus became clear, was already in an advanced state of decay by the year 200; and it was also increasingly less "Roman". We hear that, "Already before the 'age of the Antonines' [in the second century] it had been discovered as Tacitus remarked that emperors could be made elsewhere than in Rome," and, as the above writer drily remarked, "By the third century AD they were generally made elsewhere." In that century, we know, "there were not only military emperors from the frontier: there were also Syrian, African and half-barbarian emperors; and their visits to Rome became rarer and rarer."[3] And the advent of "half-barbarian" emperors was paralleled by an increasingly half- or fully barbarian army. From the third and even second century historians noted the recruitment into the Roman legions not only of great numbers of "semi-barbarians" such as Gauls and Illyrians, but of actual barbarians, such as Germans and Sarmatians. Indeed, so far had this custom gone by the fourth century that by then several distinguished Roman families boasted a barbarian ancestor many generations earlier.

The crisis of the third century naturally became the subject of

1 Hugh Trevor-Roper, *The Rise of Christian Europe* (2nd. ed., London, 1966), p. 27
2 Ibid.
3 Ibid p. 47

intense debate amongst historians. Nowadays it is often regarded as having an economic origin, and scholars talk of inflationary pressures and such like. This may be partly true; but what seems undeniable is that the real problem lay deeper. There is now little dissention on the belief that by the year 100 the population of the Empire had ceased to grow and had begun to contract. The inability to hold the most outlying of the Provinces, in Dacia and Germany, is viewed as an infallible sign of a general shrinkage. This shrinkage may have had various causes, but the practice of infanticide – widespread and commonplace in the classical world – must surely have been one of the most important.[4] Official Roman documents and texts of every kind from as early as the first century, stress again and again the pernicious consequences of Rome's low and apparently declining birth-rate. Attempts by the Emperor Augustus to reverse the situation were apparently unsuccessful, for a hundred years later Tacitus remarked that in spite of everything "childlessness prevailed,"[5] whilst towards the beginning of the second century, Pliny the Younger said that he lived "in an age when even one child is thought a burden preventing the rewards of childlessness." Around the same time Plutarch noted that the poor did not bring up their children for fear that without an appropriate upbringing they would grow up badly,[6] and by the middle of the second century Hierocles claimed that "most people" seemed to decline to raise their children for a not very lofty reason, love of wealth and the belief that poverty is a terrible evil.[7] During the third century successive emperors made efforts to outlaw infanticide, though how successful they were remains unclear. What seems certain is that even if infanticide became less important in the third and fourth centuries, the birth-rate remained stubbornly low, for the Romans also practiced very effective forms of birth control. Abortion was also practiced, and caused the deaths of large numbers of women, as well as infertility in a great many others.[8] Quite possibly, by the end of the first century, the only groups in the Empire that was increasing by normal demographic process were the Christians and the Jews.

---

4 See eg. William V. Harris, "Child Exposure in the Roman Empire," *The Journal of Roman Studies*, Vol. 84 (1994)

5 Tacitus, *Annals of Imperial Rome*, iii, 25

6 Plutarch, *Moralia*, Bk. iv

7 Stobaeus, iv, 24, 14

8 For a discussion, see Rodney Stark, *The Rise of Christianity: A Sociologist Reconsiders History* (Harper Collins, 1996), pp. 95-128

Taking this into account, several writers, by the early years of the twentieth century, began to suggest that Rome's adoption of Christianity in the fourth century may have had, as one of its major goals, the halting of Rome's population decline. Christians had large families and were noted for their rejection of infanticide. In legalizing Christianity therefore Constantine may have hoped to reverse the population trend. He was also, to some degree, simply recognizing the inevitable.[9] By the late third century Christians were already a majority in certain areas of the East, most notably in parts of Syria and Asia Minor, and were apparently the only group (apart from the Jews) registering an increase in many other areas. This was achieved both by conversion and by simple demographics. The Jews too, by that time, formed a significant element in the Empire's population – and for the same reason: They, like their Christian cousins, abhorred the practice of infanticide and abortion. It has been estimated that by the start of the fourth century Jews formed up to one tenth of the Empire's entire population. Whether or not Constantine legalized Christianity therefore, it would appear that in time the Empire would have become Christian in any case.[10]

The question for historians was: Did Constantine's surmise and gamble prove correct? Did the Christianization of the Empire halt the decline? On the face of it, the answer seemed to be "No!" After all, less than a century later Rome herself was sacked, first by the Goths and then, several decades later, by the Vandals. And by 476 the Western Empire was officially dissolved. However, by the latter years of the nineteenth century more and more evidence began to emerge, much of it from archaeology, which seemed to suggest that Roman civilization did not end in the fifth century. Some of the most important work in this field was done by Austrian art historian Alois Riegl, who did much to redefine the fifth and sixth centuries as late antiquity, rather than part of the Dark Ages, as they had previously been habitually designated. In his seminal *Die spätrömische Kunstindustrie nach den Funden in Österreich-Ungarn* (1901), he argued that the art of the fourth, fifth and sixth centuries did not represent a collapse of classical standards, but

---

9 Ibid.

10 By the same token, demographic trends in modern post-Christian Europe would suggest that, within another forty years, or perhaps less, Europe will become Muslim, since the latter group is the only one on the continent producing above replacement levels of children. This is a simple demographic fact; yet to even state it in this age of political correctness is to invite a charge of "racism" or "xenophobia" or some other equally inappropriate and frankly idiotic accusation.

a continuation and development of what went before. Partly under the influence of Riegl, more and more historians began to view the early Germanic kingdoms of the fifth and sixth centuries as clients of the Empire rather than destroying conquerors. Documents of the time, they noted, showed that the "barbarian" princes seem to have done everything in their power to preserve Roman institutions and laws. They regarded themselves as functionaries of the Empire, and they accepted Roman titles bestowed upon them by the Emperor in Constantinople. The gold coins they issued were struck with the image of the Byzantine Emperor, and many of the offspring of these "barbarian" kings were raised and educated in Constantinople. Artistic and intellectual life seemed to have flourished under them, as did the economy and the cities built earlier in the time of the Caesars; whilst a widespread and prosperous trading network continued to connect western Europe with the great centers of population and culture in the Eastern Mediterranean. This much became clear: by the late fifth and sixth centuries a recognizably "classical" civilization still existed in Italy, Gaul, Spain and North Africa – as well, of course, as in Byzantium and throughout the eastern Mediterranean. The one exception was Britain, which had been more or less lost to the Roman world in the fifth century – yet even here, in the only province where the Germanic invaders actually imposed their language – there began to emerge evidence of a much more robust Roman survival than had previously been imagined.

And yet, having said all that, scholars could hardly ignore the fact that classical civilization did indeed die, and die completely, throughout western Europe and North Africa. This seemed to have occurred sometime between the mid-seventh and early eighth centuries. Cities were abandoned, literacy plummeted, royal authority declined and local strongmen, or "barons," seized control of the provinces. The Middle Ages had begun. But the fact that the Germanic kings had presided over prosperous and apparently flourishing late "Roman" societies for two centuries – without destroying them – merely brought forth the question, more and more urgently: What then did finally destroy those societies?

This was the conundrum facing medieval historians in the early years of the twentieth century. One of those who turned his attention to the problem was Belgian historian Henri Pirenne. Originally specializing in Belgian history, from 1915 onwards Pirenne began to look at the wider European picture; and by the middle of the 1920s he had arrived at a radical conclusion: classical civilization had not been destroyed by the Goths, Vandals, or Huns, or indeed by the Christian Church. It was destroyed by a people who it had, even then, become fashionable to credit with saving Western Civilization: the Arabs. The evidence, as Pirenne was at pains to show in his posthumously published *Mohammed et Charlemagne* (1938) seemed incontrovertible. From the mid-seventh century trade between the ancient centers of high culture in the Levant and the West seemed to have come to an abrupt halt. Luxury items originating in the eastern Mediterranean, which are mentioned routinely in the literature until the end of the sixth century, disappear completely by the mid-seventh century, at the latest. The flow of gold, which the West derived from the East, seemed to have dried up. Gold coinage disappeared, and with it went the towns and urban settlements of Italy, Gaul and Spain. Documents of the period made it very clear that these, especially the ports, owed their wealth to the Mediterranean trade. Worst of all, perhaps, from the perspective of culture and learning, the importation of papyrus from Egypt seemed to have entirely ceased. Pirenne stressed that fact that this material, which had been shipped into Western Europe in vast quantities since the time of the Roman Republic, was absolutely essential for a thousand purposes in a literate and mercantile civilization; and the ending of the supply would have had an immediate and catastrophic effect on levels of literacy. These must have dropped, almost overnight, to levels perhaps equivalent to those in pre-Roman times.

* * *

Pirenne held that the disappearance of such Levantine products in the middle of the seventh century pointed to only one possible conclusion: that the Arabs, whose well-known predilection for piracy has been documented for centuries, must have, through their raiding and freebooting, effectively terminated all trade in the Mediterranean, thus isolating western Europe both intellectually and economically. Prior to that, he noted, the whole of the West was heavily under the influence of Byzantium, and was becoming increasingly so. He stressed that the Germanic kings of the Gaul and Spain regarded themselves as functionaries of the Eastern Emperor, who was, for them, still the "Roman" Emperor. They accepted titles bestowed upon them by Constantinople and the coins they minted bore the image of the Emperor. When the office of Emperor of the West was abolished in 476, Odoacer sent the insignia of the office to Constantinople.

So all-pervasive was the power of Byzantium, said Pirenne, than no Germanic ruler dared assume the imperial purple and declare himself Emperor. Although Constantinople lacked the military resources necessary to establish real control of the western provinces (Justinian's attempt was only partly successful), her vast wealth gave her effective control. Whilst she could not send her own armies to punish recalcitrant princes, she could hire whatever military assistance she needed from other "barbarian" chiefs. So complete was Constantinople's control that only once before the seventh century did a Germanic monarch issue coinage with his own image, rather than that of the Emperor. This was in the time of the Frankish king Theodebert I, who found himself at war with Justinian in Italy in 546-8. This singular display of independence on the part of a "barbarian" monarch was, noted Pirenne, bewailed by Procopius, who viewed it as a deplorable sign of decadence and decline. The next time a Germanic king showed such independence was in the 620s, during the reign of Chlothar (or Chlotar) II. Chlothar II was a contemporary of the Emperor Heraclius, in whose time Byzantium first came into conflict with the Arabs. From the time of Chlothar II onwards, no western monarch would ever again mint coins bearing the image of the Byzantine Emperor.

The significance of this fact was stressed at length by Pirenne. Evidently the impact of the Persian and Arab assaults on Byzantium during the first half of the seventh century was so great that the provinces of the west were able to detach themselves both politically and culturally from the Empire. We know that within the few decades between the 620s and 640s, the Empire lost much of Anatolia, all of Syria, and Egypt – by far the richest and most populous of her provinces. Constantinople herself was besieged by an Arab fleet between 674 and 678 and again in 718.

With the Empire now weakened apparently beyond repair, the Germanic kings of the West, said Pirenne, began to assert their independence. This was signaled by the minting of coins bearing their own images; and it was to end in the formal re-establishment of the Western Empire under a Germanic king – Charles the Great, king of the Franks. Thus for Pirenne the detachment of the West from the East, politically, culturally and religiously, was a direct consequence of the arrival on the world stage of Islam. "Without Mohammed," said Pirenne, "Charlemagne is inconceivable."

LATE ANTIQUITY ACCORDING TO CONTEMPORARY ACCOUNTS

P irenne's conclusions were the result of many years' research.
As a historian he was well aware of the importance of archaeology, and he did employ archaeological evidence, particularly with
regard to coinage and its development. Yet, as a product of his age,
he was still more inclined to emphasize written history; and it was
primarily from medieval and late classical documentary material that
he drew his conclusions. In the century before his time more and more
texts of the fifth, sixth and seventh centuries had become available
and translated into modern languages, and these are quoted at length
throughout *Mohammed and Charlemagne*. Perhaps his most important
source is Gregory of Tours (538 - 594), whose description of the social, political and religious life of the period provide a vivid account
of the lives and actions of kings, prelates, and private individuals. Pirenne noted the existence of a flourishing artistic and intellectual life
in the fifth and sixth centuries, and he quotes the work of Boethius,
Cassiodorus, and others as prime examples of the high level of culture
at the time.

He notes the enthusiasm with which the "barbarian" Franks,
Goths and Vandals adopted Roman culture and institutions. He emphasizes the numerical insignificance of the Germanic peoples, and
notes that their languages left virtually no trace on the Latin tongues
of Italy and Spain, and very little trace on the Latin language of Gaul.

He cites the archaeology, as it was then known. The major monuments left by the Goths, Franks and Vandals are called to the witness-
stand.

The evidence of coinage is quoted at some length. Pirenne noted
that the Germanic kings of the fifth and sixth centuries employed gold
currency emblazoned with the image of the Emperor in Constantinople, and he contrasts this with the debased currency of the late seventh to eleventh centuries. Indeed, as he emphasized, from the middle
of the seventh century, coinage largely disappears from Europe and is
replaced by a barter economy.

* * *

Pirenne begins by emphasizing an important point: The barbarians did not simply march into the Empire and appropriate territories; they were invited in as *foederati*, as allies, and very often this is exactly how they behaved – even during the most disturbed century, the fifth. Thirty years after Wallia defeated the Vandals and Alans, the Visigoths again, this time along with the Franks and Burgundians, proved themselves loyal allies of Rome by helping Atius overcome the Huns: thus saving Western Europe from Attila's tyranny. In Pirenne's words, "The military art of the Romans and the valour of the Germans collaborated. Theodoric I, king of the Visigoths, in fulfilling Ataulf's ambition to become the restorer of the Empire, was slain."[1] Crucially, he notes that in these years, "if the Barbarians had wished to destroy the Empire they had only to agree among themselves, and they must have succeeded. But they did not wish to destroy it."[2]

When, about three decades later, the Western Empire was actually abolished, it was not, as some have imagined, an earth-shattering event. In fact, the abolition went almost unnoticed and was merely, in the words of Trevor-Roper, "a political event."[3] This, said Pirenne, was an internal *coup d'état*, not the destruction of an empire. Odoacer, who now became king of Italy, was a barbarian, it is true, but he was not the ruler of a separate tribe or people, he was a commander of the Imperial forces. And it was as commander of those forces that he dismissed Romulus Augustulus and sent the Imperial insignia back to Constantinople. Zeno, the Emperor of the East, "went so far as to recognize Odoacer as a patrician of the Empire." The simple fact is, "nothing was changed; Odoacer was an Imperial functionary."[4] To those who, in spite of all the evidence, continued to insist that the abolition of the Western Empire was an epoch-making event, Pirenne noted that just over a decade later, the Eastern Emperor contrived to have Odoacer himself removed from office. He sent Theodoric, king of the Ostrogoths, into Italy, after granting him the title of patrician of Rome. Finally, in 493, when Odoacer was captured and assassinated, Theodoric, being "duly authorized" by Zeno, took over the government of Italy. He remained king of his own people, the Ostrogoths, but not of the Italians. These he governed as a functionary of the Emperor.

It is true, of course, that by the end of the fifth century the whole

1 Henri Pirenne, *Mohammed and Charlemagne* (English ed., London, 1938), p. 31
2 Ibid.
3 Trevor-Roper, op cit., p. 71
4 Pirenne, op cit., p. 32

of the territory of the Western Empire was de facto ruled by barbarian kings: Ostrogoths in Italy; Vandals in Africa; Seuves in Galicia; Visigoths in Spain and Gaul south of the Loire; Burgundians in the valley of the Rhone, and Franks in the rest of Gaul. If they had really wished to extirpate Roman society, culture and tradition, they were now in a position to do so. But, as Pirenne emphasized again and again, they did not. On the contrary, over the next century and a half they did everything in their power to preserve Roman civilization, fostering its language, art, law, custom, architecture and learning. Indeed, the cultural impact of the newcomers upon the lands of the Western Empire was, with the exception of some outlying regions such as Britain, the Rhineland and Bavaria, where the Roman or Romanized population was largely replaced, was minimal. In the other regions, in Italy, Gaul, Spain and North Africa, the Barbarians formed a tiny ruling minority, which depended on the vastly superior indigenous population for almost everything. And by the middle of the sixth century intermarriage between the numerically superior Romans and the Barbarians became common, with the result that in a very short time the Germans began to lose all that made them distinct from the great mass of the Romans. Pirenne stressed the extreme superficiality of their cultural impact upon western Europe. Their languages left no trace at all in the Latin-based languages of Italy or Spain, and a paltry 300 words in French.[5] And the fact that any trace was left in French is perchance explained by the common border Gaul shared with the German homelands – a border many hundreds of miles long. Even without a Germanic invasion, the peoples of Gaul would have picked up some German words.

The Germans, Pirenne noted, were as swift to embrace Roman law as they were the Latin language. By the start of the sixth century, no trace of Germanic law survived anywhere in western Europe, except among the Anglo-Saxons in Britain and those Germans who remained east of the Rhine.[6]

As well as sharing in the language and culture, Pirenne found that the Germans seem to have participated in the general moral laxity which is said to have characterized Roman society in late antiquity.[7]

The virtually complete Romanization is perhaps illustrated most graphically in the case of Theodoric, king of the Ostrogoths and ruler

---

5 Ibid., p. 40

6 H. Brunner, *Deutsche Rechtsgeschichte*, Vol. 1 (2nd ed., Leipzig, 1906), p. 504

7 Pirenne, op cit., p. 42

of Italy between 493 and 526. At the age of seven, his father gave him as hostage to the Emperor,[8] and he was educated in Constantinople until he was eighteen years of age. "Zeno made him magister militum and patrician, and in 474 even went so far as to adopt him. He married an imperial princess. In 484 the Emperor made him consul. Then, after a campaign in Asia Minor, a statue was raised to him in Constantinople. His sister was lady-in-waiting to the Empress."[9]

In 536 Evermud, his son-in-law, surrendered without even token resistance to Belisarius, preferring to live as a patrician in Constantinople rather than defend the cause of his fellow Barbarians.[10] His daughter Amalasuntha was completely Romanized.[11] Theodahat, his son-in-law, boasted that he was a follower of Plato.[12]

Other "Barbarian" rulers were comparable. Thus Pirenne found that among the Burgundians the noble figure of Gondebaud (480-516), who "in 472, after the death of Ricimer, succeeded to him as patrician of the Emperor Olybrius, and on the death of the latter had Glycerius made Emperor. ... According to Schmidt, he was highly cultivated, eloquent, and learned, was interested in theological questions, and was constantly in touch with Saint Avitus."

"It was the same among the Vandal kings. And among the Visigoths, the same development may be remarked. Sidonius praises the culture of Theodoric II. Among his courtiers he mentions the minister Leo, historian, jurist and poet, and Lampridius, professor of rhetoric and poet. It was Theodoric II who in 455 made Avitus Emperor. These kings were entirely divorced from the old traditions of their peoples...

"And among the Franks there was the royal poet Chilperic.

"As time went on the process of Romanization became accentuated. Gautier remarks that after Genseric the Vandal kings re-entered the orbit of the Empire. Among the Visigoths, Romanization made constant progress. By the end of the 6th century Arianism had everywhere disappeared."[13]

* * *

8 L. Hartmann, *Das Italienische Königreich*, Vol. 1, p. 64 (in *Geschichte Italiens* in Mittelalter, Vol. 1)

9 Pirenne, op cit., pp. 43-4

10 Hartmann, op cit, Vol. 1, p. 261

11 Ibid. p. 233

12 Procopius, ed. Dewing (The Loeb Classical Library), vol. III, pp. 22-24

13 Pirenne, op cit., p. 44

Pirenne stressed that the Germanic kings were national kings only to their own peoples. Their Roman subjects, who were nominally at least still subjects of the Emperor in Constantinople, were ruled by Roman law and by their own institutions. "For the Romans they [the Germanic kings] were Roman generals to whom the Emperor had abandoned the government of the civil population. It was as Roman generals that they approached the Romans, and they were proud to bear the title on such occasions: we have only to recall the cavalcade of Clovis when he was created honorary consul. Under Theodoric an even simpler state of affairs prevailed. He was really a Roman viceroy. He promulgated not laws but edicts only.

> "The Goths constituted the army merely. All the civil magistrates were Roman, and as far as possible the entire Roman administration was preserved. The Senate still existed. But all the power was concentrated in the king and his court ... Theodoric assumed merely the title of rex, as though he wished his Barbarian origin to be forgotten. Like the Empress, he lived in Ravenna. The division of the provinces was retained, with their duces, rectores, praesides, and the municipal constitution with its curiales and defensores, and the fiscal organization. Theodoric struck coins, but in the name of the Emperor. He adopted the name of Flavius, a sign that he had adopted the Roman nationality. Inscriptions call him semper Augustus, propagator Romani nominis. The king's guard was organized on the Byzantine model, and so was all the ceremonial of the court. The organization of the judiciary was entirely Roman, even for the Goths; and the Edict of Theodoric was thoroughly Roman. There were no special laws for the Goths. As a matter of fact, Theodoric opposed the private wars of the Goths, and their Germanic barbarism. The king did not protect the national law of his people."[14]

And so it goes on. Pirenne notes that under Theodoric the Goths constituted the garrisons of the cities, who were in receipt of a salary, and they were forbidden to undertake civil employment. "They could not exert the slightest influence upon the Government, apart from those who, with the Romans, constituted the king's entourage." They were, notwithstanding the fact that their king was the ruler of the

---

14 Ibid. pp. 46–7

land, "in reality foreigners, though well-paid foreigners." They were a military caste, whose profession furnished them with a comfortable livelihood.

Even among the Vandals of North Africa, the only Germanic people – apart from the Anglo-Saxons of England – who entered the empire as real invaders, the Roman system of government prevailed. Genseric was not a Roman official like Theodoric, but his entire governmental system was Roman, or became Roman. "He struck coins with the image of Honorius. The inscriptions were Roman. Genseric's establishment at Carthage was like Theodoric's in Ravenna: there was a *palatium.* ..."[15] It seems that the Vandal kings even continued to send presentations of oil to Rome and Constantinople.[16] Cultural life was unchanged. "Under Genseric the *termi* of Tunis was constructed. Literature was still practiced. Victor Tonnennensis still believed in the immortality of the Empire."[17]

Spain and Gaul presented a similar picture. "Among the Visigoths, before the conquest of Clovis, the kings lived in Roman fashion in their capital of Toulouse, and later, in Toledo. The Visigoths established in accordance with the rules of 'hospitality' were not regarded as juridically superior to the Romans. The king addressed his subjects as a whole as *populus noster.*"[18] Everything about the Visigothic kingship was Roman. "The king appointed all his agents. There were both Germanic and Roman dignitaries at his court, but the latter were by far the more numerous. The prime minister of Euric and Alaric II, Leo of Narbonne, combined the functions of *quaestor sacri palatii* and *magister officiorum* of the Imperial court. The king had no bodyguard of warriors, but *domestici* of the Roman type. The dukes of the provinces and the *comites* of the cities were mainly Romans."

"In the cities the *curia* was retained, with a *defensor* ratified by the king. ... For a time the Visigoths appear to have had, in the *millenarius*, a separate magistrate, like the Ostrogoths. But under Euric they were already amenable to the jurisdiction of the *comes*, who presided in the Roman fashion with the assistance of *assessores*, who were legists. There was not the faint-

---

15 Ibid. p. 48

16 Albertini, "Ostrakon byzantin de Négrine (Numidie)," in *Cinquantenaire de la Faculte des Letteres d'Alger*, (1932), pp. 53-62

17 Pirenne, op cit., pp. 48-9

18 Ibid. p. 49

est trace of Germanism in the organization of the tribunal."[19]

Pirenne goes on to note that the Code of Euric, drawn up in 475 with the purpose of regulating relations between the Goths and the Romans, was "completely Romanized," whilst the Breviary of Alaric (507), which affected the Romans, was "an example of almost purely Roman law." "The Roman taxes were still collected, and the monetary system was also Roman."[20] Yet this was not all, for, "As time went on, the Romanization became more marked." Whilst, "At first the royal insignia were Germanic ... these were later replaced by Roman insignia. ... The old military character of the Barbarians was disappearing."[21] Not only were the Germans under the influence of the Romans with whom they lived, they were constantly under fresh influences deriving from Constantinople. All the signs, Pirenne notes, were that the Visigoth monarchy "was evolving in the direction of the Byzantine system."[22]

So it was too among the Burgundians. After obtaining possession of Lyons, they were on the best of terms with the Empire. Their kings were completely Romanized. "Their courts were full of poets and rhetoricians. King Sigismond boasted that he was a soldier of the Empire, and declared that his country was part of the Empire."[23] These kings had a *quaestor Palatii* and *domesticii*. Sigismond was a tool of Byzantium, who received the title of patrician from the Emperor Anastasius. The Burgundi fought against the Visigoths as soldiers of the Emperor.

> "Thus, they regarded themselves as belonging to the Empire. They reckoned their dates from the accession of the consul — that is to say, of the Emperor; the king was magister militum in the Emperor's name.

> "In other respects the royal power was absolute and unique. It was not divided; when the king had several sons he made them viceroys. The court was peopled mainly by Romans. There was not a trace of warrior bands; there were pagi or civitates,

---

19 Ibid. p. 50
20 Ibid. p. 51
21 Ibid.
22 Ibid. p. 52
23 Hartmann, op cit, Vol. 1, pp. 218-9

with a *comes* over them. He had beside him, in order to administer justice, a *judex deputatus*, who was likewise appointed by the king, and who dispensed justice in accordance with the Roman usages."[24]

Even the Frankish Merovingians, whose territories stretched far into the German heartlands east of the Rhine, were thoroughly Roman in their laws and administration. "The Frankish State, until its submission to the Carolingians, was essentially Neustrian and Roman, from the basin of the Seine to the Pyrenees and the sea. However, the Franks who had established themselves there were very few in numbers."[25] Among the Merovingians, nearly all if not all the king's agents were recruited among the Gallo-Romans. Even the best of the generals of that period, Mummolus, appears to have been a Gallo-Roman.[26] "Even in the governmental offices by which he was surrounded the king had Gallo-Roman *referendarii*."[27]

All of these kings and monarchies were immensely wealthy, and it was a wealth they employed not only in military enterprise but also in patronage of the arts and literature, as we shall see. In Pirenne's words, "No prince of the West, before the 13th century, can have been so rich in money as these kings. The description of their treasuries calls up the image of a river of gold."[28] "To regard them, as they have been regarded, merely as great landed proprietors is a manifest error, of which the only explanation is that they have been compared with [and equated with] the kings who came after them. But the fact is that owing to their wealth in money they were far more akin to the Byzantine kings than to Charlemagne."[29] As well as an enormous revenue derived from manufacture and trade in their own domains, they drew enormous subsidies from Byzantium. We know that the Emperor Maurice sent 50,000 gold *solidi* to Childebert as payment for his alliance against the Lombards.[30] We note also the enormous dowry given

---

24 Ibid. p. 53

25 Ibid. p. 55

26 Ferdinand Lot, Christian Pfister and Francois L. Ganshof, *Histoire du Moyen Age*, Vol. 1 (Paris, 1929), p. 271

27 Pirenne, op cit, pp. 56–7

28 Ibid. p. 59

29 Ibid.

30 Gregory of Tours, Historia Francorum, vi, 42

to Riguntis in 584,[31] and the 6,000 gold *solidi* of alms given by Childebert to the Abbe of Saint-Germain for the poor. Pirenne notes that
these, along with the munificence of Dagobert I, who covered the apse
of Saint-Denis with silver, "give us some idea of the wealth of the
Frankish kings."[32]

The Ostrogoth and Visigoth kings were even richer.

Another, and crucially important feature of these states, is that
they were secular:

> "The entire administration, in all its phases, was secular." [We
> know that], "Although the kings were generally on good terms
> with the bishops, not one of the latter filled a governmental
> office: and here was one of the great differences between this
> period and the Middle Ages. On the other hand, many of the
> bishops had been royal *referendarii*. Here we have a striking
> contrast with the policy of Charlemagne, which was based on
> the *missi*, half of whom were necessarily bishops, or that of
> Otto, who entrusted the reins of government to the Imperial
> bishops. The fact is that on the morrow of the invasion the la-
> ity … was still educated.

> "The profane Merovingian State was therefore very definitely
> unlike the religious Carolingian State. And the same may be
> said of all the other States: Ostrogothic, Visigothic, Vandal,
> Burgundian. In this respect, then – and this is the essential
> point – the ancient order of things continued. The king him-
> self was a pure layman, and his power did not depend upon
> any religious ceremony."[33]

At a later stage, with the commencement of the real Middle
Ages, this situation changed radically, and the state become "religion-
ized", with kings depending heavily upon the Church both for legiti-
macy and for the day to day running of the state bureaucracy. Why
this occurred is a point of crucial importance, and we shall return to
it at a later stage.

All during the sixth century, and for a time in the seventh, the
Emperor in Constantinople was recognized as master of the world.

---

31 Ibid. vi, 45
32 Pirenne, op cit., p. 60
33 Ibid. p. 61

"... the Barbarian kings regarded him [the Eastern Emperor] as their master, striking his effigy on their coins, and they solicited and obtained titles and favours from him. Justinian adopted Theodebert, as Maurice afterwards adopted Childebert."[34] Even after Justinian's death and the loss of Italy and many other western territories, "the Empire was still the only world-power, and Constantinople was the greatest of all civilized cities."[35] In fact, throughout the fifth and sixth centuries, the lands of the West were undergoing a process of Byzantinization. This process had begun even before the formal abolition of the Western Empire in 476, but gathered pace in the final years of the fifth and during the sixth centuries. "Its [Byzantium's] fashions and its art were spread throughout the West by means of navigation. It obtained a foothold in Rome, where there was a host of Greek monks, and everywhere in Southern Italy. Its influence was perceptible in Spain, and of course throughout Africa. In Gaul the *cellarium fisci* was reminiscent of the Byzantine commerciaries."[36]

Agriculture was changed little or nothing by the invasions. The appearance of the countryside and the cities remained virtually unaltered. Paulinus of Pella, who was ruined by the Gothic invasion, relates that he was saved by a Goth, who bought a small estate which he owned in the neighborhood of Marseilles. "One could hardly wish for a better illustration of the way pillage was followed by social equilibrium. Here was a deserted estate, yet the invaders did not seize it. As soon as the Germans were established in the country in accordance with the rules of *hospitalitas*, society became once more stabilized."[37] And in fact the great Gallo-Roman and Hispano-Roman estates survived. "There were still enormous *latifundia*. ... The great landowners retained their villae, their fortresses." Even in Africa, the Vandals merely replaced the old proprietors: they lived in the Roman villas. Everywhere these estates remained prosperous. Gregory of Tours mentions one Chrodinus who established villas, planted vineyards, erected farm buildings, and organized estates.[38] In Pirenne's words, "Prestations were always paid in money, which shows that goods were circulating, that they were sold in the open market. There is no sign

---

34 Ibid. p. 63

35 Ibid. p. 73

36 Ibid. pp. 73-4

37 Ibid. p. 75

38 Gregory of Tours, vi, 20

yet of the closed economy of the mediaeval *curtes*."[39] He notes that in Provence during the Merovingian epoch the system of tenure was entirely Roman: "Great quantities of cereals were moved from place to place." In 510 Theodoric sent quantities of corn to Provence on account of the ravages of war in that region.[40] There was a vigorous trade in cereals. Despite of his own enormous resources, Gregory the Great made purchases of grain. In 537-538 a *peregrinus acceptor* made important purchases in Istria. He seems to have been a corn-merchant.[41]

It was the same throughout the former territories of the Western Empire: "Africa, under the Vandals, must have retained the prosperity which was derived from the cultivation of cereals and the olive, since it was still prosperous when the Byzantines returned to it. It does not appear that the aspect of Gaul was in any way less civilized. It seems that the culture of the vine was continued wherever it existed in the time of the Romans. If we read Gregory of Tours we do not by any means obtain the impression of a country in a state of decadence; unless it had been prosperous the landowners could hardly have been so wealthy. "The retention of the Roman *libra* affords indirect proof of the stability of the economic situation."[42]

We learn that on the large estates there existed workshops which produced various goods, including cloth, tools and pottery of various types. These workshops had already existed during the later years of the Empire.

"The population had retained the form which had been impressed upon it by the fiscal organization, although this had been greatly diminished by the almost complete curtailment of the military and administrative expenditure. In this respect the Germanic conquest may perhaps have been beneficial to the people. On the whole, the great domain had retained the essential social and economic element. Thanks to the domain, the economic basis of the feudal system already existed. But the subordination of the greater part of the population to the great landowners was manifested as yet only in private law. The *senior* had not yet interposed himself between the king

39 Pirenne, op cit., p. 77

40 R. Buchner, *Die Provence in Merowingischer Zeit* (Stuttgart, 1933), p. 30, n.1

41 Cassiodorus, *Variae*, xii, 22. M.G.H. SS. Antiq., Vol. XII, p. 378

42 Pirenne, op cit. p. 78

and his subjects. Moreover, although the constitution of society was predominantly agrarian, it was not exclusively so. Commerce and the cities still played a considerable part in the general economic, social, and intellectual life of the age."[43]

* * *

International commerce seems to have been vibrant during this period; and the Mediterranean still acted, as it had in the Age of the Empire, as a conduit for goods and ideas. Merchandise of all kinds, but especially luxury items, flooded into western Europe from the East. The great bulk of this trade continued, as it had been under the Empire, to be carried on by Syrians. Great trading companies and families, with depots in Alexandria, Rome, Spain, Gaul and Britain, as well as on the Danube, were a vital element in the economic life of the time. "The invasions," says Pirenne, "did not in any way alter the situation. Genseric, by his piracies [in the first half of the fifth century], may have hindered navigation a little, but at all events it was as active as ever when he had disappeared:

> "Salvian (d. circa 484), doubtless generalizing from what he had seen at Marseilles, spoke of the *negociatorum et Syricorum omnium turbas quae majorem ferme civitatum universarum partem occupant.*

> "This Syrian expansion is confirmed by the archaeologists, and the texts are even more significant.

> "In the sixth century there were large numbers of Orientals in Southern Gaul. The life of Saint Caesar, Bishop of Arles (d. 524), states that he composed hymns in Greek and Latin for the people."[44]

There were also many Orientals in northern Gaul, and we have Gregory of Tours testimony to the existence of Greek merchants in Orleans. These advanced, singing, to meet the king.[45] Large numbers of Syrians, it seems, settled in Gaul, where they are mentioned

---

43 Ibid., p. 79

44 Ibid., p. 80

45 Gregory of Tours, viii, 1

in many inscriptions of the fifth and sixth centuries.[46] One of these is in the chapel of Saint Eloi in Eure, near the mouth of the Seine.[47] Pirenne notes that the latter "was doubtless trading with Britain."[48]

As we shall see, the links between the Byzantine East and Britain under the Anglo-Saxons, were spectacularly confirmed by the discoveries made at the Sutton Hoo burials, discoveries made after Pirenne's death.

In Gaul, Gregory of Tours mentions a negotiator of Bordeaux, who possessed a great house in which was a chapel containing relics.[49] Another such merchant was Eusebius of Paris, who purchased the Episcopal dignity and then, finding fault with his predecessor's *scola*, constituted one of his own, which comprised only Syrians.[50] Pirenne notes that the population of Narbonne in 589 consisted of Goths, Romans, Jews, Greeks and Syrians.[51]

Evidence indicates that there were substantial communities of Syrian traders throughout Western Europe during the fifth and sixth centuries. Procopius mentions, for example, the existence in Naples, during the time of Justinian, of a great Syrian merchant, Antiochus, who was the leader of the Roman party in that city.[52]

As well as Syrians, Greeks and Egyptians, there were many, very many, Jews. These were particularly numerous in Spain, but there were also large communities of them in Italy, Gaul, and even in Germany along the Rhine. Pirenne notes for example that when Naples was besieged by Belisarius, the Jews formed a great part of the merchant population of the city.[53] The existence of sizeable Jewish communities in Ravenna, Palermo, Terracina, and Cagliari, is also mentioned by various writers.[54] The "immense majority" of the Jews, both in Italy and elsewhere, were engaged in commerce.

On the whole, there is a superabundance of evidence to show that during the fifth and sixth centuries, trade within the territories of the

---

46 Edmond Leblant, *Inscriptions chrétiennes de la Gaule antérieures au VIIIe siecle*, Vol. 1 (Paris, 1856), pp. 207 and 328

47 Ibid. p. 205, no. 125

48 Pirenne, op cit., p. 81

49 Gregory of Tours, vii, 31

50 Ibid., x, 26

51 Pirenne, op cit., p. 81

52 Procopius, v, 8, 21

53 Pirenne, op cit., pp. 82-3

54 Ibid., p. 83

Western Empire was of great importance, and that some of this trade was carried on by native merchants, some of whom "were assuredly very wealthy." Pirenne notes that "it is a very long time before we hear of such wealthy merchants again."[55] Some of these merchants, like the Syrians, Greeks and Jews, were involved in the sea-borne trade with the Eastern Mediterranean; a trade that was apparently lively and even growing. "I think we can say that navigation was at least as active as under the Empire."[56]

What did this trade bring into western Europe? It brought a great variety of things, but most especially luxury items. It also brought many of the essentials of civilized life – including, crucially, large quantities of papyrus from Egypt. Thus Pirenne notes that the Royal Diplomas of the Merovingian kings, preserved in the Archives Nationales of Paris, are written on papyrus.[57] The disappearance of papyrus in Western Europe, and its replacement by the extremely expensive parchment, is one of the crucial markers that stand at the dividing line between the classical civilization of late antiquity and that of the medieval age. This occurred, as we shall see, in the middle of the seventh century.

Contrary to popular opinion, which imagined a decline in urban life after the dissolution of the Western Empire, the cities, said Pirenne, actually prospered under the Germanic kings:

"The cities [of this time] were both ecclesiastical and commercial in character. Even in the cities of the North, such as Meaux, there were street with arcades which were sometimes prolonged into the suburb. These arcaded houses must have given the cities an Italian appearance, even in the north. They doubtless served to shelter shops, which were generally grouped together; according to Gregory of Tours, this was especially the case in Paris.

"In these cities, besides the merchants, lived the artisans, concerning whom we have very little information. Saint Caesarius speaks of their presence at Arles, in the 6th century. The glass industry seems to have been important; the Merovingian

55 Ibid., p. 103

56 Ibid., p. 95

57 Ibid., p. 92

tombs contain many objects made of glass."[58]

Pirenne cites evidence which convinced him that the cities of the West during this period remained as large as they had been during the later Empire: "The cities had, of course, suffered from the invasions. Bridges had broken down and had been replaced by bridges of boats. But all the cities still existed; moreover, the bishops had restored them. And there is no doubt that just as they were the centres of civil and religious administration, they were also the permanent commercial centres of the country. Here again the ancient economy was continued. We find nothing resembling the great fairs of the Middle Ages – such as those of Champagne."[59] Again, "On reading Gregory of Tours ... we obtain the impression of a period of urban commerce. The *conventus* of the merchants were held in the cities. We hear nothing of the countryside. It is certainly an error, as Waitz has already pointed out, to regard the innumerable localities whose names were impressed by the *monetarii* on the Merovingian coins as the sites of markets. What we do find existing in the Merovingian period, as in antiquity, are *portus* – that is to say, *étapes* and wharves or landing-places, but not markets. The king levied market-tolls (*tonlieux*) in the cities and in the *portus*. These were the ancient Roman market-tolls, payable in the same places."[60]

* * *

One of the defining characteristics of the medieval age was its relative poverty. The money-based system that had prevailed under the Roman Empire disappeared, along with international trade; and this was replaced by local, barter-based economies. There was very little money in circulation, and whatever there was, tended to be silver, rather than gold, as under the Empire. What, then, was the state of the monetary system under the Germanic kings? Did it display any of the characteristics of the feudal age? According to Pirenne, it most certainly did not. As a matter of fact, he claimed, the monetary system in western Europe seems to have been affected little or not at all by the Germanic invasions. The Germanic kings continued to use the Roman gold solidus, and continued to strike coins bearing the

58 Pirenne, op cit., p. 103
59 Ibid., p. 104
60 Ibid., p. 105

effigies of the Emperors.[61] "Nothing attests more clearly to the persistence of the economic unity of the Empire. It was impossible to deprive it of the benefit of monetary unity. … [in the fifth and sixth centuries] The Syrian navigators, on disembarking in the ports of the Tyrrhenian Sea, found there the currency to which they had been accustomed in the ports of the Aegean Sea. What is more, the new Barbarian kingdoms adopted, in their coinage, the changes introduced in the Byzantine currency."[62] All during these centuries, and right up until the middle of the seventh century, the central currency was the gold solidus.

Gold alone was the official currency during the fifth and sixth centuries, a point that Pirenne stresses again and again. "The monetary system of the Barbarians was that of Rome."[63] This was in stark contrast to that of the Middle Ages which, beginning in the Carolingian period, was based on silver, and silver alone. "Silver monometallism" is the term used by Pirenne to describe it.

The Anglo-Saxons constituted the only exception to the rule: Among them silver was the principal metal employed.[64] We note however that in Britain, and only there, the Barbarian Invasions effectively terminated Roman civilization – or, at the very least, produced a far more definitive break with the past than occurred in Gaul, Italy and Spain. Latin was replaced by a Germanic language, and Christianity was – apart from in the far west – extinguished. Yet even in Britain a few gold coins were struck in the southern part of the country; that is to say, as Pirenne remarks, "in those parts which maintained commercial relations with Gaul."[65] There is also reason to believe that these coins were the work of Merovingian minters.[66]

The Merovingian kings themselves struck pseudo-Imperial coins, the series of which closes with the reign of Heraclius (610-641), the first Emperor to come into hostile contact with the Arabs.[67]

---

61 Gunnar Mickwitz, Geld und Wirtschaft im *Romischen Reich des IV. Jahrhunderts nach Christi* (Helsingfors, 1932), p. 190

62 Ibid., p. 107

63 Ibid., p. 108

64 Ibid.

65 Ibid.

66 Arthur Engel and Raymond Serrure, *Traité de numismatique du Moyen Age*, Vol. 1 (Paris, 1891), p. 177

67 Maurice Prou, *Catalogue des monnaies mérovingiennes d'Autun*, (Paris, 1888), pp. xxvii and xxviii

The significance of this cannot be overstressed, and we shall return to the topic when we come to examine the re-establishment of the Western Empire under the Ottonian kings of the mid-tenth century – a full three centuries after the Germanic rulers of the West had symbolically terminated their allegiance to Constantinople by ceasing to place the Emperor's image on their coins. This western Roman currency can, as a rule, be distinguished at a glance from the Imperial currency. Yet while differing from the coinage struck in the East, they bear a close resemblance to one another; and it is rarely possible to say whether they were struck by the Visigoths, the Burgundians, or the Franks. Only rarely before the early seventh century did the name of a Germanic king appear on a coin, and the first instance of this occurred (to the horror of Procopius) when Theodebert I was making war in Italy against Justinian, in 539-540. These coins are in fact so much finer than any other Frankish issues that experts believe Theodebert had them struck in Italy. It was only in the reign of Chlothar II (584 – 630) that the name of the king replaced that of the Emperor in the mints of Gaul. The formula *Victoria Augustorum* was replaced by *Victoria Chlotarii.*[68]

Throughout the fifth and sixth centuries large amounts of gold coins were minted, in numerous locations, throughout Gaul, Spain and Italy. "These constant mintages," says Pirenne, "and what we know from other sources concerning the kings' wealth in gold, and the wealth of the Church and of private individuals, proves that there was a very considerable stock of gold in the West; and yet there were no gold mines, and we cannot suppose that much gold can have been derived from auriferous sands and gravels. How then can we speak of 'natural economy' in the presence of these large amounts of liquid treasure?[69]

An idea of the amount of gold in circulation can be had not only from the archaeological finds, but from documentary evidence. Thus we hear that Bishop Baldwin of Tours distributed 20,000 gold *solidi* to the poor, whilst gold is mentioned as used profusely in the decoration of garments. There was, as might be expected, a great deal of gold in the possession of private individuals, as is proved by the continual confiscations of gold by the king.[70]

The Gothic and Frankish kings put their treasure to good use. It

---

68 Ibid. p. xxxix
69 Pirenne, op cit., p. 111
70 Ibid.

provided opulent dowries for their daughters, gifts to friends, and lavish alms to the poor. They also lent money at interest, as one Frankish king is on record as doing with the Bishop of Verdun. Pensions were paid to needy ecclesiastics, and lavish churches were raised and decorated. Mention here should be made of the apse of Saint Denis, which was covered in silver. There were in fact great quantities of currency in circulation, and people sought to invest it to their advantage. This was in fact a proto-capitalist economy. Pirenne quotes a case illustrating what he describes as "the trade in money." A Jewish man named Armentarius, together with a co-religionist and two Christians, came to Tours to demand the securities they had advanced to the *vicarius* Injuriosus and Count Eonomius, who had promised to repay the amounts with interest (*cum usuris*). These "tax-farmers" had also lent money to the *tribunus* Medard, who was also requested to make payment. The three powerful debtors invited their creditors to a banquet, in course of which they were set upon and assassinated. Pirenne emphasizes the striking feature that these businessmen lent their money at interest: *cum usuries*. "This is a proof, and a proof of great importance, of the fact that under the Merovingians interest was regarded as lawful. Everybody lent money at interest, even the king, who authorized a loan, at interest, to the city of Verdun."[71]

Here again we see a situation quite different to that which pertained in the Middle Ages, when the Church forbade the practice of usury. It is true, of course, that even during the period in question, the sixth century, the Church forbade the taking of interest; but it is equally evident that as yet it lacked the authority to enforce the ban. Prelates might berate kings and private citizens who took interest, but they could do little more than berate. The Church's influence was of course important; and it is true that most Christians did heed the warnings of the priests. Even at this time most bankers and moneylenders were Jews. But not everyone involved in this kind of activity was; and this tells us a great deal about the time.

It was a time of wealth; it was a time of opulence. Cities, or at least towns, flourished, as they had under the Caesars, and life continued remarkably unchanged from the latter epoch. It was a money and not a barter economy; and the fundamental unit was the gold *solidus*. With this wealth luxury items were imported into the west in great quantities: fabrics, jewelry, spices, wines, and very many other of the things which made life pleasant for the urban elite.

---

71 Ibid., p. 115

Where then, Pirenne asked, did all this wealth originate? Some at least came from Byzantium, and we know that on occasion the Emperor sent subsidies of up to 50,000 *solidi* to individual rulers in the West. Some also must have been booty taken in wars. Yet we must agree with Pirenne that, such was the opulence of the western kingdoms, that "commerce alone could have brought this continual stream of gold into the West."[72]

And here we must stress another point: The wealth of the Germanic kingdoms, by the end of the sixth century, showed no signs whatever of exhaustion. On the contrary, if anything, these states were becoming ever more wealthy and powerful; a wealth and power which, as we shall see, brought with it a flowering of literature and the arts. This did not seem to be an age of decadence, in any way whatsoever; but an age which showed every sign of being the start of a new flowering of civilization.

This was an epoch that could scarcely have been more different from the Middle Ages. Nothing marks it as an age of barter: "All the features of the old economic life were there: the preponderance of Oriental navigation, the importation of Oriental products, the organization of the ports, of the *tonlieu* and the impost, the circulation and the minting of money, the lending of money at interest, the absence of small markets, and the persistence of a constant commercial activity in the cities, where there were merchants by profession. There was, no doubt, in the commercial domain as in other departments of life, a certain retrogression due to the 'barbarization' of manners, but there was no definite break with what had been the economic life of the Empire. The commercial activities of the Mediterranean continued with singular persistence. And the same may be said of agriculture, which, no doubt, was still the basis of the economic life, but beside which commerce continued to play an essential part, both in daily life – by the sale of spices, clothing, etc – and in the life of the State – by virtue of the resources which the *tonlieu* procured for it – and in social life, owing to the presence of merchants and the existence of credit."[73]

72 Ibid., p. 112
73 Ibid. pp. 116-7

A LINGERING DEATH OR A
VIOLENT END?

I nitial reaction to Pirenne's thesis was muted, and what reaction there was tended to be hostile. This is not surprising, given the fact that, should what Pirenne was saying be true, the reputation of virtually every medieval scholar then alive was at risk. It cannot be stressed too forcefully just how radically against the grain of contemporary academic thought Pirenne went. Far from seeing the Arabs as the destroyers of classical civilization, scholars had increasingly, over the previous half century, come to regard them as its saviors. More and more they had come to believe that whatever classical learning survived in Europe during the three or four dark centuries between the seventh and eleventh, had done so only though the good offices of the Arabs. This tendency to applaud Arab civilization is traceable to the Enlightenment, though the ground was arguably laid during the Reformation, when Protestant northern Europe detached itself politically and ideologically from the Catholic south. After this, historians in (especially) the English-speaking world came to see the Christian (and therefore Catholic) Middle Ages as a time of darkness and superstition. With the Enlightenment, this tendency spread to France; and among the contemporaries of Voltaire and Diderot, the Islamic world was increasingly viewed as something altogether more cultured – and exotic – than the "dark and obscure" civilization which seemed to have taken hold of Europe after the fall of Rome. Furthermore, by the middle of the eighteenth century scholars had come to realize just how much medieval Europe, from the late tenth century onwards, owed to the Arabs. Scholars discovered that a whole plethora of technical and scientific terms, words such as algebra, alcohol, alkali, antimony, alembic, zenith, nadir, amalgam, etc, were of Arabic origin.[1] They read of European scholars of the tenth century onwards, such as Gerbert of Aurillac, who went to great lengths in their quest to acquire the learning of the Arabs and the Moors. Indeed the more they investigated, the more profound the influence of Islamic civilization seemed to have been. Christendom, it appeared, had been little more than a backwater in the tenth and eleventh centuries, whereas the "House of Islam"

---

1 R. A. Newhall, *The Crusades* (London, 1927), pp. 90-94. See also the works of H. A. R. Gibb.

seemed to be enjoying a Golden Age. In time, some scholars began to see almost all European science and learning as an Arab creation, or at least something that appeared only under the influence of the Arabs. This opinion took root in the nineteenth century, and by the early years of the twentieth century had become, in some quarters at least, part of received wisdom. Take for example the words of one prominent historian and social anthropologist in 1919:

> "It was under the influence of the Arabian and Moorish revival of culture, and not in the fifteenth century, that the real Renaissance took place. Spain, not Italy, was the cradle of the rebirth of Europe. After steadily sinking lower and lower into barbarism, it [Europe] had reached the darkest depths of ignorance and degradation when the cities of the Saracenic world, Baghdad, Cairo, Cordova, Toledo, were growing centres of civilization and intellectual activity."[2]

Again, "It is highly probable that but for the Arabs modern European civilization would not have arisen at all; it is absolutely certain that but for them, it would not have assumed the character which has enabled it to transcend all previous phases of evolution."[3] In support of these statements, the writer lists a number of Arab inventions, discoveries and innovations. He refers to the astronomers Al-Zarkyal and Al-Farani, who postulated that the orbits of the planets was elliptical rather than circular, as Ptolemy believed.[4] He notes how Ibn Sina (Avicenna) is said to have employed an air thermometer, and Ibn Yunis to have used a pendulum for the measurement of time.[5] He points to the work of Al-Byruny, who travelled forty years to collect mineralogical specimens, and to that of Ibn Baitar, who collected botanical specimens from the whole Muslim world, and who compared the floras of India and Persia with those of Greece and Spain.[6] He lauds the Arab achievement of having introduced the zero into mathematics, and points to the Arab invention of algebra, which was to revolutionize mathematics.[7] As if all this were not enough, he asserts that the Arabs

---

2 Robert Briffault, *The Making of Humanity* (London, 1919), pp. 188-189

3 Ibid., p. 190

4 Ibid., pp. 190-191

5 Ibid., p. 191

6 Ibid., p. 198

7 Ibid., p. 194

invented the empirical method itself, which stands at the foundation of all modern science, and points to the achievements of Arab chemists, or alchemists, whose "organized passion for research … led them to the invention of distillation, sublimation, filtration, to the discovery of alcohol, or nitric acid and sulphuric acids (the only acid known to the ancients was vinegar), of the alkalis, of the salts of mercury, of antimony and bismuth, and laid the basis of all subsequent chemistry and physical research."[8]

Warming to his theme, the writer continues:

"The incorruptible treasures and delights of intellectual culture were accounted by the princes of Baghdad, Shiraz and Cordova, the truest and proudest pomps of their courts. But it was not as a mere appendage to their princely vanity that the wonderful growth of Islamic science and learning was fostered by their patronage. They pursued culture with the personal ardour of an overmastering craving. Never before and never since, on such a scale, has the spectacle been witnessed of the ruling classes throughout the length and breadth of a vast empire given over entirely to a frenzied passion for the acquirement of knowledge. Learning seemed to have become with them the chief business of life. … caravans laden with manuscripts and botanical specimens plied from Bokhara to the Tigris, from Egypt to Andalusia. … To every mosque was attached a school; wazirs vied with their masters in establishing public libraries, endowing colleges, founding bursaries for impecunious students. … It was under the influence of the Arabian and Moorish revival of culture, and not in the fifteenth century, that the real Renaissance took place. Spain, not Italy, was the cradle of the rebirth of Europe. After steadily sinking lower and lower into barbarism, it had reached the darkest depths of ignorance and degradation when the cities of the Saracenic world, Baghdad, Cairo, Cordova, Toledo, were growing centres of civilization and intellectual activity. It was there the new life arose which was to grow into a new phase of human evolution. From the time when the influence of their culture made itself felt, began the stirring of a new

8 Ibid., p. 197

life."[9]

These words were written a year after the end of the First World War and just over a decade before the launch of Pirenne's radically alternative viewpoint: they would have been endorsed by the great majority of professional academics at the time – and indeed they are endorsed by the majority of academics to this day, as a whole plethora of recent publications make perfectly clear. Thus David Levering Lewis' *God's Crucible: Islam and the Making of Europe, 570-1215* (2008), echoes Briffault's sentiments to the letter, as does John Freely's *Light from the East: How the Science of Medieval Islam helped shape the Western World* (2010). Along with major works such as these, every year sees the publication of quite literally hundreds of papers in academic publications and the popular media on a similar vein, as well as the appearance of numerous like-minded television documentaries. These are supplemented by countless lectures and symposia expounding an identical viewpoint. As just one example among many we may mention the paper delivered in April, 2010, in London by Dr. Peter Adamson, professor of ancient and medieval philosophy in King's College, London. The title of the lecture, "How the Muslims Saved Civilization: the Reception of Greek Learning in Arabic," speaks for itself.

For what appears to be the majority of academia then, on both sides of the Atlantic, the view is that by the beginning of the seventh century Europe had sunk into a profound Germanic barbarism, from which it had to be rescued by a tolerant and enlightened Islam. This is precisely the view of Robert Briffault and others of the pre-Pirenne epoch. It is true, of course, that not all contemporary academics are in agreement; yet it has to be admitted that the above perspective is still the prevailing one, especially in Europe: which means, of course, that Pirenne's ideas have been generally rejected. The process of how this came about is worth looking at.

The first shots were fired by Alfons Dopsch, who argued that, though classical civilization survived the Barbarian Invasions, and the invaders had indeed made attempts to preserve Roman institutions and learning, still they were unable to save these, which were in any case in terminal decline.[10] The barbarians themselves, he said, inadvertently speeded that decline by their own ignorance of Roman society

---

9 Ibid., p. 188

10 A. Dopsch, *Wirtschaftliche und soziale Grundlagen der europäischen Kulturentwicklung* (Vienna, 1918-20)

and by their frequent internecine wars. Thus, although Roman civilization survived till the seventh century, it was only in a debased and decadent form. The strength and vitality that had made Rome great had long since gone. The Muslims then did not so much destroy classical civilization as put it out of its misery.

Dopsch's critique tended to be echoed by scholars of French and German origin, and throughout the 1940s and 50s there were several further attempts by Continental scholars to rebut particular aspects of Pirenne. As with Dopsch, historians in general have never quite been able to get the notion out of their heads that the Germanic invaders were somehow incapable of being civilized. This was Daniel C. Dennett's approach in his 1948 article, "Pirenne and Muhammad."[11] Dennett, like Dopsch, did not deny that Graeco-Roman civilization and Roman institutions survived in Gaul, Italy and Spain into the late fifth and sixth centuries, but they survived, he said, only in a weakened and enfeebled state. Any major shock to the system was liable to finish them off, and this came, claimed Dennett, in the sixth century, with a series of plagues, famines, and wars, which effectively delivered the coup de grace to classical culture even before the rise of Islam. Indeed, said Dennett, it was the very weakness of classical civilization in Europe and elsewhere that elicited the Islamic Conquests in the first place.

Precisely the same line was taken just four years later by Anne Riising, and indeed by a whole host of authors during the 1950s and '60s.[12] Thus in 1953 one prominent historian could write of the "gradual decline of civilization in Gaul, which had been ongoing since the third century."[13] The said decline, we are informed, "became more rapid in the Merovingian period." "The Franks," the writer explains, "were essentially warriors ... [who] had no interest in urban life."[14] Their kings, we are told, "did not consider the encouragement of trade and commerce by keeping roads and bridges in repair, policing the trade routes, and protecting merchants and their goods, any part of their royal function," and "Although the ancient cities on the Mediterranean coast retained some sea-borne commerce, trade almost disappeared in

11 Daniel C. Dennett, "Pirenne and Muhammad," *Speculum: Journal of Mediaeval Studies*, Vol. XXIII (April 1948), No. 2.

12 Anne Riising, "The fate of Pirenne's thesis on the consequences of Islamic expansion," *Classica et Medievalia* 13 (1952), 87–130

13 Sidney Painter, *A History of the Middle Ages, 284–1500* (Macmillan, 1953), p. 67

14 Ibid., p. 67

the interior. By the end of the Merovingian era, Gaul was essentially an agricultural region with a localized agrarian economy. There was little money in circulation and few traders moved along the roads."[15]

The overwhelming impression given here, and in countless similar and even more recent publications, is of a long and painful decline – a gradual descent into anarchy and illiteracy under the auspices of a barbarous people who had no real understanding or appreciation of civilized life. And though the above writer does concede that, until the time of Gregory of Tours (late sixth century), there was little sign of civilizational decline in Gaul, yet, "after that generation [of Gregory of Tours] disappeared, learning became extremely rare and literacy rather uncommon."[16]

By the 1960s more writers were prepared to take up the cudgels. Thus in 1964 French historian Robert Folz could write that "... the towns of Gaul [of the fifth and sixth centuries] certainly suffered from the economic depression which had characterized the whole of the west from about the third century onwards."[17] Evidence which for Pirenne was of great importance, such as the continued use of gold in coinage, is reinterpreted. "We must not be deceived here by outward appearances," Folz warns. "As in Roman times, Gaul had continued since the fifth century to have a gold standard. But the precious metal had become more and more rare, and was hoarded; from the middle of the seventh century, no more gold coinage was struck. It was replaced by silver, in the form of the *denier* or the *sceatta*, a coin of Anglo-Saxon origin, which gives an early indication of the growing importance of exchange with the north."[18]

So, what for Pirenne was evidence of a sudden and violent break with the past – namely the abandonment of the gold standard and the reorientation of trading relations away from the Mediterranean towards the north – was for Folz simply the logical conclusion of a process that was already at an advanced stage. He admits that, "The trade carried on between west and east by way of the Mediterranean still continued [during the fifth and sixth centuries]. Silks, spices and ivory were unloaded in the ports of Provence to supply the needs of wealthy customers. Olive oil was needed for food and lighting, and Egyptian papyrus was used to write on ... But this was an unbalanced trade,

---

15 Ibid., pp. 67-8

16 Ibid., p. 68

17 Robert Folz, *The Coronation of Charlemagne* (English ed., London, 1974), p. 6

18 Ibid.

which had to be paid for in gold. Its volume continued to decrease; in any case it could not be called very great. The chief middlemen were foreigners, especially Syrians and Jews, the latter being particularly active in the towns of the south – Marseille, Arles and Narbonne."[19]

Interestingly, it is only at this point that Folz mentions Pirenne and his thesis. After providing a brief summary, he asks: "What are we to make of this theory?" There would be no need, he says, to "involve the reader in the controversy surrounding Pirenne's great book," and it would be enough, he says, "to say that his claim cannot be fully substantiated."[20] "I remarked," he continues, "that the bonds between the west and the east had been growing weaker since the third century, and that the west was slowly turning its attention northwards. It is thus impossible to speak of a sudden reversal of the situation resulting from the arrival of the Arabs."[21]

This then was the main thrust of opposition to Pirenne from the 1940s onwards, and it is an argument which has resurfaced with many variants again and again over the past sixty years. By the mid- 1940s it was joined by another and equally perennially recurring theme: namely that the Muslims did not disrupt trade in the Mediterranean at all and that, if anything, their arrival in the mid-seventh century signaled the start of a new age of trading and prosperity. Thus for example in 1947 French historian and numismatist Maurice Lombard argued that Europe benefited from the arrival of Islam (rather than suffered from it) because the Muslim desire for European slaves initiated a lively trade which brought huge amounts of gold to the continent. As proof of this he cited the hoards of Muslim *dirhems* found in Scandinavia and European Russia.[22] In the same vein Scandinavian numismatist Sture Bolin argued that Islamic trade with northern Europe during the eighth to tenth century was the basis of the Carolingian Renaissance, and held that "an examination of the hoards from Carolingian times will show fairly directly how close the connections were between the Frankish and Arab worlds ..."[23]

This argument too was marshaled by Folz: "Mediterranean

19 Ibid., p. 6

20 Ibid., p. 7

21 Ibid.

22 Maurice Lombard, "L'or musulman du VIIe au XIe siècles. Les bases monetaires d'une suprematie économique," *Annales ESC* 2 (1947), 143-60

23 Sture Bolin, "Mohammed, Charlemagne and Ruric," *Scandinavian History Review* 1 (1952).

trade," he assures us, "does not [contrary to Pirenne] appear to have ceased at this point." It may, he concedes, have been slightly impeded by piracy, "But trade between east and west continued nevertheless; it was only the trade-routes that changed."[24] He notes that "From that time onwards [mid-seventh century] silks and spices reached the west via Italy, where they were brought from the great market of Constantinople, or from Moslem Spain, which received them by sea or overland along the African coast route."[25] Folz also argues that the slave-trade, which admittedly brought slaves from Europe to the Islamic world, also became an important source of revenue for the European economies. The end result of all this, he says, is that, "Far from being the cause of a break in the activities of the Mediterranean countries, Islam was more probably responsible for a revival of their trade ..."[26]

Notwithstanding the popularity of this argument, one which is widely heard to this day, it has always had major problems. To begin with, even Pirenne's harshest critics had to admit that many products of Levantine and Oriental manufacture do indeed disappear from western Europe after the mid-seventh century. This is true, for example, of papyrus, as well as of a whole host of foodstuffs, such as spices of various kinds; and it speaks of some disruption at least. Furthermore, the disappearance of gold currency from the mid-seventh century and its replacement by a very much reduced silver coinage also points towards impoverishment and blockade. And even the most enthusiastic Islamophiles could scarcely argue that the "new" trade initiated by Islam, which was concerned almost entirely with the acquisition of European slaves, could be described as a normal commercial activity. Without exception, the slave trade, wherever it occurs, is accompanied by raiding, piracy, and general banditry; and all these things are recorded in Europe from the mid-seventh century onwards.

A further problem for Pirenne's critics was concerned with chronology: the fact that very few of the Muslim coin-hoards found in Scandinavia and Russia could be securely dated before the tenth century. From that time onwards, it was true, fairly large quantities of Islamic coinage occurred, but there was nothing, apparently, before then.[27] That, at least, was the narrative accepted until the 1990s, at

24 Robert Folz, op cit., p. 7

25 Ibid., pp. 7–8

26 Ibid., p. 8

27 See eg. Philip Grierson, "Commerce in the Dark Ages: a critique of the evidence," *Transactions of the Royal Historical Society* (5th series) 9 (1959), 123–40. In view of

which time archaeologists established that at least one major Scandi-navian settlement in Russia, at Staraja Ladoga, was actively trading with the Islamic world in the seventh century; and this was underlined by the discovery of several hoards of Arab coins dating from the mid-seventh century. These are remarkable developments which raise the prospect that the entire chronology of the Viking Age, as well as that of Islamic trading relations with Scandinavia, needs to be radically reconsidered.[28]

But irrespective of when Islamic gold first appeared in northern Europe, European states continued to mint almost all coins in silver – and even these were pitifully scarce in comparison with the number of coins recovered from the Roman and Visigothic/Merovingian peri-ods. In short, as Europe entered the eleventh and twelfth centuries it continued to have a predominantly rural and barter economy. The only conclusion to be drawn was that, notwithstanding the gold reaching the North from the Islamic slave trade, it was insufficient to generate a money-based economy, and the quantity of gold must have been very small in comparison with the quantities arriving from the Near East during the fifth and sixth centuries. These circumstances furthermore gave added weight to the argument that the source of this gold (the buying and selling of slaves) did not represent a normal pattern of trade: the gold was an inducement to piracy – a piracy which, in itself, prevented any normal form of trading and economic activity along the Mediterranean coastlands of Europe.

Another counter-Pirenne argument also suffered from chrono-logical problems: This was the arrival of new technologies and knowl-edge in Europe from the Islamic world. These too however only made an impact in the late tenth and eleventh centuries, and since they do not date from the actual "Dark Age" (seventh to mid-tenth centuries), they are not strictly relevant to Pirenne's thesis and cannot be used in argument against him. Furthermore, even the new technologies of the tenth-eleventh centuries do not necessarily constitute proof of any substantial contact: a single learned or skilled individual might be the means by which a new science or technology is transmitted from one

---

the fact that Muslims were interested in acquiring European slaves from the very beginning – the seventh century – it is seen as somewhat strange that archaeologi-cal evidence for that trade only appears in the tenth century. We shall encounter this puzzling gap of three centuries in the historical process again and again as we proceed.

28 See H. Clarke and B. Ambrosiani, *Towns in the Viking Age* (St. Martin's Press, New York, 1995)

civilization to another, and the spread of such technologies, which undoubtedly occurred in the tenth, eleventh, and twelfth centuries, cannot be regarded as proof of the existence of any meaningful economic
contact between the Christian and Islamic worlds.

Notwithstanding these objections, the arguments of Lombard
and Bolin in particular did have a powerful impact, and led to a consensus amongst a large segment of academia that Pirenne had essentially
been disproved. It is true that whilst not everyone was convinced, and
Pirenne did find support among many prominent historians, among
them Hugh Trevor-Roper,[29] in general the tone of debate continued to
be hostile throughout the sixties and seventies. And a new phase of the
battle was initiated in the 1980s with the appearance of an important
critique, by archaeologists Richard Hodges and David Whitehouse
(*Mohammed, Charlemagne, and the Birth of Europe*). This latter, which
took a detailed look at the archaeology of the Mediterranean world
and parts of Northern Europe between the sixth and tenth centuries,
proved to be extremely influential in sidelining Pirenne. Because of
the importance of this volume, we shall devote the next two chapters,
plus parts of several others, to a detailed examination of it. Suffice to
note here that such was the impact of Hodges' and Whitehouse's work
that by the mid-eighties enormous numbers of books and articles
dealing with late antiquity and the early Middle Ages made no mention of Pirenne or his theory, and on the contrary reiterated opinions
that could almost have been written by Robert Briffault in the 1920s.

* * *

By the 1980s then Pirenne and his thesis was generally consigned
to the archives of interesting but flawed historical ideas. Yet even as
this was happening the controversy about the early Middle Ages and
the transition from Graeco-Roman civilization took a somewhat unexpected turn. Increasingly, from the middle of the twentieth century
onwards, a new breed of "revisionist" historian emerged to challenge
the very notion of a Dark Age at all. This was partly prompted by the
discoveries of archaeology, but also by a re-examination of the documentary material and a general questioning of certain clichéd views
(such as those of Briffault) which had passed as accepted fact for such
a long time. The new perspective was exemplified by Denys Hay when

---

29 See, Hugh Trevor-Roper, op cit.

he wrote, in 1977, of "the lively centuries which we now call dark."[30] For Hay and others it had become clear that, contrary to what had been taught for many years, intellectual life did not ossify or contract between the fifth and tenth centuries; nor did the church discourage learning or research. Indeed, in many ways it became increasingly apparent that Christianity played a revitalizing role in the Roman world, simultaneously creating a more humane environment, halting the Empire's long-standing demographic decline, and encouraging literacy and learning. The knowledge of the ancients, it was now apparent, had not been lost nearly as completely as had hitherto been imagined. Documentary evidence showed a surprising familiarity among the scholastic thinkers of the early Middle Ages with an enormous body of Latin and Greek literature, including secular pagan writers, whose work it had been customary to believe was entirely lost to the West before the Renaissance. Nor, it became apparent, was the spirit of rational enquiry nearly as moribund as people like Briffault had imagined. It was noted for example that Gerbert of Aurillac, the future Pope Silvester II, had in the latter tenth century made important contributions in various fields of scientific research, and was credited with the construction of the first mechanical clock. Another savant of this supposedly "dark" age had made experiments with flying machines, whilst various others had written treatises on geography, natural history and mathematics.[31] The caricatures which had for so long misled the public with regard to the Middle Ages were one by one exposed for the fictions that they were. One of the most glaring of these was the belief that, prior to Christopher Columbus, Europeans had thought the earth was flat. The source of this particular fiction was traced by Jeffrey Burton Russell (*Inventing the Flat Earth: Columbus and Modern Historians*) to several anti-Christian writers of the nineteenth and early twentieth centuries, most importantly Washington Irving, John Draper and Andrew White.[32] In the above volume Russell shows in detail how writers even of the darkest epoch of the "Dark Age" had an extremely good idea of the earth's shape and of its size – thanks to the calculations of Eratosthenes in the third century BC, which they

---

30 Denys Hay, *Annalists and Historians* (London, 1977), p. 50

31 Stanley L. Jaki, "Medieval Creativity in Science and Technology," in *Patterns and Principles and Other Essays* (Intercollegiate Studies Institute, Bryn Mawr, Pennsylvania, 1995), p. 81

32 Jeffrey Burton Russell, *Inventing the Flat Earth: Columbus and Modern Historians* (Praeger Paperback, 1991)

were well aware of. Science and learning, as Edward Grant as well as many other writers found, was actually encouraged by the Church, and the old view of the Christian faith acting as a dampener on scientific enquiry had to be abandoned.[33]

Archaeology too began, in some respects at least, to show an astonishing continuity between the world of late antiquity and the Middle Ages. Thus for example it was noted that Merovingian architecture in Gaul during the sixth and early seventh centuries bore a striking resemblance to the Romanesque architecture of France during the tenth and eleventh centuries.[34] It was very clear that there existed a direct line of connection between the two, which formed part of a single artistic and technical tradition. A seminal work was that of Peter Brown, whose *The Making of Late Antiquity* (1978) offered a new paradigm for understanding the changes of the time and challenged the post-Gibbon view of a stale and ossified late classical culture, in favor of a vibrant and dynamic civilization.

In recent decades then quite literally dozens of authors have nailed their colors to the mast and published work decrying the very existence of a Dark Age. So prominent has this school become that it is now, to some degree, part of received wisdom; and to talk of a Dark Age is, in many quarters at least, to invite scorn. These writers have emphasized, in a thousand publications, how archaeology has demonstrated the existence of vibrant and demographically expanding societies throughout Europe during the sixth and seventh centuries. These were, in part at least, heavily under the influence of Rome and Byzantium; though they were also heavily "native" in their inspiration. The astonishing culture that appeared in Ireland and Britain during these centuries, with its dramatic "Hiberno-Saxon" art, was surely not the signature, these writers hold, of a decadent and dying society. Architecture in stone too, throughout the former territories of the Western Empire, which had all but disappeared by the fifth century, reappeared in the sixth and seventh centuries, even in places like Anglo-Saxon England, where the Germanic migrations had effaced Roman civilization in a most thorough way. And this architecture looked distinctly Roman in appearance. Continuity too is seen in the survival of Latin as the language of learning and of the church.

So overwhelming and striking has been the evidence for the sur-

---

33 See eg. Edward Grant, *God and Reason in the Middle Ages* (Cambridge, 2001)

34 V. I. Atroshenko and Judith Collins, *The Origins of the Romanesque* (Lund Humphries, London, 1985)

vival of classical culture that by 1996 Glen W. Bowerstock could write of "The Vanishing Paradigm of the Fall of Rome." Bowerstock went through the archaeological evidence in detail and came to the conclusion that Roman civilization (and even in some aspects the Roman Empire) never really fell at all, but simply evolved into the culture we now call "medieval," a culture which was, however, much more "Roman" than has until recently been admitted or realized.[35] More recently, a plethora of publications, many of which look in some depth at the archaeology, have argued passionately in the same vein, and we may cite Peter S. Wells' *Barbarians to Angels* (New York, 2008), Chris Wickham's, *The Inheritance of Rome: Illuminating the Dark Ages 400 – 1000* (2009); and Ken Dark's *Britain and the End of the Roman Empire* (Stroud, 2001), as among the most influential.

Denying the very existence of a Dark Age, the "Revisionists" have always tended (whenever they have considered it) to refute the contention of Pirenne that Islam plunged Europe into an economic and cultural limbo in the seventh century. But in spite of the very clear continuity they trace from the seventh to the tenth and eleventh centuries, they have been signally unable to account for one glaring fact: the apparently almost complete disappearance of archaeology for three centuries between the mid-seventh and mid-tenth centuries. This was a problem highlighted at various times during the twentieth century both by Pirenne's supporters and critics. Indeed, for the latter group it was the very completeness of the disappearance during the seventh century which convinced them that western societies had to have been already in decline in the latter years of the sixth: otherwise the thoroughness of the disappearance, the very totality of the demographic collapse, is beyond explanation or comprehension. This was a theme taken up in 2005 by Bryan Ward-Perkins, whose *The Fall of Rome and the End of Civilization*, took a more or less traditional view of late antiquity, returning fully to the opinions of people like Briffault, who imagined the Germanic peoples savages incapable of civilized life.

The Ward-Perkins book in fact fully underlines the apparently insoluble dichotomy at the heart of the whole Dark Age debate: How is it that a civilization as sophisticated as that of the Romans could disappear – apparently completely – for several centuries, only to reappear, admittedly in a greatly transformed state ("Romanesque"), in the

---

35 Glen W. Bowerstock, "The Vanishing Paradigm of the Fall of Rome," *Bulletin of the American Academy of Arts and Sciences*, Vol. 49, No.8 (May, 1996)

tenth and eleventh centuries? Ward-Perkins himself of course would deny almost any continuity from classical Rome, and would see the Latin elements in medieval civilization as entirely superficial. For him Romanesque culture was the creation of semi-literate peasants and savage chieftains who, from the tenth century onwards merely copied the ruined buildings of the Romans, which still littered the landscape. Yet even the Revisionist school struggles to explain the real or apparent lack of building in stone, and indeed of almost all archaeology, in the three hundred years stretching from the mid-seventh to mid-tenth centuries. Whilst the Revisionists tend to ignore this embarrassing gap, for Ward-Perkins it is proof positive that the barbarians really did destroy Roman civilization, a process they began in the fifth century and completed in the seventh. (Ward-Perkins will have none of Pirenne's talk about Arab culpability: The Arabs he sees as urbane and cultured.)

It would be tempting to ignore Ward-Perkins as a curious throwback; an academic dinosaur unable to "move on" to a new paradigm. Yet this would be to overlook the persuasiveness of his argument and the great influence he is having, as well as the very real problem which his work highlights and keeps us focused on: for whatever view we take, and no matter how favorable our opinion of the "barbarians," late Roman civilization did indeed die in the seventh century, and its disappearance was accompanied by the disappearance of most traces of human life and culture for several centuries.

In much of his book, Ward-Perkins does little other than state the obvious – pointing out again and again that the Roman Empire actually fell in the fifth century, and that its fall was violent. He concedes that the Germanic invaders made real attempts to adopt the sophisticated civilization of the Romans – including its religion, laws, customs, institutions, art and language – but insists that their efforts were a failure. The Germans, he says, did not commit murder, but they were guilty of manslaughter. Interestingly, he points too to the demographic and civilizational collapse in the East, which of course occurs not in the fifth but in the seventh century. Here he stresses that this collapse was a direct result of the Persian and more especially Arab invasions. By analogy, he suggests that the collapse in the West, two centuries earlier, was the result of the barbarian wars. The advent of the Germans in the West, in the fifth century, did not of course result in the complete disappearance of cities and archaeology that the Persian and Arab invasions of the seventh century seem to have produced further east. Yet in the picture presented by Ward-Perkins the devastation of the West in the fifth century is almost complete, and for him the Dark Age there did not begin in the seventh century, as almost all historians now assert, but in the fifth, and coincides precisely with the arrival of the barbarians.

Because of the importance of Ward-Perkins' work, it is incumbent upon us to examine his assertions in some detail. We shall have occasion to return to him in various places throughout the present volume, but for the moment a brief look at some of his most challenging arguments will be sufficient.

To begin with, he reiterates the sheer violence of the Barbarian Invasions during the fifth century. No one would or could contradict him on this point. The arrival of the Germans (and Asiatics), no matter how we try to put it, was violent and disruptive. But it is what happened after the fighting died down that is important; and the evidence for this is most clearly to be seen in the archaeology. Archaeology indeed is the nub of the issue. And at a first reading, it may appear that the evidence Ward-Perkins musters is impressive, even convincing. He notes, for example, that shortly after 400 the majority of the high-quality artifacts which were typical of life under the Romans disappear from the western provinces. He admits that, both in Britain and Gaul, as well as in Spain and Italy, imported luxury items continued to occur in the fifth and sixth centuries. Along with these, native craftsmen continued to produce jewelry and other high-status items of great expertise and beauty, during the same epoch. Yet for Ward-Perkins these do not represent evidence of a thriving culture and economy; rather, they are the rare goods of a highly-stratified society which has, in all other respects, reverted to an extremely primitive level. The "cultural complexity" which he attributes to the Roman period, and which was characterized by a widespread literacy and a sharing in high culture by the common man, had disappeared. In short, Europe was already, in Ward-Perkins' view, medieval.

That, in a nutshell, is the Ward-Perkins thesis; and, it has to be admitted that, on a superficial level it does appear convincing. However, a closer look reveals serious flaws in his methodology. Indeed, his methods and selection of evidence are so flawed that the informed reader must question his good faith. The most serious weakness is in his complete neglect of everything that happened in the Roman Empire before c. 400. Reading Ward-Perkins one gets the impression that it was "business as usual" in the Empire until the barbarians suddenly and inexplicably burst on the scene near the end of the fourth century. Yet all research over the past century and a half has emphasized that this was most emphatically not the case. The decline of Rome, as we have noted above, is now seen as in full swing since at least the year 200, when there is evidence of population stagnation and economic decline on an enormous scale. After that time, few if any great monuments were constructed, and Rome began the long process of imperial contraction, with the abandonment of Dacia in the middle of the third century and parts of Germany at the same time. It is true that, in the territories which remained in the Empire, the appearance of normality, on a superficial level, persisted until the fifth century. This was due to the power of the Roman state, which continued to station huge numbers of troops (who were increasingly of barbarian origin) in the northern provinces. And this brings us to the second major flaw in Ward-Perkins' argument.

Ward-Perkins places great emphasis upon the fact that, in the years after 400, a great deal of "cultural complexity" disappeared from the western provinces. The scarcity of copper coinage, for example (he admits the continued vigorous minting of gold and silver currency at the time), and the declining occurrence of quality pottery, are seen by him as infallible signs that commercial activity amongst the poorer classes (apart from subsistence farming) ceased. However, he fails to recognize that societies can be prosperous and expanding without the use either of coinage or high-quality pottery. The Egyptians had neither during their long history, and, had it not been for their habit of burying their most precious goods with their dead (and the erection of sumptuous tombs and temples), we might now imagine the ancient Egyptians to have been little more than primitive barbarians. The use of small denomination currency in the northern provinces until the 430s or 440s was entirely driven by the presence there of Roman garrisons, whilst the withdrawal of the legions in the middle of the fifth century meant the end of this money economy along the Rhine and Danube frontiers, as well as in northern Gaul and Britain. Thus it was the presence of the legions, and that alone, which had maintained the appearance of "cultural complexity" in these territories between the years 200 and 400. But this most emphatically did not mean that these regions were at that time economically prosperous. The presence of the legions maintained the illusion of normality until around 430, after which the illusion vanished, and the real situation revealed itself.

Yet the withdrawal of the Roman state would not necessarily

have been an economic catastrophe. Populations seem to have remained steady, or even – as Christianity took root – expanded. Furthermore, the loss of spending-power signaled by the disappearance of the legions appears actually to have encouraged local manufacturers, who had hitherto been hindered by the ready availability of high-quality imports from the Middle East and North Africa. That this is the case is seen both in the increasing size of rural and even urban settlements at the time, as well as in the vibrant glassmaking, pottery and metallurgical industries which appeared in Merovingian Gaul towards the end of the fifth century (of which more will be said presently). It is seen too in the adoption of new technologies such as the moldboard plough, which were devised precisely to break in new and more difficult land to feed an expanding population. None of this evidence is examined or even mentioned by Ward-Perkins; and his attempts to portray the Visigothic and Frankish states in Spain and Gaul as barbarous principalities verges on the ridiculous.

Ward-Perkins' ideas and arguments will be encountered again as we proceed. For now, all we need say is that, notwithstanding the weaknesses of his position, he has proved extremely influential, and is far from being alone in his views. Indeed a whole genre of publications now exists diametrically opposed to the Revisionist notion of classical continuity.[36] For Ward-Perkins has dovetailed nicely with what has now become the "traditional" view of the Middle Ages and of early Islam, which saw the former as barbarous and ignorant and the latter as urbane and cultured. Just as the Revisionists redoubled their efforts to abolish the Dark Age, a whole plethora of historians of the Islamic world have cast their hat into the ring in reiterating the existence of a European Dark Age – a darkness from which the West had to be rescued by Islam. The events of September 2001 have arguably heightened the passion and rhetoric of the debate: they have certainly made it more relevant and of more interest to the general public. Thus over the last decade there has been a rush of books by Islamophiles such as David Levering Lewis, John Freely and Thomas F. Glick which could, in most respects, have been written by Robert Briffault in the

---

36 Yet another angle on the problem of the Dark Age, or possible solution to it, appeared in Germany in the 1990s: This being that the Dark Age never existed at all, and that the almost three centuries between 614 and 911 were inserted into the calendar by mistake. A summary of this controversial thesis is contained in the final chapter.

1920s, and which mark a full return to the notion of a barbarous post-Roman West; and so complete has the sidelining of Pirenne become (in the English-speaking world at least) that a recent history of the Mediterranean by John Julius Norwich (*The Middle Sea*) can fill several hundred pages without the slightest reference to Pirenne. So, what for Pirenne was the "central event" of European history (the closing of the Mediterraean by the Arabs in the seventh century), is now seen by a large segment of academia as something of no importance whatsoever.

The Islamophiles have not, of course, had it all their own way, and there has also been a fairly robust restatement of the Islamic world's shortcomings, particularly with regard to its attitude to science and learning. Thus for example 1993 saw the release of Toby E. Huff's *The Rise of Early Modern Science: Islam, China and the West*, in which the author argued that Islam's world-view was essentially inimical to the rise of science as we know it, and that was why it fell behind Europe in the eleventh or twelfth century, and remained behind ever since; whilst Bat Ye'or has argued (*The Dhimmi: Jews and Christians Under Islam* (Fairleigh Dickinson University Press, 1985)) that Islam ill deserves the reputation for openness and tolerance it has gained in some quarters; and that religious minorities such as Jews and Christians suffered a very severe form of oppression during the centuries of Islamic rule in the Middle East and North Africa. Other, more controversial authors, such as Robert Spencer, have in recent years released a plethora of works arguing that Islam, from its very inception, was essentially intolerant and backward, and could never have produced either an Enlightenment or an Age of Science.[37] Yet none of these authors have specifically defended Pirenne's thesis, which was that Islam actually produced a dark age.

* * *

And so the arguments have raged back and forth. When all is said and done, however, the rejection of Pirenne remains almost absolute. That rejection is based upon a single proposition; one that has appeared in a variety of guises and headings over the past seventy

---

37 Some of Robert Spencer's most popular titles are: *The Myth of Islamic Tolerance: How Islamic Law Treats non-Muslims* (Regnery, 2005); *The Politically Incorrect Guide to Islam (and the Crusades* (Regnery, 2005); *Religion of Peace? Why Christianity is and Islam isn't* (Regnery, 2007)

years, but whose essential elements are always the same and may be summarized thus: Classical civilization, though still alive at the end of the sixth century, was badly weakened by the Barbarian Invasions, and was in an advanced state of decay. This decay had reached a critical stage by the end of the sixth century, and by the time of the Islamic invasions in the middle of the seventh century classical culture was already in effect dead. Islam did not then impede trade or trading contact between Europe and the Middle East; on the contrary, it opened up a whole new world of commercial enterprise during the seventh and eighth centuries, a process which eventually led to the revival of Europe.

THE ARCHAEOLOGY OF ITALY AND NORTH AFRICA

T he questions raised by the Revisionists who deny that Europe experienced a Dark Age and who insist that Roman civilization survived into the Middle Ages is one that shall be revisited as we proceed throughout our study. We shall also have occasion to return to the apparent disappearance of material remains throughout Europe during the seventh to tenth centuries, as well as to the important question of the nature of Islam and the nature of Islam's impact upon Europe during the seventh century. For the moment, however, it is incumbent upon us to examine in some detail the arguments presented by Henri Pirenne's most influential critics. These, after all, revolutionized the debate, and largely sidelined Pirenne in the 1980s. But how valid were their arguments?

We have seen that, as a rule, those who attacked Pirenne agreed with him regarding the reality of a European Dark Age. For them, however, the Dark Age was not caused by Islam, but by the inherent decadence of Roman or Mediterranean civilization at this time. The Muslims, they held, did not destroy a thriving and expanding classical culture but merely replaced a decrepit and dying relic.

The most comprehensive, complete and thorough assault on Pirenne came in 1982 with the publication of Richard Hodges' and David Whitehouse's *Mohammed, Charlemagne and the Origins of Europe*. In this book Hodges and Whitehouse, two archaeologists with extensive field experience, reiterated the criticisms outlined above and sought to provide these with archaeological support. Perhaps because of the emphasis they placed upon archaeology – which is, after all, a form of "hard" science – Hodges' and Whitehouse's book proved to be extremely influential (notwithstanding its brevity), and remains one of the cornerstones of the anti-Pirenne camp.

In *Mohammed, Charlemagne and the Origins of Europe*, Hodges and Whitehouse concluded that classical civilization did survive the fall of the Western Empire, but that it survived in a weakened and enfeebled state. They argued that during the fifth and sixth centuries the population of the western provinces declined dramatically, and that by the year 600, or very shortly thereafter, virtually all trade between the western Mediterranean and the East had ceased. This was several decades before the arrival of the Arabs on the world stage, and it meant essentially that the Arabs had nothing to do with the collapse of late Roman culture.

Echoing earlier criticisms of Pirenne, Hodges and Whitehouse also pointed to the thriving trade which existed between the Arab world and the Far East during the seventh to eleventh centuries, as well as between the Arab world and Scandinavia (and some parts of southern Europe) during the ninth to eleventh centuries. This latter trade brought much gold and luxury products to Europe in the critical years of the Dark Age and gave the lie, so they held, to Pirenne's claim that the Arabs had terminated all trade between Europe and the East at this time.

We need to look at both these assertions in some detail.

Hodges' and Whitehouse's conclusion that the western Mediterranean and western Europe was in some kind of economic and cultural death-spiral before the appearance of Islam was based primarily upon archaeological data from Italy and North Africa. Spain is not mentioned by the authors and Gaul is covered in little more than a page or two. North Africa is represented primarily by Carthage, with only passing reference to other regions and settlements. In Italy and Carthage, say the authors, archaeology reveals a declining and dying civilization at the end of the sixth century. Carthage, they note, "was the capital of the imperial province of Africa until it fell to the Vandals in 438. Before this most of the vast crop of North African corn destined for Italy passed through Carthage, as did huge quantities of olive oil."[1] In other words, Carthage was a major centre of late Roman civilization during the fourth and fifth centuries, and the evidence of excavations from the city must be seen as of central importance to our knowledge of the epoch. They note that large-scale excavations during the 1960s and '70s sponsored by UNESCO made it possible to re-examine the traditional narrative regarding Carthage's decline – namely, the narrative which held that Carthage only declined after the Arab Conquest. The American and British teams in particular concentrated on the latest phases of the city's occupation; in the process handling vast amounts of pottery, including hundreds of thousands of amphorae sherds and high-quality African Red Slip tableware.

---

1 R. Hodges and D. Whitehouse. *Mohammed, Charlemagne and the Origins of Europe,* (London, 1982) p. 26

Analysis of this pottery, in conjunction with parallel studies of coins, induced M. J. Fulford and John Riley to offer alternative interpretations of Carthage's final centuries.[2] Hodges and Whitehouse quote Fulford as follows:

"In the early fifth century (c. 400-425), only about 10 per cent of the amphorae can be assigned to East Mediterranean sources. This percentage is doubled by c. AD 475-500 and, in the groups deposited at about the time of Belisarius' invasion ... 25-30 per cent of all the amphorae can certainly be attributed to sources in the East Mediterranean."

Riley arrived at the same conclusion, though both he and Fulford found that the proportion of imported amphorae dropped dramatically after 534. By around 600 it was found that the incidence of eastern Mediterranean amphorae was negligible.[3] Fulford found that Vandal coinage issued in Carthage was widely circulated around the Mediterranean, and that by contrast, after Justinian re-established an imperial mint at Carthage coins from regions in the eastern Mediterranean found at the city amounted to a tiny fraction of the numismatic collection as a whole.[4] "The impression" conveyed by all of this, according to Hodges and Whitehouse, is that "Carthage enjoyed a buoyant economy in the late fifth and early sixth centuries [under the Vandals]," but that after its reincorporation into the Empire by Justinian the city went into decline.[5] The authors note that, "The last phase of occupation in several buildings near the city wall betray the pitiful condition of Carthage in the seventh century." We are told that,

"The British excavators uncovered a comparatively well-preserved mud-brick building, L-shaped in form, dating from the late sixth or early seventh century. After its abandonment the zone was used as a burial ground. Henry Hurst, the excava-

2 M. J. Fulford, "Carthage: overseas trade and the political economy, c. AD. 400-700," *Reading Medieval Studies* 6 (1980), 68-80; J. A. Riley, "The pottery from the cisterns 1977. 1, 1977.2 and 1977.3," in J. H. Humphrey (ed.), *Excavations at Carthage 1977 Conducted by the University of Michigan*, (Ann Arbor, 1981), pp. 85-124

3 R. Hodges and D. Whitehouse, *Mohammed, Charlemagne, and the Origins of Europe* (London, 1982), p. 28

4 Ibid., p. 28

5 Ibid.

tor, writes that 'late burials occur commonly within the former urban area of Carthage, as in other sites of Byzantine Africa, and are conventionally interpreted as representing a late stage of decline, economically and in terms of population, when large areas of the city were redundant and the traditional regulations relaxed.' A further building over this graveyard has been interpreted as the home of refugees from the Arabs, who arrived in the province in 695-8. By then, the city was only a shadow of its former self and must have resembled the decaying industrial towns with which, today, we in the West as beginning to become familiar."[6]

* * *

So much for North Africa. In Italy, which is the only other region of the West examined by Hodges and Whitehouse, the authors claim to find the same pattern of economic stagnation and decay. Whilst they freely acknowledge that the great basilicas and palaces of Ravenna and Rome (and several other parts of Italy) built during the fifth and sixth centuries signal at least some continuity with classical traditions of fine art and architecture, for them these represent merely the last flickerings of light in the glowing gloom. After the time of Justinian, they argue, in the middle of the sixth century, such achievements become extremely rare in Italy, and by the year 600 they cease completely.[7] The termination of major architectural works, they hold, is reflected in the archaeology of individual settlements and communities.

An example that they cite of the latter is Luni, a small Roman port near La Spezia on the Adriatic, where excavators found that "material trampled into the thin floor surfaces [of the buildings] ... indicates that 'Byzantine' copper coinage continued in use until about 600."[8] In addition, we are told, eastern Mediterranean amphorae and Syrian glass were being imported. "After about 600, on the other hand, the material standard of life appears to have suffered a further decline – imports from other parts of the Mediterranean are rare, although analysis of the refuse implies that there was no significant alteration in

---

6 Ibid., p. 30

7 Yet even Hodges and Whitehouse could scarcely deny that magnificent churches continued to be erected in Italy well into the seventh century; though they cease after about 630 or 640.

8 Ibid., p. 31

the diet."[9] Interestingly, Bryan Ward-Perkins, the excavator of Luni, was of the opinion that the town's impoverishment in the seventh century was due in large measure to the decay of the classical drainage system in the food-growing territorium.[10] Much of this territory reverted to marsh. "It is clear," say Hodges and Whitehouse, "that Luni was barely operating as a port when the Lombards ousted the last Byzantine governor in 640."[11]

This "decaying" of the classical drainage system, accompanied by the silting-up of harbors and the burying of late Roman settlements under a layer of subsoil, is a phenomenon encountered throughout the Mediterranean at the end of the classical period, and is a topic we shall return to at a later stage.

At this point, Hodges and Whitehouse take a retrospective look. "These glimpses of late Roman trade suggest two working hypotheses. First, the arrival of the 'barbarians' in the late fourth and fifth centuries damaged, but did not destroy, the commerce of the central and western Mediterranean: Rome continued to import oil and wine (and many other things) after the Gothic invasion; under the Vandals, Carthage may actually have experienced a boom in trade with the East; Luni was still receiving foreign goods in the sixth century. ... Secondly, however, the situation had changed completely by about 600: Carthage had virtually ceased trading with the East and at Luni imported luxuries disappeared."[12]

Hodges and Whitehouse admit that "these are large hypothesis built on flimsy evidence," though immediately afterwards they promise to supply more compelling data in future sections and chapters. In fact, the only other evidence they do provide centers around a series of settlements in southern Etruria, in Rome's immediate hinterland, which were excavated in the 1960s and 70s. Archaeologists, led by Bryan Ward-Perkins, the Director of the British School at Rome, found, between the third and sixth century, a sharp decline in the occurrence of a type of high quality imported pottery known as African Red Slip Ware. The decline was fairly precipitous after about 250, and by 600 only a few sites contained the expensive ceramics. "In round figures,

---

9 Ibid., pp. 31-2

10 See Catherine Delano Smith, Derek Gadd, Nigel Mills and Bryan Ward-Perkins, "Luni and the 'Ager Lunensis': the Rise and Fall of a Roman Town and its Territory," *Papers of the British School at Rome*, Vol. 54 (1986), 81-148

11 Hodges and Whitehouse, op cit, p. 32

12 Ibid

therefore, the total number of small-holdings and villas known to have been occupied in the Roman Campagna seems to have fallen by well over 80 per cent between the first century and the mid-fifth century. The decline began in the second and third centuries and for a while ran at just under 30 per cent per 100 years. It accelerated to more than 50 per cent for every hundred years between the third and fourth centuries and thereafter continued, but at a slower pace."[13]

The authors considered the various alternatives as to what this might mean:

> "How can we explain this phenomenon? The possibilities are: (1) quite simply, a decline in the use of ARS [African Red Slip Ware] (our evidence, remember, consists entirely of the distribution of potsherds); (2) a change in the pattern of settlement involving the replacement of many small sites by fewer large ones; (3) migration from the countryside to the country towns; (4) migration to Rome; (5) a decline in the population of the countryside and the country towns and of Rome itself."[14]

According to the authors, "None of the first three possibilities satisfactorily explains what happened." What then is their explanation? "We are left," they say, "with (4) migration to Rome and (5) an overall reduction of population. The present evidence suggests that these were important factors. All the information from the South Etruria survey tells the same story: an uneven, but continuous decline in the number of rural sites known to have been occupied which, if we are correct in rejecting explanations (1)-(3), represents an uneven, but continuous decline in the rural population. Rome, on the other hand, if the figures for the dole … are even remotely indicative, also experienced an overall decline, but with periods of growth in the fourth century and the second quarter of the fifth."[15] "These observations," they continue, "are consistent with the view that an overall reduction in the size of the population may have taken place between the second or third century and the mid-fifth century (and after), but that on two occasions the population of Rome was 'topped up' by immigrants from the Roman Campagna. This reduction in the total population may well have been smaller than the reduction in the number of identified sites

---

13 Ibid., p. 40

14 Ibid.

15 Ibid., p. 42

implies, but we find it difficult to believe that no reduction took place."[16]

In summary, the authors conclude that, "By 600 the Western Empire was in the final stages of political and economic decay, and within the space of only one more generation the Eastern Empire too experienced a shift towards political and economic collapse. In other words, the transformation of the Mediterranean was well advanced before the first Arab incursion. By the time Carthage was besieged (in 698) the city was a shadow of its former self, and its decay appears to be typical of cities, large and small, all over the Mediterranean. The creation of an Islamic empire in the later seventh and early eighth centuries was partly a product, not a cause, of the economic transformations detected by Pirenne."[17]

Other chapters of the book explore the thriving trade which existed between the Islamic world and South Asia during the seventh to eleventh centuries, as well as between the Islamic world and northern Europe at roughly the same time. These chapters need not concern us for the present, and shall be dealt with at a later stage.

---

16 Ibid.

17 Ibid., pp. 169-70

THE ARCHAEOLOGY OF ITALY AND NORTH AFRICA (PART II)

A t first glance, the evidence presented by Hodges and White-house from Carthage and central Italy appears impressive. Excavations in both areas seem to have uncovered a terminal decline in economic activity and even in population during the fifth and sixth centuries. Yet a closer look reveals deep flaws in the authors' thinking.

Let's look first of all at Carthage.

According to Hodges and Whitehouse, Carthage was in a pitiable state by the beginning of the seventh century. They quote Henry Hurst, who noted that, "late burials occur commonly within the former area of Carthage, as in other sites of Byzantine Africa, and are conventionally interpreted as representing a late stage of decline, economically and in terms of population, when large areas of the city were redundant and the traditional regulations requiring burial areas to be outside the city walls were relaxed."[1] Hurst here does not specifically date this degraded epoch before the Islamic invasion, but Hodges and Whitehouse nonetheless strive to portray it as such by their comment: "A further building over this graveyard has been interpreted as the home of refugees from the Arabs, who arrived in the province in 695-8. By then, the city was only a shadow of its former self and must have resembled the decaying industrial towns with which, today, we in the West are beginning to become familiar."[2]

It is striking that Hodges and Whitehouse produce no evidence to support their contention that the decaying city uncovered by Hurst, the last phase of the settlement, was a pre-Islamic city. In fact, evidence to be examined below would strongly suggest that this declining and crumbling Carthage was all that remained of the once-brilliant metropolis in the immediate aftermath of the Islamic conquest.

The proposition that the classical economy and Mediterranean trade terminated around 600 – the idea upon which Hodges and Whitehouse's thesis ultimately stands or falls – presents a glaring problem: What caused this termination? Pirenne at least proposed a mechanism – Muslim fleets of raiders and pirates – by which economic

---

1 Henry Hurst, "Excavations at Carthage 1977-8. Fourth interim report," *Antiquaries Journal* 59 (1979), 44-6

2 Hodges and Whitehouse, op cit, p. 30

activity could have been interdicted. Hodges and Whitehouse offer no such mechanism. What happened around the year 600 to cause such a collapse? Since deep antiquity western Europe had maintained economic relations with the eastern Mediterranean. Spanish and British tin, as well as bronze from central Europe and amber from the Baltic, have been found in the tombs of the pharaohs and the cities of the Assyrians. Even the most corrupt and decrepit political institutions will presumably allow some kind of economic activity – if only out of self-interest. Was there nothing in western Europe after 600 that the peoples of the Levant required; and was there nothing that the Levant could supply that the wealthy classes who ruled Spain, Gaul, Britain and Italy would want? Such a scenario strikes one a profoundly improbable; yet this is precisely what is proposed by Hodges and Whitehouse.

The only attempt at explanation comes on page 53, where they suggest that Europe in the sixth century may have had a parallel in sixteenth century South America, "where the conquistadors not only slaughtered on a massive scale, but also destroyed the traditional social and economic systems." The result of this, they say, "was indeed generalised demographic collapse." "In the Mediterranean," they continue, "the structure of Roman society and its economy were undermined, and its wealth was absorbed by two centuries of intermittent warfare."

This hardly constitutes an explanation of anything. The very point of Pirenne's study was to show that the structure of Roman society and its economy were not undermined at all in the fifth and sixth centuries; and the survival of undefended Roman villas into the late sixth century suggests that he was absolutely right. As regards the two centuries of intermittent warfare in the fifth and sixth centuries, these were hardly unusual. Rome had arguably been involved in far more destructive internecine wars during the first and second centuries BC and the second and third centuries AD. Yet these had not caused the collapse of Roman civilization.

If we return to the question of Carthage, we detect striking flaws in Hodges' and Whitehouse's methodology and conclusions. They emphasize, for instance, the decline in the occurrence of foreign amphorae and coins in the decades after Justinian's reconquest of the city. Yet this does not necessarily imply a dying society. After all, the authors themselves admit that between circa 400 and 425 only about 10 percent of amphorae found at the city were of eastern origin: Which means, essentially, that by the last decades of the sixth century the situation had reverted to what it was in the first decades of the fifth. Furthermore, the excavator himself, Fulford, did not see in this evidence of a terminal decline. He suggests that "once the province was released from its obligation to Rome [after 425 under the Vandals], it was possible to sustain a lively trading relationship with various parts of the Mediterranean. ... However, once Justinian reconquered the city and it was again burdened with taxes, commercial life diminished and the corn sold for private luxuries under the Vandals was requisitioned to meet the needs of the state."[3]

In other words, this was an economic recession, not a collapse of civilization.

Even more serious, however, is Hodges' and Whitehouse's failure to spell out the criteria by which the coins and amphorae were dated. Their statement is simply that virtually all eastern coins and amphorae disappear from Carthage by "about 600." The operative term here is "about," and I would suggest that with this word the authors are committing an act of legerdemain on their readers. Everyone agrees that Carthage continued to function as a Roman-style city until its conquest by the Arabs in 698. Presumably then from 533, when Justinian brought the region back under imperial control, until 698, the metropolis continued to use amphorae and imperial coinage. If the "dramatic decline" in eastern coins and amphorae covers all the years from 533 to 698, rather than 533 to 600, as Hodges and Whitehouse strive to imply, then all becomes clear. The Persian conquest of Syria in 614 and Egypt in 619 (plus devastation of Asia Minor in the years between) severely disrupted commerce throughout the whole Levant from that time onwards. The coins of Heraclius, the Emperor of the time, are regularly found in great hoards; and the latest of these, dating from 619 or 620, are virtually the last Byzantine coins found anywhere in the Near East for another three hundred years.[4] This being the case, it is clear that if the total tally of coins and amphorae takes in all the years between 533 and 698, then we should not be surprised to find a "dramatic" decline. The more years that are added after the real point of disappearance, namely 619 or 620, then the lower the average number of foreign amphorae and coins there will be.

If we combine Hurst's explanation for the decline in the years

---

3 Ibid. p. 28

4 See for example Cyril Mango, *Byzantium: the Empire of New Rome* (London, 1980), pp. 72-3

between 533 and 620, with the knowledge that imperial commerce virtually disappears after the violent events of the latter year, then all is explained. There was no "gradual decay" of classical civilization at Carthage; there was a sudden and dramatic disruption, a disruption caused by violent events further to the east.[5]

Fig. 2: Interior of Sant' Apollinare, Ravenna, mid-sixth century

Concomitant with the claim that trade between the western Mediterranean and the east ended around 600, Hodges and Whitehouse, we have seen, argued that the population of western Europe and the western Mediterranean had been falling dramatically since the third century – a process that continued into the sixth and early seventh centuries. They admitted to a brief economic (and perhaps population) recovery in the West during the late fifth and early sixth centuries, but asserted that by the mid-sixth century this had come to an end, and all western societies went into terminal decline.

The demographic question is fundamental to understanding Hodges' and Whitehouse's thinking. That there was a serious problem, one that can be traced back to the second or perhaps even the first

---

5 More recently, Ward-Perkins, one of Hodges' and Whitehouse's most important sources, has admitted that a vibrant classical civilization existed in North Africa well into the seventh century. See *The Fall of Rome and the End of Civilization* (2008), pp. 124 and 130-2

century, is beyond question. As we saw earlier, the Romans themselves were well aware of this issue, and the population decline has been confirmed, in the western provinces at least, by the evidence of archaeology, which shows shrinking cities and a cessation of new building, from the late second century onwards. We have seen too how Constantine's legalizing and fostering of the Christian faith may have had, as one of its goals, the amelioration of the birth-rate problem. None of this is denied. The crucial question is this: Did the decline which commenced in the second or third century continue into the fifth and sixth; and did Christianity and the Christianization of the Empire fail to halt it? According to Hodges and Whitehouse, the answer is, Yes. We have seen how, using evidence primarily from central Italy (Spain, as we have seen, is ignored, and Gaul as well as Britain are barely mentioned), the authors claimed to find grounds for believing that the population of the western provinces had declined by perhaps 80% between the middle of the third and the end of the sixth centuries. If true, such a circumstance would certainly confirm the authors' conviction that classical civilization was terminally ill and hardly needed to be killed off by the Arabs. But an assertion of such sweeping implications needs abundant proofs, whereas the authors' argument is in fact based on little more than the evidence from Italy, particularly from the Roman Campagna, alluded to in the previous chapter. Archaeologists, we recall, found a sharp decline in the occurrence of the high quality imported pottery known as African Red Slip Ware from the third to seventh centuries. The decline began around 200, was fairly precipitous after 350, and by 600 only a few sites contained the expensive ceramics.

Hodges and Whitehouse considered the various alternatives as to what this might mean, but came down in favor of the idea that it indicated a dramatic fall in population as a whole. And from this they extrapolated that the whole of western Europe and North Africa was involved in a similar process. They admitted, in passing, that a great many other academics had considered this question and addressed it at length; and that almost invariably they had rejected the notion of a demographic collapse taking in the whole of western Europe. Of these only two names are mentioned: C. R. Whittaker and C. J. Wickham. Hodges and Whitehouse make no attempt to explain Whittaker's and Wickham's thinking, though they quote Wickham's statement that "generalised demographic collapse is a difficult enough process to imagine, let alone ... locate in the evidence," as well as his claim that "historical sources ... in the eighth century, primarily the *Liber Ponte-*

ficalis, give no impression that the countryside had been abandoned."[6] From this, Hodges and Whitehouse give the impression that Whittaker's and Wickham's rejection of the idea of population collapse was based solely on a reading of early medieval documents. But this was far from being case. In fact, both Whittaker and Wickham considered the archaeological evidence from Italy in detail, and they duly noted the decline in African Red Slip Ware between the fourth and sixth centuries. However, they also (unlike Hodges and Whitehouse) considered the political history of Rome between the third and sixth centuries; and, having done so, concluded that the occurrence of luxury items in villas surrounding Rome concurs precisely with what we know of the Eternal City's fortunes during this epoch. They emphasized that between the fourth and sixth centuries the balance of power in the Roman Empire shifted decisively to the East, with the founding of Constantinople in 324. By the beginning of the fifth century, Rome was no longer even the capital of the Western Empire, her place having been taken by Ravenna. The city was then sacked twice in the same century; in 410 by Alaric and his Visigoths, and in 455 by Genseric (or Geiseric) and his Vandals. With the abolition of the Western Empire in 476 the prestige of the city suffered further, and after the invasion of Italy by the Lombards in 568, Rome seems to have been reduced to little more than an average-sized provincial town.

The country villas around Rome which imported luxuries like Red Slip Ware in the second and third centuries were owned by members of the Roman aristocracy. With the precipitate decline of that aristocracy, along with Rome's fortunes (and population), in the fourth to sixth centuries, we would expect, said Whittaker and Wickham, nothing else than a dramatic drop in the wealth of the settlements around the city. And that is precisely what we do find. It is important to remember that Rome, unlike other great cities of antiquity such as Alexandria and Constantinople, did not occupy a position that would naturally have guaranteed her wealth and prosperity. She stood at no trading crossroads; she owed her vast wealth and population to her military prowess and to her political importance. With the decline of these, her population would naturally have dwindled.

We should note at this point that, from at least the first century, Rome's population was inflated by hundreds of thousands of economically inactive persons. Aside from the aristocrats themselves, there

---

6 C. J. Wickham, "Historical and topographical notes on early medieval South Etruria: part II," *Papers of the British School at Rome* 47 (1979), 66-95

were armies of bureaucrats and courtiers surrounding the Emperor, huge numbers of soldiers, and a vast host of unemployed plebeians, who had to be supported by a social security system, which the Romans named the "dole." This vast unproductive population could only be maintained by the importation into the city, on an annual basis, of enormous quantities of grain and other foodstuffs from Egypt and North Africa. Clearly Rome, at the height of the Empire, housed a population that was far and away in excess of anything that could be maintained by normal systems of trade and agriculture. With the decline of the city as a political power, the great majority of this population would naturally have disappeared.

Italy, then, and particularly central Italy, was far from being typical of the provinces and territories that made up the Western Empire. To attempt to use the fate of the wealthy settlements in the environs of Rome as a microcosm for what happened in Gaul, Spain, and North Africa in the fourth to sixth centuries, as Hodges and Whitehouse did, can only strike one as disingenuous.

The situation in Italy was untypical also in the damage done from the middle of the sixth century onwards by Justinian's disastrous war against the Ostrogoths, and by the subsequent conquest of the Peninsula by the Langobards. Both these events caused enormous disruption, a disruption we would naturally expect to be reflected in the archaeological record. The Langobard invasion marked the last barbarian conquest of a western European territory, and it can only have resulted in conditions very similar to those that obtained in Italy during the earlier invasions of the Visigoths under Alaric.

Fig. 3. Campanile of Sant' Apollinare, Ravenna. Reckoned to be early seventh century.

Thus Italy was the exception rather than the rule in late sixth century Europe. And the idea that western Europe as a whole was a depopulated wasteland in the late sixth century is flatly contradicted by the archaeology, which we shall examine in due course, and by the copious written sources, which tell of thriving economies and trade in the Frankish regions of Gaul and Germany and in the Visigothic territories of Spain.

Furthermore, we cannot be sure of the true scale of the population collapse (outside of Rome) even in Italy. It is true that the number of wealthy villas, which could afford African Red Slip Ware, declined dramatically. This would indicate a reduction in the number of villas, probably as a result of a few landowners buying more and more land; but such a situation does not necessarily indicate a reduction of the overall population. We must presume the big landowners would have wished to profit from their holdings. Empty and uncultivated land does not produce wealth. Agriculture at the time was extremely labor-intensive, so there must have been substantial populations of tenant farmers upon the estates. These peasants would have left little in the way of archaeology to mark their existence. Just a hundred and fifty years ago Ireland supported an enormous population of tenant farmers, who labored for a small number of big landowners. Of this population scarcely a trace now remains, for they had few metal tools and their shacks were frequently built of little more than turf. Yet they produced vast wealth for the landed gentry of the country.

It is by no means impossible that the same situation pertained in Italy during the sixth and early seventh centuries.

There is one other factor to be considered. During the Empire, large numbers of people, both in the cities and in the countryside, were supported, one way or another, by the state. As we noted earlier, the legions, together with their ancillary staff, injected huge amounts of cash into the provinces, though with the abolition of the Western Empire and dissolution of the state's apparatus, this cash-flow came to an abrupt end. Yet it was this currency which enabled local tradesmen and other middle-ranking classes to purchase a few of life's luxuries, such as high-quality pottery from Africa. The end of the Roman state would thus naturally have signaled a decline in the occurrence of luxury imports in the provinces; but this would certainly not prove a relapse into barbarism or a population apocalypse. Indeed, the new political situation may actually have stimulated local manufacturers and artisans, whose business had hitherto been depressed by cheap high-quality imports. That such an economic upturn did in fact occur towards the end of the sixth century is seen in the proliferation of new church-building which marked the decades immediately before and after the year 600. This was true of territories ruled both by the Langobards and the Byzantines. Thus Rome alone counts six surviving seventh century churches. These are: Sant' Agnese fuori le Mura; San Giorgio in Velabro; San Lorenzo in Miranda; Santi Luca e Martina; Santa Maria in Domnica; and Santa Maria ad Martyres. Outside of Rome the picture is similar, with new churches and civic structures continuing to appear until the middle of the seventh century. The Langobard queen Theodelinda (c. 570-628) was a particularly active builder, who is known to have commissioned numerous churches in Lombardy and Tuscany. Amongst these we may note the celebrated Cathedral of Monza (603), as well as the first Baptistry of Florence. The famous Treasure of Monza, housed in the Cathedral, contains the Iron Crown of Lombardy and the theca persica, enclosing a text of the Gospel of John.

Fig. 4. Interior of Sant' Agnese fuori le Mura. The ceiling is Renaissance, but the main structure is early seventh century.

On the whole, the early years of the seventh century seem to have been an extremely active and innovative epoch of Italian architecture. It was then, for example, that there appeared the campanile, ("bell tower"), a remarkable and striking feature of church design.[7] Some of these, such as those at Sant' Apollinare in Ravenna, are extremely large and elaborate, complete with arched windows at various levels. Such bell-towers spread quickly throughout Europe and were the inspiration for similar structures in Gaul and the famous Round Towers in Ireland, two regions that also seemed to experience a remarkable revival of art and architecture in the late sixth and early seventh centuries.

Fig. 5. Mosaic from apse of Sant' Agnese fuori le Mura, Rome, built by Pope Honorius I, 625-638. The illustration shows Honorius holding a model of the church, with Saint Agnes.

None of this is mentioned by Hodges and Whitehouse.

Perusal of the archaeology of this epoch does not then leave one with the impression of a declining and exhausted civilization. It is true, however, that after the middle of the seventh century all building

---

7 According to the Encyclopaedia Britannica, the appearance of the campanile is "variously dated from the 7th to the 10th century." Here again is that curious three-century hiatus or gap whose beginning and end seem to echo each other. Encyclopaedia Britannica; Micropaedia, Vol. 2 (15th ed.) "Campanile."

and indeed archaeology of any kind becomes extremely scarce in Italy, as it does throughout Europe.

Outside of Italy, we find a similar pattern. In Gaul, Spain, and elsewhere, there is strong archaeological evidence to show that trade and industry survived, and even flourished, in the late sixth and early seventh centuries. That the peoples of the Levant still valued the products of northern and western Europe, which they had been importing since remote antiquity, is proved beyond question by the discoveries made north of the Alps and in Britain. It is to this evidence that we now turn.

GAUL AND CENTRAL EUROPE IN THE SIXTH CENTURY

We have already seen that, following the appearance of Dopsch's and Pirenne's work, scholars gradually came to accept that the Germanic invaders of Gaul, Spain and Italy did not, after all, immediately destroy classical civilization. It was conceded that the Barbarians tried to preserve that very civilization and adopted it wholesale, often enthusiastically. But rather than going with Pirenne, who saw a sudden disappearance of the Graeco-Roman society in the seventh century, the scholarly community as a whole went with Dopsch, who saw a gradual decline of classicism throughout the fifth and sixth centuries, leading to its complete disappearance in the seventh. Crucially, they held that it had already vanished before the advent of the Arab armies.

By the 1940s and '50s archaeology began to cast its own light on the problem; and it did not seem to show a "gradual decline" of classical society at all: Rather it seemed to point to a decline in the third, fourth and fifth centuries, followed by a partial revival in the sixth and early seventh centuries, followed by a dramatic termination sometime between 630 and 650. Such being the case, it is perhaps not surprising that Hodges and Whitehouse generally ignored the archaeology of western Europe outside of Italy. But they could scarcely censor it completely from their study, and Gaul (though not Spain) is mentioned in passing. What little they do say about the former region is most instructive:

"Joachim Werner first drew attention to the north Italian and Coptic objects in cemeteries north of the Alps. Byzantine gold solidi which occur in the Coptic ladles, bowls and 'tea-pots' firmly date this transalpine commerce to between the very end of the fifth century and about 560 – the reigns of Theodoric and Justinian. Clusters of the finds have been mapped by Werner in north Switzerland, the central Rhineland and eastern and central Sweden. During this last phase of Late Antiquity transalpine trading relations seem to have been established between the Ostrogoths and the new Frankish and Scandinavian elites. ...

"Furthermore, at the same time ports in the Mediterranean were sending a few ships laden with eastern Mediterranean, Gaza and North African oils, wines and tableware to the Late Celtic Christian communities in Brittany and western Britain. Sherds of African Red Slip dishes similar to those described in the South Etruria Survey have been found in Tintagel, South Cadbury and other western British sites; at Garranes and at Clogher – two royal sites in Ireland; and at Dinas Powys in Wales. The Mediterranean amphorae have been found on many more sites besides and testify to a modest directional trade intended – we suppose – for royal and ecclesiastical strongholds anxious for imported commodities that afforded their owners prestige. What was traded in return remains obscure, but the ubiquity of these Late Roman Mediterranean imports is striking."[1]

Though Hodges and Whitehouse talk of "a few ships" laden with eastern Mediterranean goods, and a "modest" trade with the British Isles, even they would have to admit that there are few signs of a dying society here. Note too the actual expansion of classical culture into regions the Roman legions had never reached, such as Ireland and Scandinavia. All this, again, is confirmed by the literary sources, where we find familiarity with Homer and Virgil among the rocky crags of western Ireland and the Hebrides of Scotland during the sixth and early seventh centuries.

After 560, however, Hodges and Whitehouse insist that the situation changed in Gaul and Britain. From then on, they say, the west's demographic and economic decline kicked in: "The sharp decline in the Mediterranean economy monitored in and around Carthage and Rome also resulted in the closing of trade-routes to the north. From the mid to late sixth century imports from the Mediterranean are rare in northern contexts; those that occur, as in early seventh-century Kent, can be assumed to be heirlooms or gifts passed from one generation to the next and ultimately interred."[2]

What evidence do the authors bring forward to support this? The answer appears to be: precious little. They devote barely a page or two to Britain and Gaul, and the evidence they quote actually seems to prove the precise opposite of what they claim. Thus we hear how:

1 Hodges and Whitehouse, op cit, p. 88-90
2 Ibid., p. 90

"Briefly at the turn of the sixth century the territory of Provence appears to have acted as the intermediary between north and south. ... Certainly some thirty to forty years after about 580 gold solidi minted in Provence are prominent finds in the gold hoards found at Saint Martin's, Canterbury, Escharen in Holland and Sutton Hoo in Suffolk. But the prominence of Provence evidently began to wane after about 630 when king Dagobert rose to power, and it may be no coincidence that the Provencal coins after this time were rapidly devalued, and that they tend subsequently not to occur in central or northern French hoards in any significant number. ... All the evidence points to Provence as a short-lived acquirer of gold which was circulated for a decade or two in the form of currency, giving European prominence to the kingdom."[3]

The authors add, in parenthesis, "(This may coincide with the very end of Early Byzantine trade in the eastern Mediterranean ...)"[4]

So, according to Hodges and Whitehouse, the end of Provence's epoch of economic prominence – around 630 – coincides with the "very end of Early Byzantine trade." But this is thirty years after the date they previously argued that virtually all trade between East and West had terminated!

In fact, the evidence from Gaul and from northern and central Europe, as well as from the British Isles and Spain, which Hodges and Whitehouse more or less pass over, stands in striking and stark contrast to the picture of a decrepit and terminally ill society which they seek to paint of Europe in the late sixth and early seventh centuries. Indeed, it would be difficult to imagine a narrative more diametrically opposed to the one they present. Contrary to what they suggest, we find throughout Europe at this time an expanding population engaged in vigorous trade within Europe and a more modest, though increasing, trade with the Eastern Mediterranean. We find evidence of new territories being brought into cultivation and the growth of cities, both old and new. And we find clear proof of dramatic technical and scientific innovation, as well as advanced learning and scholarship of all kinds. The reality could not in fact be further from what Hodges and Whitehouse claimed.

---

3 Ibid., pp. 90-1

4 Ibid., p. 91

Let's look first of all at Gaul.

* * *

We must remember that even at the height of the Roman Empire Gaul was never an urbanized society comparable to Italy. Cities and towns were built by the Romans, but they were comparatively small. In the words of Patrick J. Geary, "During the more than five centuries of Roman presence in the West, the regions of Britain, Gaul, and Germany were marginal to Roman interests. ... The West boasted only one true city ... Rome."[5] The largest urban settlements were in the south, in Provence and the Rhône valley. All these had grown steadily in the first two centuries of Roman rule; and it is estimated that by the year 200 the largest Gaulish cities may have housed 50,000 people. However, everything changed in the third century, when they hastily fortified themselves against the threat of barbarian invasion. The area enclosed was small, much smaller than the total urban area of the previous centuries: 30 hectares at Bordeaux and Marseilles, 20 to 30 hectares at Rheims, 11 at Dijon, and about 8 or 9 at Paris. Thus we find in Gaul, as in virtually all other areas, dramatic evidence of the population decline noted throughout the Empire in the third and fourth centuries. The one exception was Trier, whose 265 hectares is explained by the fact that from early in the fourth century it became the capital of the Prefecture of Gaul.[6] We are told that, "The actual population of these cities is extremely difficult to determine."[7] One estimate has it that Marseilles, one of the largest cities of Gaul, was home at this time – the third and fourth centuries – to a mere 10,000 people. Other "cities" were much smaller. Rheims is reckoned to have had a population of around 6,000, and Châlons 900.[8] "What a contrast," says Robert Folz, "with the several hundred thousand living in Constantinople or Alexandria."[9]

The fifth century, as might be expected, saw a further decline. Urban settlements continued to exist, as the Goths and then the Franks took control of the country; but from the middle of the fifth

---

5 Patrick J. Geary, *Before France and Germany: The Creation and Transformation of the Merovingian World* (Oxford University Press, 1988), pp. 8-9

6 See Robert Folz, op. cit., p. 5

7 Patrick Geary, op. cit., p. 98

8 Robert Folz, op. cit., p. 5

9 Ibid.

century there are major changes in the countryside, where the high-quality imported products that were one of the hallmarks of Roman civilization, become extremely scarce. Above all, there is the virtual disappearance of the fine African Red Slip Ware, which had hitherto been almost ubiquitous throughout Gaul. Small denomination coinage too, especially copper currency, either disappears or becomes extremely scarce. Until that time even peasant farmers, it seems, could afford some of the luxuries of life. High culture was thus in some ways generally spread throughout the population, a phenomenon that Ward-Perkins names "cultural complexity." Yet by the end of the fifth century, luxuries such as African Red Slip Ware were enjoyed only by the upper echelons of society; infallible proof, thought Ward-Perkins, of a return to an altogether more primitive form of existence.

But such a judgment, as I indicated in Chapters 3 and 5, betrays a fundamental misunderstanding of the situation in Gaul and northern Europe in general during the Imperial epoch. Graeco-Roman civilization was only ever a veneer in those territories; all of which, even at the height of the Empire, remained overwhelmingly rural. It was the presence of the legions and the administrative apparatus of the Empire, and this alone, which provided these territories with the little cultural sophistication they enjoyed. It was the soldiers and ancillary staff, on salaried incomes, who injected cash into the northern regions – cash spread amongst the local populations in exchange for food, raw materials, and services of various kinds. With this hard currency, it is true, food-producing Gaulish peasants could afford some luxuries, such as imported pottery. Yet there was a downside: it was the very ease with which a good living could be made from supplying food-stuffs to the Roman garrisons that hindered economic diversification and tended to keep these regions agricultural. There were always local potters, of course, as well as metal-workers and artisans of various kinds, but their products tended to be utilitarian and for local consumption. Local manufacturers made no real effort to compete with the highly-polished products of the Mediterranean regions. Thus it was the very presence of the legions, with their ready cash, which impeded the economic development of Gaul and the other northern provinces – a fact admitted even by Ward-Perkins himself.[10] Yet these craftsmen could provide the basic skills upon which to construct native manufacturing industries, should circumstances ever be favorable.

The withdrawal of the legions in the fifth century, together with

---

10 Ward-Perkins, op cit., pp. 132 and 136-7

the imperial administration, meant, among other things, that circumstances were now favorable for the development of such industries; and that is precisely what we find. Archaeology indicates that from the sixth century onwards, the population decline of the third, fourth and fifth centuries is reversed; new towns and new rural settlements begin to appear; and with them come new and home-grown crafts and skills.

Fig. 6. Baptistry of Saint Jean, Poitiers, sixth century. Very large churches and cathedrals were erected by the Merovingians during the sixth and seventh centuries, but these have disappeared, either through accidents or through "renovation" and rebuilding by church authorities. Only small and relatively unimportant structures, such as the baptistery of Saint Jean, have survived.

The majority of the "lower class" rural settlements were constructed of wood, which was by far the most readily available raw material throughout Gaul and central Europe; so it is not always easy to identify such settlements for archaeological investigation. When such have been identified, they invariably reveal vibrant and increasingly prosperous communities. Such was the case, for example, at Brebières, in northern France, where, in the early 1970s, a team of archaeologists uncovered a typical settlement of the late sixth century.[11] The village

---

11 See P. Demolon, *Le village mérovingian de Brebières, Vie-VIIe siècles* (Commission départementale des monuments historiques du Pas-De-Calais, Arras, 1972)

consisted of thirty small rectangular structures, their walls supported by vertical posts. There was no trace of any larger architecture, such as a public assembly hall or a church. So, the village was relatively poor and of little consequence for the time. Yet, in addition to good quality pottery, iron implements, and stone tools, all of which could be made locally, there was evidence of trade and some wealth: Fragmentary bronze ornaments such as brooches were found in some of the houses, as were fragments of glass vessels. Both these would need to have been imported, probably from fairly remote locations. In the words of Peter Wells, "…material culture [at Brebières] is abundant and of good quality. Much of the pottery is decorated. Iron was readily available and was used to make a wide range of implements, including nails, belt buckles, and knives. Bronze was not common, but a number of personal ornaments of this valuable metal show that bronze was available and people in this community had something they could trade for it. The copper and tin that constitute bronze had to be mined elsewhere in Europe, then smelted and brought together to make the bronze alloy:

> "Spindle whorls show that people were spinning fibers to make textiles. Bone combs indicate that members of the community were making these important objects or trading valued goods for them. Like bronze, the fragments of ornate glass vessels show that the community had important outside contacts and had wealth to trade for imported luxury goods. Glass beads at the site were less costly than vessels but still required a technology to produce that was probably not practiced at Brebières. They, too, represent trade goods imported from elsewhere.

> "The archaeological evidence at Brebières shows that a typical community of this period lived a rather modest life compared to modern Western standards or the lifestyles of elites in the Roman provinces. But the people had ready access to iron, which they put to use for a wide variety of purposes. They took the trouble to decorate their pottery even though plain vessels would have contained food and drink just as well. And they were able to import into their little community a variety of desired goods from outside – bronze ornaments and decorative glass beads that they wore on their persons, and ornate

glass vessels that must have been used to hold beverages on special occasions."[12]

This then was how the peasantry lived in the late sixth century. High-status pottery from North Africa may have disappeared, but, in the absence of competition from these imports, native industries now came into their own. In the Argonne area of north-eastern France, pottery similar to the Roman terra sigillata continued to be made in the sixth and early seventh centuries; whilst as Mayen, in the middle Rhineland, the pottery industry established in Roman times survived and flourished through the Merovingian period and into the High Middle Ages.

Fig. 7 Merovingian glass, sixth-seventh century.

Again, north of Mayen, between Bonn and Cologne, rich deposits of fine clay provided the raw material for several important pottery-producing centers in the seventh century. Large numbers of kilns and pits containing fragments of misfired pottery attest to the scale of manufacturing the villages of Badorf and Pingsdorf. "Great quantities of these ceramics in settlements throughout the Rhineland, northern continental Europe, southern Britain, and even Scandinavia show how far these fine wares were traded."[13] At the same time, we know that in southern Gaul, "traditional Mediterranean pottery of late classical design continued to be produced into the eighth century."[14]

None of these Gaulish potteries produced work to rival that previously imported from North Africa. Nor was it as widely dispersed as the African Red Slip Ware had been during the third and fourth centuries. Gaulish peasants and artisans, deprived of the hard currency earlier provided by the Roman Army, simply could not afford such refinements. Yet the very existence of native potteries which attempted

12 Peter Wells, *Barbarians to Angels* (New York, 2008), p. 134

13 Ibid., p. 148

14 Geary, op cit., p. 101

to reproduce the high-quality products of the Imperial Age, prove that things "Roman" were still seen as prestigious, and the spirit of classicism lived on.

Glass-manufacture, begun in the Roman period, continued under the Franks, who even introduced new forms and techniques, and who exported their products throughout northern Europe. Frankish glass did not quite reach the high quality of the best Roman glass, but it certainly was made to very high standards, and it got better and better during the course of the sixth century.[15]

We know that, in addition to the small luxuries with which the peasants of sixth-century Gaul and central Europe adorned their persons and enlivened their lives, that they were well-fed, and, on average, slightly taller than the modern inhabitants of western Europe.[16] They had their own local metallurgical industries, but they also imported bronze products from further afield. Actually, we know that, around this time, there were thriving metallurgical industries throughout western Europe. The bronze found at Brebières and elsewhere would have come either from Cornwall in Britain or from Bohemia; whilst the production of iron, as well as the fashioning, for export, of a wide variety of tools and weapons from the metal, was practiced on a very large scale at various places in central and northern Europe during the late sixth century. This for example was the case at Helgö in central Sweden, as well as various other places:

"The abundant evidence at Helgö for the processing of iron to make tools and weapons, bronze for personal ornaments, glass for beads, antler and bone to make combs and pins, and amber for beads and amulets is replicated at other manufacturing centers throughout temperate Europe between the fifth and eighth centuries. Many of these places are on the coasts of northern Europe. Coastal manufacturing sites include Helgö's successor, Birka, in central Sweden; Lundeborg, in central Denmark; Ribe, on Denmark's west coast; Hamwic/Southampton, in southern England; Dinas Powys, in southern

---

15 Edward James, *The Franks* (Basil Blackwell, Oxford, 1988), pp. 202-3

16 Wells, op cit., p. 134. That peasants of the time, at least in some areas, were taller than late medieval and early modern inhabitants of Europe is confirmed by studies from Anglo-Saxon England and south-western Germany. See Wells, op cit., p. 139. The stature achieved at this time (sixth/seventh century) was not again attained in these parts of Europe until the twentieth century.

Wales; Dorestad, near the mouth of the Rhine; and Haithabu/ Hedeby, in southeastern Jutland. Inland sites include Klein Köris, in northeastern Germany, and the Runder Berg, in southwestern Germany. When we compare the objects make at these sites and the industrial debris in the workshops, it is striking how similar the manufacturing industries were at these commercial centers all over Europe."[17]

Of these industrial and commercial sites, the Runder Berg in southern Germany was among the most important. Here, in a former border region of the Roman Empire, which then formed an eastern province of the Merovingian state, a thriving metallurgical industry existed in the sixth and seventh centuries. The site is the most thoroughly investigated of about fifty hilltop settlements in this part of Europe dating from the fourth to the sixth centuries: "As at the sites on the coasts of the North Sea, Irish Sea, and Baltic Sea, crafts workers at the Runder Berg employed a range of different materials. They forged iron weapons and tools. Hammers, anvils, tongs, punches, and chisels show the variety of smithing implements they used. Bronze, much of it obtained from melting down old Roman vessels and re-used belt attachments, was recast into new ornaments. Models, partly fashioned objects, and molds recovered at the Runder Berg show that ornate fibulae and belt buckles were among the special personal paraphernalia fashioned there. Silver and gold work attest to the specialized manufacture of precious ornaments for elites. Glass was being shaped into vessels and beads. Antler, bone, jet, and lead were among the other materials that these craft workers fashioned into tools and ornaments."[18]

The finished products of industrial locations like the Runder Berg have been found in sites throughout Gaul and central Europe. Remarkable and finely-wrought vessels, often for use in ecclesiastical ritual, are among the best-known examples of this flourishing Merovingian artwork. And the astonishing wealth of the Frankish nobility has been dramatically illustrated by a series of burials. The first of these to come to light was that of Childeric (died 482), discovered in the seventeenth century near Tournai in Belgium. The fabulous treasures interred with Childeric, most of which are now lost,

---

17 Ibid., pp. 144–5
18 Ibid., p. 145

were the wonder of the seventeenth and eighteenth centuries.[19] More recently a large and increasing number of Merovingian burials have been located beneath famous churches and cathedrals, indicating that these monuments were founded by the Franks, usually in the sixth and seventh centuries. One of these was that of a young woman, who died around 530, located underneath the choir of Cologne Cathedral. The grave had been set within a small chapel of rectangular shape, with an apse extending eastward. The western edge of the grave was formed by part of the Roman wall that had been built around the Roman city of Cologne.[20] The jewelry and other artifacts buried with the woman display both Roman and barbarian influence. Twelve gold coins, eight of them outfitted with eyelets for suspension, were found with her. On her forehead she wore an ornamental band that included gold threads, gold beads, gold-and-garnet ornaments, and silver wire. Other treasures included: a pair of gold-and-garnet earrings; a solid gold bracelet; a gold ring was on one finger on each hand; two pairs of richly decorated fibulae; five pendants of gold and filigree decoration; three gold-and-garnet pendants in the shape of fleur-de-lis, three cloisonné beads; gold beads, and nineteen glass beads. There was also, at the foot of the grave, a feasting set comprising six glass vessels, including three high-necked bottles, two bowls, and a small beaker. A bronze basin, a drinking horn, and a wooden bucket completed the set. A fragmentary wooden box contained remains of slippers, a ceramic spindle whorl, hazelnut and walnut shells, and a date seed.

The above burial was not exceptional. Indeed, it was rather typical of the epoch. In 1953 workmen found the rich grave of a fifth century warrior near Bro in the Czech Republic. The man was interred with two elaborately decorated swords, as well as a gold bracelet and numerous other ornaments of gold, silver and garnet. His shoes were decorated with gold-and-garnet buckles and rings, very similar to objects found in Childeric's grave.[21] A grave found at Pouan in northeastern France in 1842 contained, like Childeric's tomb, ornate long and short swords, a gold bracelet and a gold finger ring with an in-

19 See eg. G. Halsall, "Childeric's Grave, Clovis' Succession, and the Origins of the Merovingian Kingdom," in R. W. Mathisen and D. Shanzer, eds., *Society and Culture in Late Antique Gaul* (Aldershot: Ashgate, 2001), pp. 116-33

20 O. Doppelfled, "Das fränkische Frauengrab unter dem Chor des Kölner Doms," *Germania*, 38 (1960), pp. 89-113

21 J. Werner, "Der goldene Armring des Frankenkönigs Childerich und die germanischen Handgelenkringe der jüngeren Kaiserzeit," *Frühmittelalterlicke Studien*, 14 (1980), pp. 1-41

scribed name – Heva.[22] A similarly rich burial in southern Germany was found in 1843. This contained a gold bracelet similar to those in the graves discussed above, three solid gold buckles with garnet inlay, and a beaker made of green glass.[23] Another extremely rich burial, of the same period, was found near Békés, in Hungary, in 1884.[24]

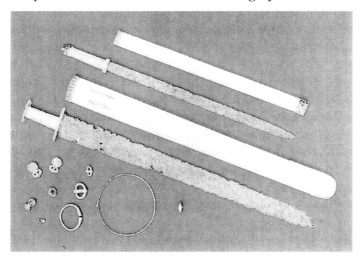

Fig. 8. Examples of Merovingian swords and other metalwork, sixth–seventh century

A large number of royal Merovingian burials, mainly from the late sixth and early seventh centuries, were located underneath the Church of Saint Denis in Paris.[25] We have even found, from the sixth and early seventh centuries, the graves of some of the craftsmen who created the jewels and weapons which accompanied the aristocrats to the otherworld. Thus a grave in a small cemetery at Poysdorf in Austria, from around 535, contained goods which showed the occupant to be a warrior and a metal smith. He was buried with an anvil, three hammers of different sizes, two pairs of tongs, a file, a whetstone, a burin made of bronze, and a black spherical stone. The stone had minute particles of silver on it, indicating that it had been used to polish silver objects. There were also two bronze models of fibulae, the final versions of which were to be of silver.[26] A grave in another small cem-

22 Ibid.

23 Ibid.

24 Ibid.

25 Edward James, op cit., p. 157

26 F. Daim and M. Mehofer, "Poysdorf," in *Reallexikon der germanischen Alterumskunde,*

etery at Kunszentmarton in Hungary, from around 610, also contained the body of a warrior metal-smith. He was buried with weapons and horse harness gear, as well as with tools and models for making metal objects; gold, silver and bronze decoration horse harnesses, belts and sword scabbards.[27]

It would be superfluous to attempt a comprehensive overview of these interments. Suffice to say that they are numerous, and growing in number by the year. With their vast wealth, they can only represent the apex of a society with a powerful economic base and a substantial technological and trading infrastructure. Viewed this way, Ward-Perkins' attempt to suggest otherwise rests on weak foundations.

Most of these burials contained some Christian artifacts and religious objects, and thus represent a transitional phase of Frankish cultural history. As Christianity took firmer root, during the seventh century, the tradition of burying goods and finery with the dead was abandoned.

Some of the treasures buried with the Frankish aristocrats were imports from far-off lands. Byzantine jewelry was found alongside glass-work from the Levant and lapis-lazuli from Afghanistan. Trade and international commerce, though it may have been slightly impeded by the invasions of the fifth century, was alive and well again. The towns and cities established by the Romans survived into the sixth century and into the High Middle Ages, often retaining their Roman names and frequently following the street plans laid down by the original Roman architects. Indeed, from the sixth century onwards the urban settlements of Gaul and central Europe, began, for the first time since the third century, to grow: "... the Merovingian bishops," we hear, "were great builders, and close to their towns they founded sanctuaries, which were often abbeys. These foundations soon became centres of new settlements as they opened hospices for travellers and pilgrims, and attracted men to till their soil. And so in the north, centre and west of Gaul – but, by a striking contrast, not in the south – the towns began to look like nebulae: the urban nucleus became surrounded by new centres of population which ... were in their turn surrounded by walls and so turned into fortified towns like Saint-Germain-des-Prés, near Paris, Saint-Médard de Soissons, Saint-Remi de

23 (2003), pp. 327-31

27 J. Werner, "Zur Verbreitung frügeschichtlicher Metallarbeiten (Werkstatt-Wanderhandwerk-Handel-Familienverbindung)," *Early Medieval Studies, I* (Antikvarist Arkiv, 38) (1970), pp. 65-81

Rheims, and many others."[28]

Thus the patterns of urban settlement did not, well into the early seventh century, differ significantly from that which pertained under the Caesars. The archaeology speaks, contrary to the impression put forward by Hodges, Whitehouse and Ward-Perkins, of continuity and growth.[29] The same period was to witness an explosion of church-building. Although the great majority of these have now disappeared, enough have survived to bear witness to the splendor that once was. It is estimated that, altogether, there were around 4,000 houses of worship in Gaul by the middle of the seventh century. In the words of one historian, "What astonishes us today is the great number of churches in Merovingian towns, few of which are thought to have had more than a few thousand inhabitants: as many as 35 churches are known or suspected from Paris, for instance."[30] Again, "the sixth and seventh centuries were clearly a great age of Gallic church-building," and "as far as the [ethnically] Frankish north-east was concerned, that process accelerated with the foundation of monasteries."[31]

From the few (generally small) Merovingian churches that survive, we know that they were heavily influenced by those of contemporary Byzantium. Indeed, it is likely many of them were executed by Greek or Italian craftsmen, for the Franks were long-standing allies of the Emperor. Several of the most opulent of these basilicas were described in detail by Gregory of Tours, and we can only regret the disappearance of these monuments – some destroyed as recently as the French Revolution – with their marble columns, stained glass windows, richly-colored mosaics, and finely-wrought statuary. Here is Gregory's take on the cathedral church of Clermont. It is, he says,

> 150 feet long and 60 feet wide across the nave and 50 feet high to the ceiling. It has a rounded apse, and on either side are elegantly made wings; the whole building is in the shape of a cross. There are 42 windows, 70 columns and eight doors. In it one is conscious of the fear of God and of a great brightness, and those at prayer are often aware of the most sweet and aromatic odour which is being wafted towards them. Round the

28 Folz, op cit

29 See eg. B. Hårdh and L. Larsson, eds., *Central Places in the Migration and Merovingian Periods* (Department of Archaeology and Ancient History, Lund, 2002)

30 Edward James, op cit., p. 151

31 Ibid.

sanctuary it has walls which are decorated with mosaics made of many varieties of marble.[32]

Another outstanding structure was the Church of the Holy Cross and Saint Vincent, built by Childebert I in Paris. Around 1000 it was described in some detail:

> It seems superfluous to describe the clever arrangement of windows, the precious marbles which support it, the gilded panels of the vault, the splendour of the walls which were covered with a sparkling gold colour and the beauty of the mosaic-covered pavements. The roof of the building is covered with gilded bronze and reflects the rays of the sun, shining so brightly that onlookers are dazzled, and call the church St. Germanus the Golden.[33]

We know that the architectural ambitions of the Merovingians did not end with church and monastery-building. Great palaces once existed, and Chilperic I (reigned 561 – 584), in true Roman fashion, built circuses in both Paris and Soissons.[34]

The overwhelming impression gained from both the written sources and the archaeology is of a vital and prospering late classical civilization extending into the mid-seventh century. Indeed, it was just at this time – the very period identified by the Hodges, Whitehouse and Ward-Perkins as marking the final death-throes of the Romanized Germanic kingdoms – that Merovingian Gaul began to experience its period of greatest prosperity and splendor. Even Hodges and Whitehouse, we saw, admitted the substantial flow of gold currency from the East through Provence during the first quarter of the seventh century; and it is agreed that the most frenetic period of church-construction and manufacture in general was precisely in the second half of the sixth century and the first half of the seventh. Patrick Geary remarked on the fact that from the late sixth century, "Products of artisanal workshops circulated regionally and even over great distances, although the mechanism of this circulation is uncertain. In the south, traditional Mediterranean pottery of late classical design continued to

---

32 Gregory of Tours, ii, 16

33 Quoted from the *Vita S. Droctovie* by Jean Hubert in *L'Art Préroman* (Paris, 1938), p. 9

34 Gregory of Tours, v, 17.

be produced into the eighth century; glass produced in the Ardennes and around Cologne found its way as far north as Frisia [northern Germany] and even Sweden; Frankish weapons, which enjoyed a great reputation across Europe, have been found throughout Francia and in Frisia and Scandinavia. Textiles also circulated between regions: Provence was particularly known for its inexpensive cloth as far away as Rome, Monte Cassino, and Spain."[35]

The reign of Chlothar II (584 – 629), who reunited the disparate territories of the Merovingian realms under his sole control, marked perhaps the apex of Merovingian prosperity. He was the first ruler of the Franks to issue coins bearing his own image, rather than that of the Emperor in Constantinople. According to Geary, the final twenty-five years of his reign (604 – 629), as well as that of his son Dagobert I, "would be the most peaceful, prosperous, and significant period[s] of Frankish history since the reign of Clovis."[36] Gold circulated freely and new structures in stone were erected throughout Gaul. We hear that from around 600, gold coins minted by the Frisians in imitation of Merovingian coins have been found in southeast England, on the western coast of Denmark from the mouth of the Elbe to Limfjord, and up the Rhine as far as Coblenz and even Lake Constance.[37]

Fig. 9. Gold coin of Chlothar II, 584-628. Chlothar II's reign was a particularly prosperous and vital period of Merovingian history. He reunited the disparate Frankish realms and inaugurated many building projects. After his time however the Merovingian kingdom entered a period of rapid decline.

After the time of Chlothar II and (possibly) his son Dagobert I, towards the middle of the seventh century, the Merovingian world went into terminal decline. Indeed, it is impossible to look into the history of this period without being reminded forcefully of Pirenne: For it is precisely in the third decade of the seventh century – the very

35 Patrick Geary, op cit., p. 101

36 Ibid., p. 151

37 Ibid., p. 178

point at which Islam began to impact on the eastern Mediterranean – that the decay began. We are told that "Chlothar II's son Dagobert (622-38) is often seen as the last of the great Frankish kings of the Merovingian dynasty.

After him came *les rois fainéants*, the 'Do-Nothing Kings', who peter off into obscurity in the eighth century ..."[38] In the words of Sidney Painter, "If one is to call any period the 'Dark Ages,' the later Merovingian period [after Dagobert I] is the one to choose."[39] From about 640 onwards material remains from the Frankish regions become scarce in the extreme. This applies as much to small things as large. Church-building, for example, previously such a prominent feature of Merovingian civilization, all but ceases. Glass-production too, which had earlier displayed a progressively advancing refinement and sophistication, now declines, and what remains is degraded. And we should note that it is widely accepted that the decline of glass manufacture was primarily due to the unavailability of vital raw materials such as soda, which had hitherto been imported from the eastern Mediterranean. With regard to glass however it is interesting to note the schematic diagram produced by Kurt Böhner, and reproduced here (fig. 10). Like everyone else, Böhner sees a rich late classical civilization, with sophisticated glass and pottery, until the seventh century, at which point we see a marked decline. But, as I have stressed elsewhere, the very division of historical periods into centuries is of course little more than a literary construct, a terminology of convenience used by historians to indicate immense generalities. The fact that what we (or Böhner) describe as "seventh century" begins with the year 600, tells us little or nothing about the actual historical processes at work at the time: all the evidence indicates that the real watershed was around 625 or perhaps 630. Thus the degraded material Böhner describes as "seventh century" is in fact material from circa 625 or 630 onwards (after the reign of Chlothar II), whilst the high quality material described by him as "sixth century" is in fact material of the sixth century and the first quarter of the seventh.

The downward course of Merovingian culture continues into the middle of the eighth century, at which point historians talk of a "renaissance" of the Frankish realms under the Carolingians. Yet the progress of scholarly investigation has shown that almost all of

38 Edward James, op cit., p. 230
39 Sidney Painter, op cit., p. 68

the material remains hitherto regarded as "Carolingian," need to be reassigned to the late tenth and eleventh centuries. This goes for both small artifacts and major structures. And so the supposedly Carolingian churches, which have hitherto generally been dated to the eighth and ninth centuries, such as the so-called Chapel of Charlemagne at Aachen, reveal themselves, on closer inspection, to be products of the late tenth or eleventh centuries.[40] When church architecture actually reappears, in the early Romanesque of the mid-tenth century, there is a pronounced impoverishment when compared to the work of the last of the Merovingians in the seventh century. The Romanesque churches are smaller and simpler, and less rich in decoration. Gone are the marble columns and colorful mosaics of the sixth and seventh centuries, to be replaced by duller sandstone and granite, with simple wall-painting replacing mosaic. The Romanesque of the tenth century does show striking continuity with the Merovingian, but it is an altogether poorer cousin.

The disappearance of archaeology, from the middle of the seventh century, is a feature we shall encounter throughout Europe and the Middle East.

So much for Gaul: The evidence gleaned thus far from excavation has tended to fully confirm what Gregory of Tours said. Frankish Gaul did not share the decline of central Italy during the fifth and sixth centuries; it was a vigorous society with a stable or even perhaps growing population. Trade prospered and Graeco-Roman civilization, far from being in decline, was spreading into the Frankish territories east of the Rhine. But if Gaul presents a picture of growth and prosperity during the late sixth and early seventh centuries, other regions did to an even greater degree.

---

40 See Heribert Illig's detailed examination of the Aachen Chapel, in *Das erfundene Mittelalter* (Econ Verlag, 1996). Here Illig shows, in literally dozens of architectural and artistic details, that the Aachen Chapel could not have been built before the mid-eleventh century.

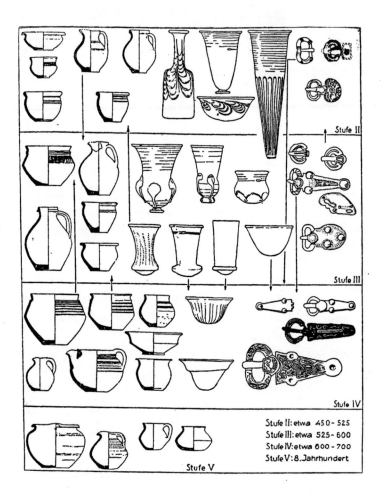

Fig. 10. Böhner's table showing development of pottery, glass and metalwork in Merovingian Gaul. The marked decline which Böhner sees from the seventh century onwards (Stufe IV) needs to be understood as beginning not in the year 600, which, as a cultural and historical marker is meaningless, but from the real watershed, which was somewhere between 625 and 640. All authorities now agree that the decline of Merovingian glasswork only began after the Arab blockade of the Mediterranean terminated the supply of raw materials from the Middle East. (After Edward James, *The Franks.*)

BRITAIN AND IRELAND IN THE SIXTH CENTURY

T he revival of the late Roman world after the adoption of Christianity is nowhere better illustrated than in Britain and Ireland. Both these regions saw a veritable "renaissance" of learning and prosperity between the fifth and seventh centuries. One of them, southern Britain, had been part of the Roman Empire, but had seen Roman civilization decline and almost disappear in the years between the third and sixth centuries. Other territories, such as Scotland (Caledonia) and Ireland, which had never been part of the Empire, were effectively incorporated into Latin civilization between the fifth and seventh centuries. Here Christianity took strong root and produced an astonishing flowering of culture. So striking was this in the case of Ireland that the island gained, in the sixth and seventh centuries, the reputation as the "Land of Saints and Scholars."

Although the two adjacent islands shared much in common, there were important differences; so it is perhaps best to deal with each separately. Let's look first at southern Britain; modern England.

* * *

We know that, of all the provinces of the Western Empire, the Province of Britannia was worst affected by the barbarian invasions of the fifth century. Here at least there is no question that Roman civilization was terminated, and that the entire region regressed into a more primitive state. Pirenne acknowledged this, and noted too that the Anglo-Saxons, unlike the Franks, Visigoths, and various other Germanic incomers, arrived as real invaders and destroyed the whole fabric of Roman life in the island. Uniquely, they transplanted their Germanic language to a new territory, completely supplanting Latin and the native Celtic language which yet survived in the countryside. The fact that very few Celtic or Latin words made their way into Anglo-Saxon also suggested a major clear-out of the native population. In addition, whilst the Visigoths, Ostrogoths, Franks and Vandals presided over a late classical civilization with urban settlements, Mediterranean trade and gold coinage, in Britain the towns largely disappeared and a barter economy, with only a little silver coinage, prevailed.

Yet in Britain, as in all other areas of the Roman Empire, the real "decline" began long before the invasions of the fifth century. It started two hundred years earlier. This has been illustrated most dramatically by the archaeology of London. We hear that, "Beginning in the third century and continuing into the fourth, there is clear evidence for major changes in what people were doing in the city [London]. Two changes are particularly evident, one involving the reuse of stone architectural elements, the other the deposition of soil over much of the formerly built-up areas."[1]

The above writer continues:

"During the third and fourth centuries, some large public structures built of stone were allowed to fall into disrepair, whereas others were carefully taken down, apparently for reuse of the stone elsewhere. Some of the stone was employed for building a new wall along the north bank of the Thames. Excavations in the 1970s in Upper Thames Street, along the course of the Roman river wall and the bank of the Thames at that time ... recovered sculpted stones and fifty-two blocks of cut stone that had been parts of standing structures. Some of the sculpted stones, carved with floral ornament and images of deities, had formed parts of monumental arch. Others, also with images of deities carved in relief, were parts of a tableau, or screen, twenty feet in length ...

"Some of the stones removed from large public structures were used for building houses for wealthy individuals during the third and fourth centuries. ... Even sculptures such as statues and tombstones were recycled as building stone. This practice of dismantling buildings to procure the stone blocks, and removing statues and gravestones to use the material for construction, seems strange to us, but it was common practice in the late Roman period and is well documented at many cities during the fourth century."[2]

Concomitant with this demolition and recycling of existing monuments, there appeared in London, as well as many other cities of the Roman world during the third and fourth centuries, a layer of

1 Wells, op cit., p. 109

2 Ibid., pp. 109-10

dark humic soil, sometimes more than a meter thick, containing cultural debris – pottery, bones of butchered animals, glass fragments, etc – mixed into it, covering occupational remains of earlier centuries. This "dark earth," as it is popularly known (not to be confused with the Younger Fill of the Mediterranean regions), was once regarded as evidence of decline and abandonment of Roman urban centers. However, for a variety of reasons, this interpretation has been dropped. It is now thought to represent not abandonment so much as a change in the urban environment. "The dark earth," says Wells, "has been found to contain remains of timber-framed, wattle-and-daub huts, along with sherds of pottery and metal ornaments datable to the late Roman period. These observations demonstrate that people who were living on the site were building their houses in the traditional British style rather than in the stone and cement fashion of elite and public Roman architecture."[3] "What are we to make of these two major changes reflected in the archaeology?" he asks. "After a rapid growth in the latter part of the first century, London emerged as a stunning center of the Roman Empire on its northern edge, with the monumental architecture, a thriving commercial center, and a military base characteristic of the greatest Roman cities. The third and fourth centuries at London are marked by a stoppage in major public architecture and a reverse of that process, the dismantling of major stone monuments, at the same time that much of the formerly urban area seems to have reverted to a non-urban character."[4]

We thus have ample evidence in the province of Britannia of the great crisis and contraction of Empire in the third century that we have noted elsewhere in Europe. Whatever may have happened on the European mainland in the late fourth and early fifth centuries, when the spread of Christianity may have revived the birth rate and halted population decline, there was to be no recovery in Britain. Here the barbarians began a war of annihilation against the native Romano-Britons, with the consequent complete disappearance of Latin civilization in the region. The five centuries which followed were a true Dark Age, with all urban settlement gone and its replacement by an illiterate and warlike culture so primitive that it even forgot how to make pottery.[5] Or so we have been told until recently. This narrative

---

3 Ibid., pp. 111-12

4 Ibid., p. 112

5 Or at least good-quality pottery, though even the poor-quality material is in short supply. See eg. Ward-Perkins, op cit, pp. 104-8 and 123

has always jarred somewhat with the written sources, which seemed to speak of a flourishing Christian society, from the mid-seventh century onwards, complete with prosperous towns like London (known as Lundenwic) and monastic institutes of learning producing artistic and literary masterpieces.

Fig. 11. Reconstruction of seventh century English Winchester Cathedral. (after M. Biddle). By the year 600 such structures, based on Roman and Byzantine architectural models, were being constructed in England. These were the first stone structures to appear in southern Britain for over two centuries.

The most recent discoveries of archaeology have tended to support the literary sources, in a rather dramatic way.[6] Excavations in London at the site of the Royal Opera House, carried out between 1989 and 1999, have revealed for the first time an extensive settlement area occupied during the early Anglo-Saxon epoch, from the sixth century onwards. "The community," we are told, "was actively involved in manufacture and trade. Ironworking was practiced, as was the manufacture of jewelry of silver and gold. Wine bottles from abroad attest to the importation of wine. Workshops of butchers, hide tanners, and bone and horn carvers have been identified. The area of modern London around Covent Garden is now known to have been the site of a

6 A thorough overview of the archaeological evidence is provided in Robin Fleming's excellent *Britain after Rome: The Fall and Rise, 400-1070* (Allen Lane, 2010)

major settlement during this early medieval period. Excavations have revealed numerous house foundations, ditches, and storage pits and substantial evidence of manufacturing and commercial activity. Indications of industry include kilns for firing pottery, decorative pins of different kinds, combs made of antler, and loom weights attesting to weaving on the site. West of Covent Garden, where Trafalgar Square now is located, were farms that produced the foodstuffs for the crafts workers and merchants. Food remains in the Covent Garden settlement indicate that wheat, barley, and rye were particularly important in the diet of the people there, along with the meat from cattle, sheep, and pigs. Other foods included beans, hazelnuts, and berries and other fruits. Particularly well represented among trade goods are imported pottery from the continent and other parts of Britain, grindstones made of basalt from the middle Rhineland, and coins from many different places."[7]

The wine bottles, pottery and coinage found in London indicate trade with Mediterranean lands; and this impression is reinforced by finds throughout southern Britain. We have seen, for example, how Hodges and Whitehouse accepted that the discovery of amphorae and other pottery from Carthage and the eastern Mediterranean in sites along the south coast of England pointed to, in their words, a limited trade with the Mediterranean regions in the fifth and sixth centuries. But the most recent evidence, especially from Tintagel in Cornwall, points to a vigorous rather than a limited commerce. We now hear of "masses of luxury imports from Spain, northern Africa, and the eastern end of the Mediterranean Sea."[8] These luxury objects, we are told, which included "large ceramic amphoras for transporting wine and olive oil, finely crafted bowls and plates, and ornate glass beakers," arrived throughout "the fifth, sixth and seventh centuries."[9] Cornwall, we know, was economically important to the Mediterranean civilizations from the Early Bronze Age onwards, owing to its high quality tin, essential for producing bronze. Evidently the region retained its importance into late Roman and Byzantine times.

The luxury products arriving here were traded throughout Britain and Ireland, and found their way to the feasting halls and fortresses of Anglo-Saxon and Celtic princes.

The wealth of these princes, who began (in England) to con-

---

7 Wells, op cit., p. 116

8 Ibid., p. 154

9 Ibid.

vert to Christianity and to foster Latin civilization from the late sixth century onwards, has been dramatically illustrated by great numbers of archaeological finds. Perhaps the most spectacular of these was at Sutton Hoo in East Anglia (south-east England). Here excavators in 1939 discovered an immensely wealthy royal ship burial, dating from around 600, complete with some of the most astonishing artwork and jewelry ever unearthed in the British Isles.

The fine quality and design of the metalwork, which shall be discussed more fully in a later chapter, indicated that it was the product of skilled and competent craftsmen, whilst the discovery of ten magnificent Byzantine silver bowls, together with two silver spoons, of the sixth century, are eloquent testimony to the vibrancy of trading and other cultural relations between Britain and the eastern Mediterranean at this time, supposedly the darkest of Britain's Dark Age.

Fig. 12. The Byzantine silverware discovered at Sutton Hoo, early seventh century.

Sutton Hoo, according to one writer, has shown that "… historians have underestimated, or at least understressed, the amount of moveable wealth that was at the disposal of a great seventh-century English king. … It is no longer possible to regard the culture of the Anglo-Saxon courts as a stunted and poverty-stricken version of the environment which surrounded the barbarian kings of larger peoples."[10] Again, says the same writer, "the discoveries greatly enlarge the range of contacts known to be possible to Englishmen of the early seventh century. … The discoveries at Sutton Hoo, like the traces of eastern influence on early English sculpture, should probably be taken as indications of peaceful, if sporadic, intercourse between England and the countries of the further Mediterranean."[11]

It should be noted that the ship burial is generally attributed to

10 Frank Stenton, *Anglo-Saxon England* (3rd ed., Oxford, 1973), p. 52
11 Ibid.

the East Anglian king Raedwald, who played a vital role in the Christianization of the Anglo-Saxons.

This fresh flowering of Latin civilization in Britain was augmented by several new and vital technologies, such as the moldboard plough, which powered an agricultural revolution that enabled new land to be brought into cultivation and consequently to support a far greater population. These technologies, which shall be discussed more fully in Chapter 9, were not infrequently popularized and spread by the monasteries, which themselves became centers of learning and technology. The growth of the monasteries was accompanied by a revival of building in stone. These structures were of late Roman design and were the first stone edifices to appear in Britain since the fourth century. The very first was Canterbury Cathedral, whose foundations were laid by Saint Augustine in 602. The original cathedral and associated buildings has of course – with the exception of the foundations – disappeared, though a little more of the church which served Augustine's suburban monastery of Saint Peter and Saint Paul has been recovered by excavation, and fragments still survive of two adjacent churches of the same period. These have all been shown to be of Italian design.[12] From then onwards church-building spread throughout England, and by the mid-seventh century we have several fairly intact examples of Saxon churches, amongst which are: All Saints' at Brixworth in Northamptonshire; Saint Martin's, Canterbury (seventh century nave with parts of possible earlier origin); and Saint Peter's on the Wall, at Bradwell-on-the-Sea, Essex (c. 654). Several others, reduced to their foundations, are also known. These structures, modest though they may be, bear eloquent testimony to the new expansion and growth which we have detected in Merovingian Gaul during the sixth century, and which we shall see again in Visigothic Spain in the same epoch. All of this is quite contrary to the view expounded by Hodges, Whitehouse and Ward-Perkins of a decrepit and dying late classical world from the second half of the sixth century.

Before moving on, we should note that the next surviving Anglo-Saxon churches date from the second quarter of the tenth century. There is nothing – or virtually nothing – attributable to the eighth, ninth, or early tenth centuries.[13] Church building reappears with Saint

---

12 Ibid., p. 111

13 The single exception is said to be Saint Wystan's church at Repton in Derbyshire, which contains a small crypt, dated from the mid-eight century, and chancel walls, supposedly dating from the ninth century.

Mary's Priory Church at Deerhurst in Gloucestershire, dated to circa 930. The new tenth century structures, notwithstanding the enormous gap of time separating them from their seventh century predecessors, bear striking resemblance to the latter and look, to all intents and purposes, as if they represent a natural continuation and progression from the earlier buildings.

Here then, once again, we find an example of that puzzling three-century long gap in the historical narrative of European civilization and society.

* * *

Unlike Britain, Ireland was never part of the Roman Empire. During the centuries of Rome's occupation of the neighboring island, Ireland had remained essentially a barbarian Celtic society, little different from the Gaul conquered by Caesar several centuries earlier. Then came Christianity. Famously, the new faith was said to have been introduced to Ireland by Saint Patrick, a native of Britain, who had apparently been captured by Irish slave-traders whilst still a boy, and forcibly brought to the land with which his life was to become so intimately connected. After escaping and training for the priesthood, he returned to the country as a missionary, where his teaching found fertile ground. Within a short time most of the island was converted; the last conquest, so it has often been said, of the Roman Empire.

Patrick is traditionally credited with preserving the tribal and social patterns of the Irish, codifying their laws and changing only those that conflicted with Christian practices. He is also credited with introducing the Roman alphabet, which enabled Irish monks to preserve parts of the extensive Celtic oral literature. The historicity of these claims remains the subject of debate and there is no direct evidence linking Patrick with any of these accomplishments. Nevertheless, they are all clearly connected with the appearance in the country of Christianity; and from Patrick's time at least Irish scholars excelled in the study of Latin learning and Christian theology. Nor was their knowledge confined to Latin: as we shall see, there exists ample evidence to show that Greek too, and the Greek writers – not all of them ecclesiastical – were taught in the Irish centers.

In effect, Ireland was now, by the late fifth century, added to Roman civilization. What the legions had failed to do, Christian missionaries accomplished within a decade or two. The Irish, previously remarkably resistant to Roman influences, now opened up. Fine ceramics, including African Red Slip Ware, as well as other *objets d'art*, began to make their appearance in the country.[14] Churches and cathedrals were erected, and monastic settlements became miniature universities. Very little of these structures has survived, but we know that, initially at least, they were of wood, or at least partly of wood. Several examples of apparently seventh century stone monastic churches, most famously the Oratory of Gallerus, provide us with a tantalizing glimpse of what once existed. Two contemporary descriptions of the larger Irish buildings have survived. The first, in an obscure seventh-century work called the *Hisperica Famina*, describes a square oratory fashioned out of massive wooden beams, with a western porch, a central altar, an ornamented roof, and four "steeples." The second is in Cogitosus' *Life of Saint Brigit*, also of the seventh century. The account is worth quoting in full:

> There (at Kildare) repose the glorious bodies of both Archbishop Conled and the noble virgin Brigit in their sarcophagi, the one to the right and the other to the left of the beautifully adorned altar. These sarcophagi are richly decorated with gold, silver and multicoloured precious stones; they have also pictorial representations in relief and in colours, and are surmounted by crowns of gold and silver. The church, however, is not the original one: a new church has been erected in the place of the old one, in order to hold the increased numbers of the faithful. Its ground-plan is large, and it rises to a dizzy height. It is adorned with painted tablets. The interior contains three large oratories, divided from one another by walls of timber, but all under one roof. One wall covered with linen curtains and decorated with paintings, traverses the eastern part of the church from one side to the other. There are doors in it at either end. The one door gives access to the sanctuary and the altar, where the bishop, with his school of clerics and those who are called to the celebration of the holy mysteries, offers the divine sacrifice to the Lord. By the other door of the dividing wall, the abbess enters with her virgins and

---

14 Nancy Edwards, *The Archaeology of Early Medieval Ireland* (B. T. Batsford Ltd., London, 1996), pp. 68-71. Prior to the fifth and sixth centuries, the number of identifiably Roman artefacts is "remarkably small." Ibid., p. 1

with pious widows in order to participate in the Supper of Jesus Christ, which is His flesh and blood. The reminder of the building is divided lengthwise into two equal parts by another wall, which runs from the western side to the transverse wall. The church has many windows. Priests and lay persons of the male sex enter by an ornamented door on the right-hand side; matrons and virgins enter by another door on the left-hand side. In this was the one basilica is sufficient for a huge crowd, separated by walls according to state. Grade and sex, but united in Spirit, to pray to the almighty Lord.[15]

A few of the famous Irish Round Towers (an adaptation of similar structures in Merovingian Gaul) are said to date from the sixth and seventh centuries.

With the adoption of the new faith (complete with its injunctions against warfare and infanticide), Ireland appears to have experienced substantial population growth. Certainly it was an epoch of expansion. Irish colonies were established along the western coasts of Britain and in Scotland (Caledonia). With the colonists came Irish missionaries and educators. Though their first efforts were concentrated in western and northern Britain, they soon moved further afield, bringing the Christian faith to previously barbarian regions such as eastern and northern Germany, and establishing monasteries and centers of learning wherever they went. Some travelled to Rome and beyond in search of precious manuscripts. The influence of Egypt, both in terms of art and religious ideas, began to be felt on the western shores of the Atlantic.

One of the best-known of these Irish missionaries was Columba, who left Ireland for western Scotland following a conflict over a book and its copy. Eventually he settled in Iona, off the coast of Scotland, where he established a monastic settlement that was to become renowned across Europe as a centre of Christian education. Columba had pledged to "convert as many souls for Christ" as he could and his new monastery was designed specifically for this undertaking. His monks were sent throughout Europe.

When King Oswald of Northumbria in England wanted a center of learning to be established for the education of Anglo-Saxon boys, he called upon the great monastery of Iona to provide him with a

---

15 Cited from Nancy Edwards, Ibid., p. 122

spiritual guide. The task was taken up by another Irish monk, Aiden, who, traditionally in 635, but probably earlier, arrived at Lindisfarne Island, which soon became the base and cradle of Celtic Christianity in north-east England. From there, the whole of Northumbria and the northern half of England was converted.

Two of the first pupils accepted into Lindisfarne were Anglo-Saxon brothers called Cedd and Chad. The elder of these two, Cedd, was sent to Mercia, in the English midlands, where he quickly transformed the region. He was so successful that when King Sigbert of the East Saxons (Essex) asked for a similar mission, it was Cedd who was sent with one companion. Cedd's first church in Essex was built of wood, but this was soon replaced by a more permanent structure using cut-stones from a nearby Roman fort. This new church, now called Saint Peter's on the Wall, was modeled on the churches of Egypt and Syria, illustrating the profound influence that the Eastern Church then exerted in the far-off regions of the west. Although generally dated to later in the seventh century, the Egyptian influence would seem to indicate that this structure must have been completed before circa 630, when, as we shall see, Arab piracy severely curtailed travel on the Mediterranean.

The monastery attached to Saint Peter's on the Wall was said to have incorporated a hospital, a guest-house and a library. All in the middle of a supposed Dark Age!

Perhaps the most notable of Ireland's scholars, as opposed to saints, of this period, was John Scotus Erigena (or Eriugena). As well as being a theologian, he was a Neoplatonist scholar and a poet. He travelled to various parts of Europe, and seems to have had a thorough knowledge of Greek, as well as Latin. About the age of thirty, we are told, he moved from Ireland to France, where he took over the Palatine Academy at the invitation of King Charles the Bald. He succeeded Alcuin of York as head of the Palace School. It is generally believed that he remained in France for at least thirty years, during which time he undertook, at the request of Byzantine Emperor Michael III the translation into Latin of the works of Pseudo-Dionysius. He also added his own commentary, thus being the first to introduce the ideas of Neoplatonism from the Greek into the Western European intellectual tradition.

Erigena was a "truly original thinker," a Christian universalist who he believed that all people and all beings, including animals, reflect attributes of God, towards whom all are capable of progressing and to which all things ultimately must return. His thought was Neo-platonist to the core, and "while recognizing the validity of authority in thought and accepting the authority of the Scriptures, he insisted upon the equal validity of reason."[16] "Authority," he wrote, "sometimes proceeds from reason, but reason never from authority. For all authority which is not approved by true reason seems weak. But true reason, since it is established in its own strength, needs to be strengthened by the assent of no authority."[17] To Erigena, hell was not a place but a condition and punishment was purifying, not penal. He was a believer in apocatastasis, which maintains that all moral creatures – angels, humans and devils – will eventually come to a harmony in God's kingdom.

Erigena based his beliefs on the Greek writings of the early Christian fathers, like Origen, and considered himself an orthodox Christian thinker. And his knowledge of Greek is a crucial chronological marker. Having travelled to the East and studied there, he must have lived and worked before the middle of the seventh century, though he is generally placed at a somewhat later date.

* * *

The sixth and early seventh centuries therefore saw the expansion, rather than the withering away, of classical Latin civilization. The great works of Greek and Roman literature were now known and debated in the formerly barbarian lands of Ireland and Caledonia. Paganized Britain, or England, was again being Romanized, this time mainly through the offices of Christianity. Churches and cathedrals, based on Roman and Near Eastern models, began to appear throughout the British Isles and in the previously savage lands of eastern Germany, on the borders of the Elbe. Around these ecclesiastical centers towns and cities began to form in regions never reached by the armies of Imperial Rome. Far from being in terminal decline, classical civilization was on the move.

Although the art and technical know-how of the peoples of western Europe in the fifth to seventh centuries is a topic we shall deal with in a separate place, it would be impossible to complete this section without mention of the astonishing craftwork that appeared in Ireland

---

16 Ibid., p. 258
17 Ibid.

and Britain at this time.

Fig. 13. Page from the Book of Kells, probably early seventh century. The Hiberno-Saxon illuminated manuscripts of this period, which used blue pigment derived from Afghanistan lapis-lazuli, are by common consent among the finest and most technically brilliant works of miniature art ever produced.

Influenced by the Anglo-Saxons in mainland Britain, Irish artists in the fifth and sixth centuries, many of them monks, developed a new decorative style, described as Hiberno-Saxon, which combined the old Celtic motifs of the region with the interlinking animals and serpents which the Anglo-Saxons had brought from Germany (ultimately under the influence of the Goths). The new style was now applied to some of the most outstanding artwork ever created. Illuminated books and metalwork, whose microscopic detail is justly celebrated, make us wonder whether the insular artists were in possession of an understanding of the magnifying lens. And the materials used in these masterpieces, such as lapis-lazuli from Afghanistan (the source of ultramarine blue), convince us that both the Book of Kells and the Lindisfarne Gospels were created before the middle of the seventh century.[18]

The quality and sheer technical competence of Hiberno-Saxon art is perhaps best illustrated by the comments of art historian J. O. Westwood: "I have examined, with a magnifying glass, the pages of the Gospels of Lindisfarne and the Book of Kells, for hours together without ever detecting a false line or an irregular interlacement; and when it is considered that many of these details consist of spiral lines, and are so minute as to be impossible to have been executed with a pair of compasses, it really seems a problem not only with what eyes, but also with what instruments, they could have been executed. One instance of the minuteness of these details will suffice to give an idea of this peculiarity. I have counted in a small space, measuring scarcely three-quarters of an inch in width, in the Book of Armagh, not fewer than one hundred and fifty-eight interlacements of a slender ribbon-pattern, formed of white lines edged by black ones upon a black ground.

Fig. 14. Round Tower at Glendalough in Ireland. These bell-towers were the Irish equivalent of the Italian campanile which appeared in the early seventh century. It would appear that the Irish began constructing their own similar bell-towers very shortly thereafter.

18 See www.irish-society.org/Hedgemaster%20Archives/book_of_Kells.htm

No wonder that an artist of Dublin, lately applied to by Mr Chambers to copy one of the pages of the book of Kells, excused himself from the labour on the grounds that it was a tradition that the lines had been traced by angels."[19]

Art historian Kenneth Clark remarked on the fact that the technical excellence of the work evinced in the Book of Kells and the Lindisfarne Gospels was never equaled. They are, he said, "almost the richest and most complicated pieces of abstract decoration ever produced," and are "more sophisticated and refined than anything in Islamic art."[20] This in spite of the fact that among the Muslims (owing to the ban on representational art), calligraphy became the primary outlet of artistic expression.

19 Westwood, quoted in Thompson and Johnson, op cit., pp. 212-3
20 Kenneth Clark, *Civilisation* (BBC publication, London, 1969), p. 11

SPAIN IN THE SIXTH CENTURY

P erhaps owing to the fact that the Islamic Emirate founded in Spain in the eighth century has captured the imagination of so many writers in the English-speaking world, Visigothic Spain has tended to be eclipsed in terms of academic attention. Even worse, many of those who speak and write of the Visigothic epoch do so only as a preliminary to a discussion of the Islamic period, and works promoting the old and clichéd view of the "barbarian" Visigoths continue to appear with depressing regularity. Oblivious to the discoveries of archaeology, these insist that Visigothic Spain was a declining and generally disintegrating society. Recent examples of the genre (and it is an enormous one) are Thomas F. Glick's *Islamic and Christian Spain in the Early Middle Ages* (originally published by Princeton University in 1979, but republished by Brill Publishers in 2005) and David Levering Lewis's *God's Crucible: Islam and the Making of Europe, 570 – 1215* (New York, W. W. Norton and Company, 2008). Both these authors present what they purport to be an examination of the Visigothic state prior to the Islamic conquest. They each endeavor to portray a divided and stratified society that was already in an advanced state of decay before the arrival of the Muslims. They admit that the ruling Visigoths formed a relatively small proportion of the population – perhaps a quarter of a million Visigoths as against about six to eight million Hispano-Romans. This we might imagine would imply that the economy should have continued more or less as it had been before the Visigothic conquest. Yet Glick and Lewis will have none of this. They argue that the country was an economic ruin when the Arabs arrived; though they demure in identifying the cause of this ruin, save from hinting darkly that natural disaster may have had a role to play. In Glick's words:

"The Hispano-Romans followed the general pattern of Mediterranean agriculture: cereal grains (wheat and barley), grapes, and vegetables grown in irrigated fields in the Ebro Valley and the Eastern littoral. What is clear is that the entire economy was in a state of profound disarray and agriculture was ruined as result of a series of natural disasters beginning in the seventh century. Perhaps we can accept at the root of this string of bad harvests, famine, and plague Ignacio Olagüe's theory of a general climatic shift in the western Mediterranean world, beginning in the third century A.D., which had the result of making the climate drier and hotter and which reached crisis proportions in the high middle ages, forcing a greater dependence on irrigation agriculture in North Africa and Spain. Medieval chronicles noted famine and plague in the reign of Erwig (680-686), when half the population was said to have perished. Plagues of locusts were reported. There can be no doubt that the constant political turmoil of late-seventh- and early-eighth-century Spain takes on more poignant meaning if set against a background of worsening harvests, prolonged drought, famine, and depopulation. Moreover, it makes more intelligible the shift in the balance of peninsular agriculture, away from dry-farming and herding, towards an increased reliance on irrigated crops, during the Islamic period. Islamic society in Spain was able to adjust to an arid ecology by directing the flow of economic resources into the technological adjustments required to increase irrigated acreage, whereas the Visigoths understood only a herding, forest ecology and could not adjust to any other."[1]

Amidst all the wordiness here the only evidence proffered for a climate shift are the medieval chronicles which "noted famine and plague in the reign of Erwig." But medieval chronicles noted famine and plague all the time, and their reliability is now regarded as suspect, to say the least. This is very poor grounds for such a sweeping statement about a national economy during a period of over two centuries. Note also the claim that the entire climate of North Africa became drier in the seventh and eighth centuries, thereby exonerating the Arabs from any responsibility for the desertification of these once-prosperous regions. Yet the loss of North Africa's agricultural base is intimately tied with the arrival in the region of the Arabs, as we shall see in this and subsequent chapters.

Glick's pronouncements on Spain's urban economy in the Visigothic period are of a type with those on agriculture. He tells us that, "Visigothic trade was largely in the hands of Jews, who formed a numerous minority, and foreigners." This, he claims, could have had re-

---

1 Thomas F. Glick, *Islamic and Christian Spain in the Early Middle Ages* (Brill Publishers, New York, 2005), pp., 30-1

percussions: "When economic recession set in, Jews were blamed and a regressive cycle of restrictive anti-Jewish legislation could only have led to more disruptions of trade."[2] We here note the phrase "could only have." And this, essentially, says it all. The author is clutching at straws, endeavoring to paint a picture of a decayed and degenerate civilization, already in the clutches of its own Dark Age before the arrival of the Muslims. "The barbarian invasions [of the Visigoths]," he claims, "were further responsible for the physical ruin of much of the urban plant built by the Romans," and "Archaeological evidence demonstrates that when the Muslim invaders arrived in 711 many Hispano-Roman cities were already largely buried in subsoil."

This latter is a reference to a layer of subsoil which in fact covers virtually all late classical settlements in the Mediterranean, from Syria to Spain and Morocco, though Glick is apparently unaware of this. We shall deal with this stratum in due course, for it is extremely important in attempting to understand the fate of Graeco-Roman civilization. But before proceeding we should note that the reference Glick provides is a Spanish one, Leopoldo Torres Balbás, who however does not blame the Visigoths for the feature: all he says is that the deposit generally marks the end of the Roman period. Yet Visigothic civilization, by any reckoning, was "Roman" in its essential features; so it is evident that the clay stratum in question cannot be used as proof that the Visigoths destroyed the Roman cities.[3] In fact, the latest archaeological consensus, as we shall shortly see, is that the Hispano-Roman cities thrived under the Visigoths. It was only after the Arab conquest that urban life disintegrated.

The impression of bad faith on the part of the author is reinforced by his pronouncements on almost every topic. Take for example his comments on mining and metallurgy under the Visigoths:

> "The economic regressiveness of Visigothic Spain is well illustrated by the failure of the Goths to carry on the vast mining enterprise begun by the Romans, who removed from Iberian pits a wide variety of metals, including silver, gold, iron, lead, copper, tin, and cinnabar, from which mercury is made. The relative insignificance of mining in Visigothic Spain is attested to by the winnowing of the full account given by Pliny to the

2 Ibid., p. 29

3 Leopoldo Torres Balbas, *Ciudades hispano-musulmanas* Vol. 1 (Ministerio de Asuntos Exteriores, n.d., Madrid), pp. 32-4, 38.

meager details supplied by Isidore of Seville, who omits any mention, for example, of iron deposits in Cantabria. The most important Roman mines have lost their Latin names, generally yielding to Arabic ones – as in Almadén and Aljustrel – probably an indication of their quiescence during the Visigothic period and their revival by the Muslims. The Goths may have allowed their nomadic foraging instinct to direct their utilization of metal resources. In some areas mined by the Romans they probably scavenged for residual products of abandoned shafts that remained unworked, and metal for new coinage seems largely to have been provided by booty captured from enemies or from older coins fleeced from taxpayers."

Take note: The only evidence Glick has that mining declined under the Visigoths is the "meagre details supplied by Isidore of Seville" and the fact that the most important Roman-age mines in Spain are now known by Arabic names. This hardly constitutes convincing evidence upon which to make such a sweeping statement; and it stands in stark contrast to the vast wealth, in gold, silver and precious stones, that the Arabs themselves claimed to have carried off from Spain.

Glick's portrayal of the Visigoths as nomadic pastoralists verges on the comic, given the fact that they had left their nomad existence behind two centuries earlier and had adapted so completely to the Roman style of life (remember they never constituted more than a tiny minority of the Spanish population) that they left not a single Germanic word in the Spanish language. The Arab chroniclers who described the conquest of Spain remarked repeatedly on the effeminacy of the Visigoths. Not, we might feel, the most attractive of characteristics, but one that is hardly typical of nomadic warriors. Glick goes on:

"Thus the failure of the Visigothic state, seen in its unbalanced economy, as well as in its disjointed and incohesive social organization, was also reflected in its technological atony, which was at the core of the elite's inability to adapt to any ecology other than that with which it was originally familiar: the men of the woods never strayed too far from there. They were unable to build on the Roman base. In 483 the duke Salla repaired the Roman bridge at Mérida; yet in 711 the Arabs found the bridge at Córdoba in ruins …"[4]

4 Glick, op cit., p. 31

On this last point, it seems never to have occurred to Glick that the Visigoths themselves destroyed the bridge to prevent the further advance of the Arab armies. This is a basic rule of warfare. Yet the comment is typical of Glick and adds further ammunition to the idea that he is pursuing an ideological agenda, and has little interest in facts. Unable to find any evidence of a decaying urban environment either in the written sources or in the archaeology, Glick clutches at straws. For the facts, as disclosed both by archaeology and contemporary written sources, as we shall now see, speak of Visigothic Spain as a prosperous and largely urban late classical civilization.

Fig. 15. View of Reccopolis, one of at least four great cities founded by the Visigoths during the sixth and seventh centuries.

It is well known that, unlike Gaul, Spain was a relatively urbanized and sophisticated society under Imperial Rome. Along with Italy and North Africa, the Iberian Peninsula had been one of the mainstays of Graeco-Roman civilization. What then happened under the Visigoths: Did it retain its pre-eminence? Written evidence certainly gives the impression of life continuing more or less as normal. One of the most important sources, the *Vitas Patrum Emeritensium*, or Lives of the Fathers of Merida, apparently written in the seventh century, provides a vivid description of everyday existence in the city of Merida, the provincial capital and seat of the metropolitan bishop of Lusitania in the sixth century. "The impression created by the Lives of the Fathers of Merida," we are told, "is that of a city [and a society] still enjoying a period of some prosperity in the sixth century ..."[5] Even the Arab invaders, who arrived in Spain several decades later, were impressed by the size and opulence of the cities. Their annalists recall the appearance at the time of Seville, Cordoba, Merida and Toledo; "the four capitals of Spain, founded," they tell us naively, "by Okteban [Octavian] the Caesar." Seville, above all, seems to have struck them by its wealth and its illustriousness in various ways. "It was," writes Ibn Adhari,

> "among all the capitals of Spain the greatest, the most important, the best built and the richest in ancient monuments. Before its conquest by the Goths it had been the residence of the Roman governor. The Gothic kings chose Toledo for their residence; but Seville remained the seat of the Roman adepts of sacred and profane science, and it was there that lived the nobility of the same origin."[6]

This can hardly be described as the picture of a society in the middle of a Dark Age! Another Arab writer, Merida, praises Seville's great bridge as well as "magnificent palaces and churches."[7]

The Iberian Peninsula has been much excavated over the past half century, and what has been found fully confirms the literary testimony. Archaeologists have uncovered a "wealth" of architectural remains, which "seem to confirm" the impression created by the written sources.[8] We are told that, "Continuity from classical antiquity into the sixth century is strikingly recorded at Merida" and various other places, and that "in Visigothic Spain elements of physical continuity with antiquity were greater than is often appreciated."[9] We hear, for example, that "the very distinctive style of sculpture of the sixth and seventh centuries, which seems to have spread to other parts of western Baetica and southern Lusitania, appears to owe something to the

---

5 Roger Collins, *Early Medieval Spain: Unity in Diversity, 400 – 1000*, (2nd ed. Macmillan, 1995), p. 88

6 Cited from Louis Bertrand and Sir Charles Petrie, *The History of Spain* (2nd ed., London, 1945), p. 7

7 Ibid., pp. 17-8

8 Roger Collins, op cit., p. 88

9 Ibid.

conscious imitation of the models of the earlier Roman past ... as well as to the influence of contemporary Byzantium."[10] "Recent excavation," we hear, "has shown that the urban centre of Merida did remain in use in the Visigothic period and that, unlike some of the former towns of Roman Britain, it did not become a deserted or semi-rustic area. The principal change lay in the way Christian buildings replaced the former secular public ones in the city centre. Traces of what appears to be a substantial civic basilica, now obscurely described as a triumphal arch, survive beside the site of the early Roman forum. Adjacent to this structure was the Church of St Mary, the Baptistery of St John and the bishop's palace. At least one other church was built across on the other side of the forum in the sixth century."[11]

Fig. 16. Church of Saint John, built by Visigoth king Recceswinth in the seventh century and fashioned entirely of cut stone.

Evidence of the same type has been found in all the cities of Iberia between the fifth and seventh centuries. Quite literally hundreds of Visigothic-period structures are known, and we must bear in mind that

10 Ibid., pp. 88-9

11 Ibid., p. 90

these can only represent a small fraction of what once existed. One of the most outstanding examples of architecture from the period, and one often quoted in the literature, is the seventh century church of St John in Baños de Cerrato, Valencia, perhaps the oldest church in Spain. In Visigoth times, this was an important grain-producing region and legend has it that King Recceswinth commissioned the building of a church there when, on returning from a successful campaign against the Basques, he drank from the waters and recovered his health. The original inscription of the king, cut in the stones above the entrance, can still be discerned. Several bronze belt buckles and liturgical objects – as well as a necropolis with 58 tombs – have been discovered in the vicinity.

The impressive Gothic Cathedral at Valencia itself also has a crypt from the Visigoth era.

Again, the elegant Ermita de Santa María de Lara, at Quintanilla de Las Viñas, near Burgos, is a masterpiece of the Visigothic architectural style. Among its outstanding features is an unusual triple frieze of bas reliefs on its outer walls. Other surviving examples of Visigothic architecture are to be found in the La Rioja and Orense regions. The so-called horseshoe arch, which was to become so predominant in Moorish architecture, occurs first in these Visigothic structures, and was evidently an innovation of their architects. Toledo, the capital of Spain during this period, still displays in its architecture the influence of the Visigoths. It should be noted too that, whilst the quality and quantity of new buildings in Spain declined during the last few centuries of Roman rule – as it did everywhere else – it showed a marked improvement under the later Visigoths. Everywhere we look there are signs of renewed prosperity and urban expansion. New cities were founded.[12] Reccopolis, for example, established by Leovigild in 578, was to become a major administrative and commercial center, and excavations at the site have dramatically illustrated the sheer wealth and sophistication of Visigoth society at the time. Indeed, all the indications are of an expanding population, something we would expect to have occurred earlier in Spain than in the other western provinces, owing to the region's extremely large Jewish population and to the very early conversion of the peninsula to Christianity. In Reccopolis

---

12 According to E. A. Thompson, there were at least four. In addition to Reccopolis, there was Victoriacum (apparently modern Vitoria); Ologicus (modern Olite); and Lugo, or Luceo. E. A. Thompson, "The Barbarian Kingdoms in Gaul and Spain," *Nottingham Mediaeval Studies*, 7 (1963), pp. 4n, 11

and elsewhere we encounter again the use of carefully fashioned stone for entire buildings – a practice that had been abandoned in Spain by the fourth century. From then on cut stone was everywhere replaced by unhewn blocks in churches and palaces, with only the corner-stones – often plundered from earlier monuments – of cut-stone. Yet by the early seventh century Visigoth architects were again using carefully fashioned stone for entire buildings; and we should note, in passing, that these structures are far superior, technically and artistically, to their successors of the tenth century Romanesque.[13] During the latter epoch the cut-stone of the Visigoths is replaced by rough, uncut stone, and the churches, generally smaller, are not nearly so richly decorated, with only very small arches and vaulting. There is all round a general impoverishment when compared to the work of the Visigoths, whose standards are only again reached around 1100.

So, we might be justified in concluding that archaeology has only reinforced the impression laid down centuries ago by the chroniclers and biographers of a prosperous and cultured society under the Visigoths. We know that a silk-making industry had taken root in the Peninsula during the sixth century – very shortly after the secret of silk-production was sequestered out of China during the reign of Justinian,[14] and we know that well into the seventh century there existed a lively economic intercourse between the Visigothic kingdom and the eastern Mediterranean. Evidence of every kind therefore leads to the conclusion that Spain under the Visigoths, like North Africa under the Vandals, experienced not a decline but a great revival of culture and prosperity. But if such be the case, how is it that Spain fell so easily to the Islamic invaders? The very rapidity and ease with which the Muslims overran the Peninsula has, after all, been – until recently – one of the most important factors in convincing scholars of the decay and decadence of the Visigothic state.

The topic of Islam's conquests, and their speed, is one that shall be dealt with fully in due course. For the present, it is sufficient to note that the lands conquered by the Muslims during the seventh and early eighth centuries were invariably the most civilized parts of the Roman and Mediterranean worlds. It was only when they reached the more barbarous and least Romanized regions, such as the north of Spain and central Gaul, that the Muslims began to face effective resistance.

---

13 See eg. Heribert Illig, *Wer hat an der Uhr gedreht?* (Econ Taschenbuch Verlag, 2000), pp. 106-10

14 See eg. Louis Bertrand, op cit.

In short, the evidence would indicate that Visigothic Spain fell (just like Syria, eastern Anatolia, and Egypt), not because it was too barbarous, but because it was too civilized. In the words of Roger Collins, "The relative speed with which most of southern and central Spain fell to the Arab armies (mostly consisting of Berbers recruited in recently conquered North Africa) is testimony more to the sophistication of the Visigothic monarchy than to the decline and decay that historians once thought was its hallmarks."[15] Again, "Once prevalent interpretations of the late Visigothic kingdom as being decadent and demoralized are now discounted."[16]

Before leaving the topic of Visigothic Spain, it is important to emphasize a crucial feature: The abundance of archaeology from Visigothic times contrasts sharply with the virtually complete absence of all archaeology from the first two centuries of the Islamic epoch. This is a fact that has only recently come to the attention of the scholarly community, and assuredly constitutes one of the greatest puzzles unearthed by excavation. We have traditionally been told that the first two centuries of the Spanish Emirate, supposedly founded in 756 by Abd' er Rahman I, constituted a veritable Golden Age of Spanish history. The following description of eighth-tenth century Cordoba, written by English historian H. St. L. B. Moss in 1935, may be regarded as fairly typical of the genre: "In Spain ... the foundation of Umayyad power [in 756] ushers in an era of unequalled splendour, which reaches its height in the early part of the tenth century. The great university of Cordova is thronged with students ... while the city itself excites the wonder of visitors from Germany and France. The banks of the Guadalquivir are covered with luxurious villas, and born of the ruler's caprice rises the famous Palace of the Flower, a fantastic city of delights."[17]

The picture Moss paints was derived from medieval Arab annalists, who spoke of a city of half a million inhabitants, of three thousand mosques, of one hundred and thirteen thousand houses, and of three hundred public baths – this not even counting the twenty-eight suburbs said to have surrounded the metropolis.[18]

15 Roger Collins, *Spain: An Oxford Archaeological Guide to Spain* (Oxford University Press, 1998), p. 23

16 Ibid., p. 20

17 H. St. L. B. Moss, *The Birth of the Middle Ages; 395-814* (Oxford University Press, 1935), p. 172

18 See eg. R. Dozy, *Histoire des Musulmans d'Espagne jusqu'à la Conquête de l'Andalousie*

Over the past sixty years intensive efforts have been made to discover this astonishing civilization – to no avail. Try as they might, archaeologists have found hardly anything, hardly a brick or inscription,
for the two centuries prior to the mid-tenth, at which point substantial
remains are indeed attested. According to the prestigious *Oxford Archaeological Guide*, Cordoba has revealed, after exhaustive excavations:
(a) The south-western portion of the city wall, which is presumed to
date from the ninth century; (b) A small bath-complex, of the 9th/10th
century; and (c) A part of the Umayyad (8th/9th century) mosque.[19]
This is all that can be discovered from two centuries of the history of
a city of supposedly half a million people. By way of contrast, consider the fact that Roman London, a city not one-tenth the size that
eighth and ninth century Cordoba is said to have been, has yielded
dozens of first-class archaeological sites. And even the three locations
mentioned in the Guide are open to question. The city wall portion is
only "presumably" of the ninth century, whilst the part of the mosque
attributed to the eighth century is said to have been modeled by Abd'
er Rahman I. However, the latter character sounds suspiciously like his
namesake and supposed descendant Abd' er Rahman III, of the tenth
century, who indisputably made alterations to the mosque (which was
originally the Cathedral of Saint Vincent).

Even when real archaeology does appear at Cordoba, from the
mid-tenth century onwards, the settlement is absolutely nothing like
the conurbation described by the Arab writers. Indeed, at its most opulent, from the late tenth to the late eleventh centuries, the 'metropolis'
had, it would seem, no more than about forty thousand inhabitants;
and this settlement was built directly upon the Roman and Visigothic
city, which had a comparable population. We know that Roman and
Visigothic villas, palaces and baths were simply reoccupied by the
Muslims, often with very little alteration to the original plan. And
when they did build new edifices, the cut-stones, columns and decorative features were more often than not plundered from earlier Roman/
Visigoth remains. A text of the medieval writer Aben Pascual tells us
that there were, in his time, to be seen in Cordoba surviving buildings,
"Greek and Roman. … Statues of silver and gilded bronze within them
poured water into receptacles, whence it flowed into ponds and into
marble basins excellently carved."[20]

par les Almoravides, Vol. 1 (Paris, 1861)

19 Collins, *Spain: An Oxford Archaeological Guide to Spain*, p. 120

20 Cited from Bertrand, op cit., p. 65

So much for the "vast metropolis" of eighth to tenth century Cordoba. The rest of Spain, which has been investigated with equal vigor, can deliver little else. A couple of settlements here and a few fragments of pottery there, usually of doubtful date and often described as "presumably" ninth century or such like. Altogether, the *Oxford Guide* lists a total of no more than eleven sites and individual buildings in the whole country (three of which are those from Cordoba mentioned above) which are supposed to date from before the first quarter of the tenth century. These are, in addition to the above three:

Balaguer: A fortress whose northern wall, with its square tower, "is almost entirely attributable" to the late-9th century. (p. 73)

Fontanarejo: An early Berber settlement, whose ceramic finds date it to "no later than the 9th century." (p. 129)

Guardamar: A ribat or fortress mosque, which was completed, according to an inscription, in 944. However, "Elements in its construction have led to its being dated to the 9th cent." (pp. 143-4)

Huesca: An Arab fortress which "has been dated to the period around 875." (p. 145)

Madrid: Fortress foundations dating to around 870. (p. 172)

Merida: A fortress attributed to Abd' er-Rahman II (822-852). (p. 194)

Monte Marinet: A Berber settlement with ceramics within "a possible chronological range" from the 7th to the early 9th century. (p. 202)

Olmos: An Arab fortress with ceramics "dated to the 9th cent." (pp. 216-7)

The above meager list contrasts sharply with the hundreds of sites and structures from the Visigothic epoch – a comparable timespan – mentioned in the same place. (It is impossible to be precise about the Visigothic period, since many sites, such as Reccopolis, contain literally hundreds of individual structures. If we were to enumerate the

Visigoth structures by the same criteria as we did the Islamic remains above, then the Visigoth period would reveal not hundreds, but thousands of finds). And we stress again that most of the above Islamic finds suffer from a problem highlighted by Hodges and Whitehouse in other parts of Europe: an almost unconscious attempt to backdate material of the tenth century into the ninth and eighth in order to have *something* to assign to the latter epoch.[21] Look for example at the fortress of Guardamar. Although an inscription dates the completion of the edifice to 944, we are told that "elements" in its construction have led to it being dated to the ninth century. What these elements are is not clear; yet we should note that such defended mosques, being essentially fortresses, must have been raised very quickly – certainly in no more than a decade. Why then are we told that this one took fifty or perhaps seventy-five years to complete? Bearing this in mind, we can say that there is scarcely a single undisputed archaeological site attributable to the first two centuries of Islamic rule; whilst there are, to date, hundreds of rich and undisputed sites linked to the Visigothic epoch! The first real Islamic archaeology in Spain occurs during the time of Abd' er Rahman III, in the third or fourth decade of the tenth century (when the Guardamar fortress was completed); and it should be noted that the life and career of the latter character sounds suspiciously like that of his namesake and ancestor Abd' er Rahman I, who is supposed to have lived two centuries earlier, at the beginning of the Islamic epoch in Iberia.

What could all this mean? There is no question that the Muslim invaders wrought great destruction in the Iberian Peninsula. Roger Collins mentions numerous settlements destroyed at the time, many of which were never reoccupied. And it is true, as we shall see, that the Arab doctrine of jihad, or perpetual war against the Infidel, led to the permanent devastation of huge areas of Spain and the destruction of the agricultural base of the region. In Chapter 11 we shall find how it was this custom of incessant and unremitting raiding which led to the formation of the subsoil layer mentioned by Glick. Yet even taking such factors into account, we have to admit that the absence of all archaeology for two centuries is not adequately explained. Not even the most destructive invaders could remove all trace of life and habitation from a territory for that period of time.

And the suspicion that some other factor is involved is reinforced by the knowledge that Spain is not the only region to experience this

---

21 Hodges and Whitehouse, op cit., p. 84

phenomenon. Indeed, the same thing is encountered throughout Europe and the Middle East. So complete is the disappearance of archaeology that we might suspect a complete and total depopulation of everything from the British Isles to eastern Persia. And the attempts of Hodges and Whitehouse to suggest a declining population throughout the territories of the classical world during the fifth and sixth centuries is at least partly explained by the subsequent apparent wipe-out of all settlement by the late seventh and early eighth centuries. As the authors themselves note, repeated attempts to discover any trace of urban life for these years have resulted in complete failure: "... all these efforts," they remark, "provide us with an invaluable body of negative evidence against the continuity of towns after 600, and the case for discontinuity of urban life is very strong indeed."[22] They even note the somewhat desperate attempts of archaeologists to backdate material of the tenth century into the ninth, simply to have something from that century. "For two decades," they write, "urban archaeologists have doggedly searched for traces of seventh- to ninth-century occupation above Roman levels, simply to verify isolated historical references to the existence of an *urbs* or a *municipium*. Thwarted by the absence of early medieval deposits, there is the constant temptation to attribute tenth-century layers to the ninth century and so to recover at least something in the bid to prove urban continuity."[23] The authors concede that, "the excavated areas are tiny percentages of the Roman or later medieval settlements," and leave open the possibility that something more substantial might be found in the future. That was in 1982; yet we can state that in the almost thirty intervening years nothing more substantial has been found. Indeed, the progress of excavation has only powerfully reinforced the negative evidence mentioned above, and as every new site is examined, it becomes increasingly less likely that we will ever find much from these truly "dark" centuries. And even the pitifully few monuments or artifacts hitherto assigned to the "dark centuries," such as Charlemagne's chapel at Aachen – supposedly built around 800 – have, upon closer inspection, been shown to date from other ages entirely. Thus dozens of architectural and stylistic features show that the Aachen chapel could not have been built before the eleventh century.[24] The same can be said for settlements. Until recently, for example, Professor Ferdinanrd Opll, of Vienna, held that in Vienna a

---

22 Ibid.

23 Ibid.

24 See esp. Heribert Illig, *Das erfundene Mittelalter*

small community had continued to exist throughout the seventh to tenth centuries, but in August 2010 he finally admitted: "For more than 300 years, old Vindobona [Vienna] was deserted ... Wolves were searching the ruins for prey."[25] Professor Karl Brunner of the same department has for years insisted that the entire Danube valley between Linz and Vienna was uninhabitable for three centuries.

It cannot be stressed too strongly that this apparently complete demographic collapse is found not only in Europe, but also in the Eastern Empire (from the 630s onwards) and in the Islamic lands (also from the 630s onwards). And whether or not there was a massive demographic decline in western Europe in the decades that preceded 600 – as Hodges and Whitehouse suggest – there is no question of any such decline in the East, where bustling and densely populated cities of the 610s and 620s have been excavated. After the 630s these are as depopulated as western Europe.

What, we might ask again, does all this mean? How could the whole of Europe and the Middle East lose virtually its entire population for three centuries? And even worse: how could these regions then, in the mid-tenth century, be re-peopled by settlers whose material culture is strikingly similar to that of their seventh-century predecessors?

This is one of the great puzzles of modern archaeology, and it is one that will be revisited frequently as we proceed through our investigation.

25 H. Lackner, "Multikulti in Ur-Wien. Archäologie. Historiker schreiben die Geschichte Wiens neu: Anders also bisher angenommen, war die Stadt zu Beginn des Mittelalters 300 Jahre lang eine menschenleere Ruinenlandschaft," in *Profil*, Wien (2010), 31

SCIENCE AND LEARNING IN THE WEST

P irenne devoted considerable space in *Mohammed and Charle-magne* to an examination of intellectual and cultural life in the western provinces during the fifth and sixth centuries, where he showed a striking continuity of classical attitudes and institutions. There were some towering figures during this epoch, men such as Boethius, Cassiodorus, and Benedict. Furthermore, the general impression conveyed in the literature is of a well-educated populace, where learning was not at all confined to members of the clergy. There was a thriving literature, consisting largely of poetry, which was consumed by an evidently avid reading public. The theatre flourished, even in Vandal North Africa. The philosophers, both Greek and Latin, were discussed and widely known. One of the sons of the Ostrogoth king Theodoric boasted that he was a follower of Plato. And as Christianity spread into those areas never controlled by Rome, such as Ireland, so profane Latin culture followed in its wake. Both Virgil and Homer were known and discussed in the west of Ireland in the sixth century and books were highly valued. In one famous incident a war was fought over the ownership of a book's copy (the first ever recorded incident of copyright) during the lifetime of Saint Columba, in the late sixth century. A little later Irish thinkers such as Scotus Erigena, a Neoplatonist, were making important contributions of their own.

Perhaps the greatest figure of this age however was Boethius, a man whom we can indisputably place alongside characters like Cicero and Seneca. We are told that "Few men have contributed so much to the intellectual sustenance of posterity as Boethius did."[1] He seems to have been born in Rome in 480 (the same year as Saint Benedict), into the distinguished family of the Anicii. Both his parents counted Roman Emperors among their ancestors. His profound knowledge of Greek has led to the supposition that, as a young man, he studied in Athens and perhaps Alexandria. Since his father is recorded as proctor of a school in Alexandria around 470, the younger Boethius may have received some grounding in the classics from him or another close relative.

---

1 James W. Thompson and Edgar N. Johnson, *Introduction to Medieval Europe, 300-1500* (New York, 1937), pp. 221-2

Boethius was to be celebrated throughout the Middle Ages, during which time he occupied a central position. His best known work is the *Consolation of Philosophy*, parts of the which are reminiscent of the Socratic method of Plato's dialogues, as the spirit of philosophy questions Boethius and challenges his emotional reactions to adversity. The *Consolation* was translated into Old English by King Alfred, and into later English by Chaucer and Queen Elizabeth. Many manuscripts survive and it was extensively edited, translated and printed throughout Europe from the 14th century onwards.

Boethius' stated goal was to translate all the works of Aristotle and Plato from the original Greek into Latin, and then to synthesize the two masters, thus producing a unified philosophy. His completed translations of Aristotle's works on logic were the only significant portions of Aristotle available in Europe until the twelfth century. However, some of his translations (such as his treatment of the *topoi* in *The Topics*) were mixed with his own commentary, which reflected both Aristotelian and Platonic concepts. He also wrote a commentary on the *Isagoge* by Porphyry, which highlighted the existence of the problem of universals: whether these concepts are subsistent entities which would exist whether anyone thought of them, or whether they exist only as ideas. The ontological nature of universal ideas was one of the most vocal controversies in medieval philosophy.

Besides these advanced philosophical works, Boethius is also reported to have translated important Greek texts for the topics of the *quadrivium*. His loose translation of Nicomachus' treatise on arithmetic (*De institutione arithmetica libri duo*) and his textbook on music (*De institutione musica libri quinque*, unfinished) became the corner-stone of medieval education. His translations of Euclid on geometry and Ptolemy on astronomy, if they were completed, no longer survive.

In his *De Musica*, Boethius introduced the threefold classification of music, namely: (1) *Musica mundana* — music of the spheres/world. (2) *Musica humana* — harmony of human body and spiritual harmony. (3) *Musica instrumentalis* — instrumental music (incl. human voice). He also wrote theological treatises, which generally involve support for the orthodox position against Arian ideas and other contemporary religious debates. His authorship was periodically disputed because of the secular nature of his other work, until the 19th century discovery of a biography by his contemporary Cassiodorus which mentioned his writing on the subject.[2]

---

2 *Encyclopedia Britannica*, Micropaedia Vol. 2, "Boethius".

Boethius has been called by Lorenzo Valla the last of the Romans and the first of the scholastic philosophers. Nonetheless, there is nothing medieval in his thinking: He is entirely a man of classical antiquity, and it is evident that the great transformation which brought Graeco-Roman culture to an end had, in his age, not yet occurred. He was a Christian, and yet, "while accepting the principle of revealed faith, he was not averse to using his own reason to buttress it."[3] Indeed, his thinking is so pervaded by the rationalism of Greece that his Christianity, notwithstanding the fact that the Church considers him a saint, has long been questioned.[4] Such hypotheses however are unnecessary. Christian civilization of the fifth and sixth centuries was not the Christian civilization of the Middle Ages, and the influence of the ancients, of the "pagan" thinkers of classical antiquity, had not yet been sidelined. It was still perfectly acceptable for a writer to be a Christian and a follower of Plato. In the words of one author, "... while eager and courageous spirits were contending for the Faith ... throughout the Empire, men (and some of them Christian men) were writing and speaking as though no thing as Christianity had come into the world. And the age that witnessed the conversion of Constantine and inherited the benefits of that act was an age that in the East listened to the interminable hexameters of Nonnus' *Dionysiaca*, which contain no conscious reference to Christianity; that laughed over the epigrams of Cyrus; that delighted in many frankly pagan love-stories and saw nothing surprising in the attribution of one of them (the *Aethiopica*) to the Christian bishop Heliodorus; that in the West applauded the panegyrists when they compared emperor and patron to the hierarchy of gods and heroes."[5]

The other great mind of the time was Cassiodorus. Cassiodorus was born at Scylletium, near Catanzaro in southern Italy, of a family that was apparently Syrian in origin. He began his career as councilor to his father, the governor of Sicily, and made a name for himself while still very young as learned in the law. During his working life, as *quaestor* between 507 and 511, as a consul in 514, then as *magister officiorum* under Theodoric and his successor, Athalaric, Cassiodorus

---

3 Thompson and Johnson, op cit., p. 222

4 Carl Stephenson, *Medieval History: Europe from the Second to the Sixteenth Century* (Harper and Row, New York, 1962), pp. 78-9. There exists a large literature on this topic.

5 H. F. Stewart, "Thoughts and Ideas of the Period," in *The Cambridge Medieval History: The Christian Empire*, Vol. 1 (2nd ed., 1936), p. 596

kept copious records concerning public affairs. At the Gothic court, his literary manner, which appears overly stylized and rhetorical to a modern reader, was accounted so remarkable that, whenever he was in Ravenna, significant public documents were often entrusted to him for drafting. Ultimately he was appointed praetorian prefect for Italy, effectively the prime ministership of the Ostrogothic civil government and a high honor to finish any career. His promotion seems to have coincided with Boethius' execution, though, understandably enough, he makes no mention of this in his writings.[6]

Athalaric died in early 534, and the remainder of Cassiodorus' public career was engulfed by the Byzantine reconquest and dynastic intrigue among the Ostrogoths. His last letters were drafted in the name of Witigis. Around 537-38, he left Italy for Constantinople where he remained almost two decades, concentrating on religious questions. He noticeably met Junilius, the quaestor of Justinian and his experiences in the East may have contributed to an increasing interest in religion and spirituality.

It may be said of Cassiodorus that he spent his career trying to bridge the cultural divides that were causing fragmentation in the sixth century between East and West, Greek culture and Latin, Roman and Goth, and Christian people with their Arian ruler.

His great project, for which he is mainly remembered, was his attempt to create an institution for the preservation, study and duplication of copies of Christian and classical literature.[7] He realized his plans "through the establishment at Squillace of a monastery, which he called Vivarium, from the fish ponds (*vivaria*) on its grounds."[8] Here he spent the remainder of his long life with his monks, guiding them in their work. During this time he collected "from Italy and North Africa Greek and Latin manuscripts of such wide variety and scope that his monks had a considerable library to work with."[9] Like his predecessor Boethius, he treasured the intellectual inheritance of Greece and Rome and thus "set a standard and example for the Benedictine monks to follow."[10] And follow they did, as we shall see: Just as he had hoped, the monasteries became the repositories of all knowledge, not just centers of Christian meditation; and the monks of the Benedictine

---

6 www.en.wikipedia.org/wiki/Cassiodorus

7 Thompson and Johnson, op cit., p. 206

8 Ibid

9 Ibid.

10 Ibid., p. 207

order in particular preserved for us the great bulk of ancient literature that we now possess.

Other important intellects of the period were the following: Arator, who entered the service of the state under the reign of Athalaric, becoming *comes domesticorum* and *comes rerum privatarum*. He entered the Church, apparently during the siege of Rome by Vitiges, and in 544 he publicly recited his poem *De actibus apostolorum* in the Church of San Pietro-in-Vinculi.

Venantius Fortunatus, born between 530 and 540, studied grammar, rhetoric and jurisprudence at Ravenna. In 560 he moved to Gaul, where he came to the attention of Sigebert of Austrasia and other important personages. At Poitiers he made the acquaintance of Saint Radegunda, who had just founded the monastery of the Holy Cross. He became a priest there, and he died Bishop of Poitiers. His poems were mainly panegyrics, the most notable of which he dedicated to Chilperic and Fredegond. He lauds the Roman eloquence of Caribert, and praises Duke Lupus, a Roman who took pleasure in attracting to the court of his master those of his compatriots who, like Andarchius, were distinguished for their learning.

Roman men of letters were also prominent at the court of the Vandals. Dracontius addressed a poem entitled *Satisfactio* to King Gunthamund (484-496). He was a pupil of the grammarian Felicianus, and there is evidence in his work that individual Vandals attended the classes of the grammarians in company with the Romans. His family had retained possession of their estates under the Vandals, but was himself later persecuted by Gunthamund, who had him thrown into prison on account of a poem in which he seems to have celebrated the Emperor to the king's disadvantage.

Under Thrasamund (496-523) and Hilderic (523-530) flourished the poets of the Anthology: Florentinus, Flavius Felix, Luxorius, Mavortius, Coronatus and Calbulus, who, although Christians, wrote in the style of pagan antiquity. Their poems celebrate the magnificent *termi* of Thrasamund and the monuments erected at Aliana. In these poems Christianity and Christian sentiments are found side by side with frankly pagan sexual innuendo.

This is hardly what we would expect of an intolerant theocracy.

* * *

An extremely important cultural innovation of the East, which was to have a profound impact upon the intellectual life of Europe from the sixth century onwards, was monasticism. Monasticism began in Egypt, where the austerities of Saint Anthony, who took up residence first in the tombs near Thebes and then in a remote part of the Eastern Desert, were imitated by a host of other devout believers. By the mid-fourth century many religious-minded young men, heeding the call of Saint Basil the Great, began to live in monastic communities devoted to the same austere life of prayer as the hermits, yet without the complete isolation of the latter. Living in a community of faith, it was realized, had some distinct advantages over the life of the anchorite.

Initially, monks did not see themselves as educators or men of letters: they were merely followers of Christ who wished to tread the path of spiritual perfection by relinquishing all worldly desires and possessions, as he had instructed. Nonetheless, even by the fourth century we find them involved in study and education. Saint John Chrysostom tells us that already in his day (circa 347 – 407) it was customary for people in Antioch to send their sons to be educated by the monks.

Monasticism probably began in the West during the fourth century, and it made great headway in particular in Ireland. The story of western monasticism however really begins with Benedict of Nursia, Saint Benedict, a contemporary of Boethius and Cassiodorus. Around 525 he established twelve small communities of monks at Subiaco, thirty-eight miles from Rome, before heading fifty miles south to Monte Cassino, where he established the great monastery that would forever be associated with him. It was here that he formulated his famous Rule, the excellence of which was reflected in its almost universal adoption throughout Western Europe in the centuries that followed. Under the Rule of Benedict, the monks lived a life of prayer, work and study, and subsisted at a level comparable to that of a contemporary Italian peasant.

Although the monk's purpose in retiring from the world was to cultivate a more disciplined spiritual life, in the end the Benedictine Houses would play a much wider and historically-significant role. The monks may not have intended to make their communities into centers of learning, technology and economic progress; yet, as time went on, this is exactly what they became. Indeed, one can scarcely find a single endeavor in the advancement of civilization during late antiquity and the early Middle Ages in which the monks did not play a central role.[11] It is well-known, of course, that they preserved the literary inheritance of the ancient world (much more completely, in fact, than was previously realized), yet they did much more. According to one scholar, they gave "the whole of Europe … a network of model factories, centers for breeding livestock, centers of scholarship, spiritual fervor, the art of living … readiness for social action – in a word … advanced civilization that emerged from the chaotic waves of surrounding barbarity. Without any doubt, Saint Benedict was the Father of Europe. The Benedictines, his children, were the Fathers of European civilization."[12]

We could fill volumes enumerating the achievements of the Benedictines. That they single-handedly preserved much of ancient literature is well-known. Not so widely known is the enormous quantity of that literature that they saved. We are accustomed to think that, following the collapse of the Western Empire, most of the literary heritage of Greece and Rome was lost in the west and was only recovered after contact with the Arabs in Spain and Italy during the eleventh century and after the fall of Constantinople during the fifteenth. Yet this notion is quite simply untrue. The great majority of the literature of Greece and Rome that has survived into modern times was preserved by the monks of the sixth and seventh centuries and was never in fact forgotten. Thus for example Alcuin, the polyglot theologian of Charlemagne's court, mentioned that his library in York contained works by Aristotle, Cicero, Lucan, Pliny, Statius, Trogus Pompeius, and Virgil. In his correspondences he quotes still other classical authors, including Ovid, Horace, and Terence. Abbo of Fleury (latter tenth century), who served as abbot of the monastery of Fleury, demonstrates familiarity with Horace, Sallust, Terence, and Virgil. Desiderius, described as the greatest of the abbots of Monte Cassino after Benedict himself, and who became Pope Victor III in 1086, oversaw the transcription of Horace and Seneca, as well as Cicero's *De Natura Deorum* and Ovid's *Fasti*.[13] His friend Archbishop Alfano, who had also been a monk of Monte Cassino, possessed a deep knowledge of the ancient writers, frequently quoting from Apuleius, Aristotle, Cicero,

---

11 For a discussion, see Stanley L. Jaki, *The Savior of Science* (William B. Eerdmans, 2000)

12 Réginald Grégoire, Léo Moulin, and Raymond Oursel, *The Monastic Realm* (Rizzoli, New York, 1985), p. 277

13 Cited from Charles Montalembert, *The Monks of the West: From St. Benedict to St. Bernard*. Vol. 5, (London, 1896), p. 146

Plato, Varro, and Virgil, and imitating Ovid and Horace in his verse.

By the end of what is generally termed the early Middle Ages (ie by the tenth and eleventh centuries) we find that monasteries all over Europe were in possession of substantial libraries stacked with the works of the classical authors, and that knowledge of Greek and even Hebrew was widespread. This is important, because it illustrates the continuity between this period and the world of late antiquity (fifth and sixth centuries), and would seem to vindicate the Revisionist historians who regard the Dark Age is little more than a mythical construct. It illustrates too that Christian Europe did not need to depend upon other societies and cultures (such as the Islamic) to reacquaint it with letters. Thus we find for example that Gerbert of Aurillac, at the turn of the tenth century, taught Aristotle and logic, and brought to his students an appreciation of Horace, Juvenal, Lucan, Persius, Terence, Statius, and Virgil. We hear of lectures delivered on the classical authors in places like Saint Alban's and Paderborn. A school exercise composed by Saint Hildebert survives in which he had pieced together excerpts from Cicero, Horace, Juvenal, Persius, Seneca, Terence, and others. It has been suggested that Hildebert knew Horace almost by heart.[14]

If the monks were classical scholars, they were equally natural philosophers, engineers and agriculturalists. Certain monasteries might be known for their skill in particular branches of knowledge. Thus, for example, lectures in medicine were delivered by the monks of Saint Benignus at Dijon, whilst the monastery of Saint Gall had a school of painting and engraving, and lectures in Greek and Hebrew could be heard at certain German monasteries.[15] Monks often supplemented their education by attending one or more of the monastic schools established throughout Europe. Abbo of Fleury, having mastered the disciplines taught in his own house, went to study philosophy and astronomy at Paris and Rheims. We hear similar stories about Archbishop Raban of Mainz, Saint Wolfgang, and Gerbert of Aurillac.[16]

The monks, from the time of Benedict onwards, established schools all over Europe. Indeed, our word "school" is related to the word "Scholastic", a term used to broadly define the system of thought

14 John Henry Newman, in Charles Frederick Harrold, (ed.) *Essays and Sketches*, Vol. 3 (New York, 1948), pp. 316-7

15 Ibid., p. 319

16 Ibid., pp. 317-9

and philosophy developed by the monks of this period. Scholastic thinking was based largely on Aristotle, and represented real continuity with the classical traditions of philosophy and rationality.

As well as teachers and educators, the monks established hospitals. These were the first institutions ever to provide free medical care to all, irrespective of financial circumstances. There were no parallels in pagan antiquity. In the words of one writer: "Following the fall of the [Western] Roman Empire, monasteries gradually became the providers of organized medical care not available elsewhere in Europe for several centuries. Given their organization and location, these institutions were virtual oases of order, piety, and stability in which healing could flourish. To provide these caregiving practices, monasteries also became sites of medical learning between the fifth and tenth centuries, the classic period of so-called monastic medicine. During the Carolingian revival of the 800s, monasteries also emerged as the principal centers for the study and transmission of ancient medical texts."[17]

As noted by the above writer, their interest in healing led the monks naturally into medical research, and in course of time they accumulated a vast knowledge of physiology, pathology, and medication. Their studies of herbs and natural remedies led them into the investigation of plants, and they laid the foundations of the sciences of botany and biology.

As part of the Rule of Benedict, the monks were committed to a life of work, study and prayer, and the work part often involved manual labor in the fields. This led to a renewed respect for this type of activity amongst the aristocracy who, by the late Roman period, had come to regard manual work with contempt. Their labors in the fields produced a deep interest in agriculture and agricultural techniques. New technologies were developed by the monks, and everywhere they introduced new crops and production methods. Here they would introduce the rearing of cattle and horses, there the brewing of beer or the raising of bees or fruit. In Sweden, the corn trade owed its existence to the monks.

When Benedict established his Rule, much of Europe was still an uncultivated wilderness. This was true primarily of those areas which had never been part of the Roman Empire, such as Germany, but even of parts of Gaul and Spain, as well as Britain and Ireland, remained in this condition into the sixth and seventh centuries. In addition, the

---

17 Günter B. Risse, *Mending Bodies, Saving Souls: A History of Hospitals* (Oxford University Press, 1999), p. 95

decline in population which the Roman Empire experienced from the end of the second century, had, by the sixth century, returned large areas of once-cultivated land even in Italy to a primeval wilderness. These areas the monks brought under cultivation, often deliberately choosing the wildest and most inhospitable tracts in which to set up their houses. Many of the virgin forests and marshes of eastern Germany and Poland were brought into cultivation for the first time by the monks. "We owe," says one writer, "the agricultural restoration of a great part of Europe to the monks." According to another, "Wherever they came, they converted the wilderness into a cultivated country; they pursued the breeding of cattle and agriculture, labored with their own hands, drained morasses, and cleared away forests. By them Germany was rendered a fruitful country." Another historian records that "every Benedictine monastery was an agricultural college for the whole region in which it was located."[18] Even nineteenth century French historian Francois Guizot, a man not especially sympathetic to Catholicism, observed: "The Benedictine monks were the agriculturalists of Europe; they cleared it on a large scale, associating agriculture with preaching."[19]

Although we can never be sure of this, it seems highly likely that the moldboard plough, as well as the horse collar and the system of crop rotation (all of which we shall mention further below), were innovations of the Benedictines.

It would be possible to fill many volumes outlining the vital contribution of the monks, particularly those of the early Middle Ages, to the founding of Europe. Their role cannot be emphasized strongly enough; yet it is one that has been curiously overlooked. In the 1860s and 1870s, when Comte de Montalembert wrote a six-volume history of the monks of the West, he complained at times of his inability to provide anything more than a cursory overview of great figures and deeds, so enormous was the topic at hand. He was compelled, he said, to refer his readers to the references in his footnotes, in order that they might follow them up for themselves.

* * *

None of the above strikes one as the signature of the decrepit and

18 Alexander Clarence Flick, *The Rise of the Medieval Church* (New York, 1909), p. 223

19 See John Henry Cardinal Newman, loc cit., pp. 264–5.

dying civilization portrayed by Hodges, Whitehouse and Ward-Perkins. Concomitant with the improvements and innovations wrought by the monasteries, the sixth century also saw the appearance in Europe of a whole series of new technologies that were to revolutionize every aspect of life. Some of these were native inventions, others were imports from Asia – the first wave of new technologies and ideas from the Far East which would, at a slighter later date (and often through the filter of the Arabs) bring to the West such life-changing products and techniques as paper-making, the windmill, printing, the compass, and gunpowder, as well as algebra and the "Arabic" numeral system with its concept of zero. It is important to stress here that, although all of the latter reached Europe from the ninth or tenth century onwards via the Arabs, none of them were Arab in origin; they derived from much further to the east, mostly from China, though several were from India. And it is vital to remember that the importation of the new technologies began long before the time of the Arabs, in the sixth or perhaps even the late fifth century.

First of the new techniques to appear – that we know of – was silk-making, which reached the Eastern Empire in the reign of Justinian (mid-sixth century). Shortly afterwards, silk-making industries were established at various places in the Mediterranean, including in Spain.

Next of the new technologies was the stirrup, introduced from Central Asia by the Avars in the second half of the sixth century. The latter tribe of nomad warriors, who entered the Hungarian Plain around 560, would have learned the idea from the Indians or the Chinese, where it was apparently devised centuries earlier. The stirrup was not an invention that impacted upon the life of ordinary citizens of the Empire, but it was extremely important militarily, and eventually led to the development of the heavily armored knight, mounted on extremely powerful horses, who formed the backbone of all medieval armies.

The above two are important in that they display the dynamism of the historical processes at work in the West during the sixth century; but their impact upon the population at large was limited. The same however cannot be said for the next innovations, which had a dramatic and far-reaching impact upon the entire population, and which revolutionized the lives of all Europeans in the following centuries.

By far the most important of these was the so-called moldboard plough.

Up until the third or perhaps the fourth century the only plough available in Europe was a simple scratch plough, known as an ard. This was a pointed piece of wood that was pulled by oxen through the top layer of soil, making a narrow ditch, or furrow, in which the farmer sowed seeds. The ard was fine for the light and shallow soils of the Mediterranean, but inefficient (if not entirely useless) in the heavy and rich soils of the North. However,

"During the fifth and sixth centuries, a whole new kind of plow was developed by local [European] engineers working to create a more efficient machine. This was the mouldboard plow, which included a series of technical elements and permitted the farmer to work heavier and more productive soils than was possible with the earlier tools. The new plow had an iron coulter, shaped like a knife, that sliced through the topsoil; a metal-tipped share that cut underneath the earth that had been sliced by the coulter; and a mouldboard, mounted obliquely behind the share, that turned over the chunks of earth as the plow moved along. The most complex plows had a pair of wheels in front of the coulter to ease the passage of the machine across the field. This new device meant that farmers could produce crops much more efficiently by plowing more quickly than had been possible before, by turning the soil rather than simply opening a small furrow and thus moving the nutrients from below into the upper layers, and by making accessible rich, heavy loams that could not be worked easily with the simple scratch plows."[20]

The writer quoted above errs in placing the invention of the moldboard plough in the fifth century. New evidence indicates that it was known in Roman Gaul and Britain in the fourth century.[21] However, it is beyond question that the new type of plough was popularized in the fifth and sixth centuries, at which time it became widespread throughout northern Europe.

It is interesting to note that in the 1960s Hugh Trevor-Roper was attributing the great expansion of Europe during the tenth and

---

20 Peter Wells, op cit., p. 131.

21 Evi Margaritis and Martin K. Jones, "Greek and Roman Agriculture", in Oleson, John Peter (ed.): *The Oxford Handbook of Engineering and Technology in the Classical World* (Oxford University Press, 2008)

eleventh centuries to the introduction of this very technology.[22] It was the latter tool, he said, which powered the growth in population evidenced by the revival of urban life and the expansion of Christendom's borders on all sides during those centuries. Since we now know however that it was introduced three or four hundred years earlier, where does that leave Hodges and Whitehouse's and a host of other writers' view that precisely then Europe was a decrepit remnant of Imperial Rome in the midst of a demographic death plunge? Furthermore, if we admit that the new plough signaled a population expansion (it was designed specifically to bring into cultivation very heavy soils that had previously resisted farming), this would tend to support the "Revisionists" who deny the existence of a "Dark Age."

Along with the arrival of the moldboard plough, there appeared in Europe the horse collar, which "allowed this faster and stronger animal to replace oxen on some farms as the draft animals pulling the plow,"[23] whilst "The introduction of the three-field system increased agricultural yields. One set of fields was planted with winter cereals – wheat, barley, or rye. One was planted with peas or beans, or sometimes with oats and alfalfa as feed for horses. The third was left fallow. Livestock could graze on the fallow fields, manuring them for planting in the next season."[24] "These three changes," the moldboard plough, the horse collar and the three-field system, "enabled farmers to feed their communities at an unprecedented level of efficiency. The new technologies were introduced at different times in different parts of Europe, but everywhere their impact was revolutionary."[25]

The development of the moldboard plough, made of good quality steel, calls to our attention the striking developments in steel manufacture in the West from the fifth century onwards. We have seen the archaeological proofs, from Runder Berg in Germany and elsewhere, of the enormous scale of iron and steel manufacture at the time, and we have seen how among the Franks the manufacture and export of weapons, especially swords, became a major industry in the sixth and seventh centuries. We hear that, "The swords used by the Franks were often of exceptional quality – hard, durable, yet extremely flexible: one can almost believe in the swords of the heroic literature, which could be bent until the tip touched the pommel, only to snap back

---

22 Trevor-Roper, op cit., pp. 113-15

23 Peter Wells, op cit., p. 132

24 Ibid.

25 Ibid., pp. 132-3

again, perfectly straight, or swords so sharp that they cut a human hair as it drifted down a river. The technique used in the best swords is known as 'pattern welding': a number of bars of different qualities of iron and steel are welded, hammered and twisted together, not only producing the necessary suppleness, but also providing the surface with attractive swirling patterns. The technique is pre-Roman and Celtic in origin, but reaches its heights in the workshops of Francia; in the sixth and seventh centuries Frankish swords seem to have been exported to much of the Germanic world."[26]

Generally speaking, in the sixth century techniques of metalworking and production developed far beyond anything known by the Romans. Goldsmiths and silversmiths, especially those working in Ireland and Britain, though also in Gaul and elsewhere, now began to produce some of the finest miniature artwork ever created. We have already seen how the manuscript makers of Britain and Ireland utilized the interlacing patterns of Hiberno-Saxon art to create astonishing designs of microscopic detail. Metal-workers of the period now reproduced the same patterns in gold and silver, creating works of miniature art that were never equaled in ancient or medieval times, and had to wait till the eighteenth century before they found rivals. Such masterpieces as the Tara Broach and the Ardagh Chalice display the skill of these jewelers in all its glory.

Along with new techniques of metallurgy, there appeared in the fifth and sixth centuries new forms of architecture, which were innovative in their design, and prefigured the masterpieces of Romanesque and Gothic architecture, which again surpassed anything achieved by the Romans. Thus for example in the late fifth century the Merovingians began building churches which "displayed the vertical emphasis, and the combination of block units forming a complex internal space and the correspondingly rich external silhouette, which were to be the hallmarks of the Romanesque."[27] Similarly, in Spain the Visigoths were producing, by the sixth century, architectural masterpieces that prefigured the Spanish Romanesque of the tenth century. New stone churches, the first buildings in that material, began, as we saw, to appear in England from the early seventh century.

* * *

26 Edward James, op cit., pp. 203-4

27 V. I. Atroshenko and Judith Collins, *The Origins of the Romanesque* (Lund Humphries, London, 1985), p. 48

All in all, we may conclude that the western regions of Europe, the former provinces of the Western Empire, as well as regions such as Ireland, Caledonia, and eastern Germany, which had never been part of the Empire, experienced a thriving intellectual life during the late fifth, sixth and early seventh centuries. Literacy appears to have been widespread, and the classical traditions of scientific and philosophical enquiry were alive and well. New agricultural and metal-producing techniques speak of a vibrant and growing economy, impelled by a rising population. Even greater scientific and intellectual feats were accomplished in the Eastern Empire at the same time, and we shall refer to some of these at a later date.

Before finishing, we should note that in the second half of the tenth century another wave of technical innovation commenced in Europe. Many of the introductions of this period, such as the windmill and paper manufacture, were derived from the East. Yet the spirit of innovation and openness was clearly but a continuation of the same phenomenon which existed in the sixth and early seventh centuries, but which then apparently disappeared in a profound and prolonged Dark Age, an epoch so impoverished and obscure that hardly a fragment of pottery or a coin has emerged from it. What could have caused such a remarkable relapse, a relapse followed three centuries later by an equally remarkable revival?

EVIDENCE FROM THE EAST

U p until the 1960s and 70s, historians tended to believe that Byzantium had somehow escaped the general disintegration that
occurred in the rest of Europe from the seventh century onwards. The
Eastern Empire, after all, did not fall to the Barbarians. No Gothic
or Vandal army ever breached the walls of Constantinople. The European provinces of the Empire were indeed periodically overrun by
barbarian hosts, but these territories were invariably recovered; and
in any case, they did not form the economic or cultural core of the
Empire. The eastern provinces however, constituting Anatolia, Syria
and Egypt, were by far the most important and populated provinces,
and these areas were never touched by the Barbarians. The Arab and
Persian assaults in the seventh century, it was conceded, may have deprived the Empire of her most important regions, but Constantinople
held onto western Asia Minor and then recovered her European territories in the Balkans. And all through this time she remained a beacon
of civilization and culture. Even Pirenne assumed that the Eastern
Empire had survived the Arab onslaught more or less unscathed; and
indeed the supposed survival of classical culture in Byzantium was
viewed as a telling argument against him. If the Arabs had destroyed
Graeco-Roman civilization in western Europe, why did they fail to do
so in the East? Byzantium would presumably have been subject to the
same economic blockade as Italy and Gaul. Why then no disintegration there? Such considerations threw many back to the traditional
belief that it was indeed the Germanic invaders of western Europe,
rather than the Arabs, who had terminated classical culture there.

The idea that Byzantium not only escaped the "Dark Age" but
actually flourished during it was widespread even into the 1950s. Thus
in 1953 Sidney Painter was able to describe the eighth, ninth and tenth
centuries at Byzantium as "three centuries of glory," and remarked
that during this time, "The Byzantine Empire was the richest state in
Europe, the strongest military power, and by far the most cultivated."[1]
We are further informed that, "During these three centuries while
Western Europe was a land of partly tamed barbarians, the Byzantine
Empire was a highly civilized state where a most felicitous merger of

---

1 Sidney Painter, op cit., p. 35

Christianity and Hellenism produced a fascinating culture."[2]

Fig. 17. Saint Demtrios, Thessalonika, begun in 629; one of the largest surviving seventh century Byzantine churches.

The above opinion, common till the middle of the twentieth century, was of course partly prompted by Byzantine propaganda, which always sought to portray Constantinople as the "New Rome" and the successor, in an unbroken line of authority, of the first Christian Emperor, Constantine. But it was also the result of habitually seeing "barbarism" solely as an innovation of the nomadic tribes of Germany and Scythia. Since Constantinople had never been overrun by these Barbarians, it could not have lost its civilized character. The failure of academics to move away from this almost reflex reaction is testimony to the failure of Pirenne's thesis to make any real inroads into the mindset of so many in the scholarly community.

Yet irrespective of the somewhat clichéd thinking prevalent in academia, discoveries in the ground have not stopped happening; and these have forced, albeit begrudgingly, a complete rethink of Byzantium's early medieval past. As a matter of fact, archaeology over the past half century has shown beyond question that the once-proud Eastern Rome was devastated during the seventh century. The same poverty and illiteracy that we find in the West we now find also in the

2 Ibid.

East. Cities decline or disappear completely and the economy of the Empire, or what remained of it, is left in tatters. Indeed, just as in the West, a "dark age" descends.

Fig. 18. Interior of Saint Demetrios.

The disclosure by archaeology of this utterly unexpected circumstance created a major problem for mainstream academia. Apart from the fact that we now knew a "Dark Age" had occurred in the East, just as in the West, it seemed an incredible coincidence that this should have occurred in both regions at more or less exactly the same time. Only a few decades earlier, the writings of Dopsch and Pirenne had compelled historians to abandon their old and traditional view of a Dark Age descending on the West in the fifth century, with the arrival of the Barbarians. They had found it difficult (if not impossible) to picture Germanic kings reigning as Christian and Roman monarchs for two centuries; and, in order to explain the Dark Age that eventually did appear without putting the blame on the Arabs, they had to postulate a gradual decline of the western provinces under the incapable and uncouth leadership of the Germans. What they did not expect was a similar decline in the eastern provinces, territories not governed by Germans, but by descendants of some of the most venerable and ancient families of Rome and Greece.

How to explain this without conceding the argument, in its entirety, to Pirenne?

The discovery of Byzantium's Dark Age in fact produced what can only be described as a remarkable volte face on the part of the academic community. What was previously regarded as flourishing and opulent was now seen as, from the end of the sixth century, decadent and indeed terminally ill. It could not be argued that the East suffered a gradual decline, for the archaeology proved, beyond question, the existence of a flourishing and wealthy Byzantine world well into the middle and even late sixth century. In the words of one prominent authority, "Archaeological evidence offers striking confirmation of the wealth of the Church [and society at large] from the fourth to the sixth centuries. All round the Mediterranean, basilicas have been found by the score. While architecturally standardized, these were quite large buildings, often a hundred feet or more in length, and were lavishly decorated with imported marble columns, carving and mosaic. In every town more and more churches were built ..." But this church-building (and indeed palace-building) did come to a complete halt well before the middle of the seventh century. How could this be explained without pointing to the Arabs? The answer seized upon was a rapid decline from the end of the sixth century onwards. The writer quoted above continues: "... more and more churches were built until about the middle of the sixth century, when this activity slackened and then ceased entirely."[3]

But the truth, as we shall see, is there was very little slackening of building activity after the mid-sixth century: new and sometimes magnificent structures continued to be raised throughout the Byzantine lands until the first quarter of the seventh century, after which it did cease entirely. But it did not, as the above writer seeks to imply, cease gradually: It came to an end suddenly and violently.

The sheer wealth and luxury of Byzantine civilization during the sixth and early seventh centuries, long hinted at in the written sources, has now been fully confirmed by excavation. I leave it to another chapter to examine this topic in detail: Suffice to note here that the opulence of the late classical cities has astonished the excavators. Let's look, for example, at the city of Ephesus. Once again, I will quote Pirenne's arch-opponents, Hodges and Whitehouse: "In the fifth century many parts of the classical city were being rebuilt, and all the signs point to an immense mercantile wealth as late as 600. The best examples of this late flowering have been found in the excavations alongside the Embolos, the monumental street in the centre of Ephe-

---

3 Cyril Mango, op cit., p. 38

sus, where crowded dwellings have been uncovered. Nearly all of them were lavishly decorated in the fifth or early sixth century, and their courtyards were floored with marble or mosaics."[4]

Again, "The sheer grandeur of the fifth and sixth centuries in Ephesus can be seen in the remains of the great Justinianic church of St. John. In architectural and artistic terms the chroniclers led us to believe St. John was close to Sancta Sophia and San Vitale in magnificence. Its floor was covered with elaborately cut marble, and among the many paintings was one depicting Christ crowning Justinian and Theodora. No less remarkable are the many mausolea and chapels of the period centred around the grotto of the Seven Sleepers. These Early Christian funerary remains testify to the wealth of its citizens in death, complementing their lavishly decorated homes by the Embolos."[5]

Tellingly, Ward-Perkins, another severe critic of Pirenne, goes much further even that Hodges and Whitehouse. Writing in 2005, and therefore from the perspective of an extra thirty years of archaeological excavation in the Byzantine region, Ward-Perkins remarks that, "throughout almost the whole of the eastern empire, from central Greece to Egypt, the fifth and sixth centuries were a period of remarkable expansion." "We know," he continues, "that settlement not only increased in this period, but was also prosperous, because it left behind a mass of newly built rural houses, often in stone, as well as a rash of churches and monasteries across the landscape. New coins were abundant and widely diffused, and new potteries, supplying distant as well as local markets, developed on the west coast of modern Turkey, in Cyprus, and in Egypt. Furthermore, new types of amphora appeared, in which the wine and oil of the Levant and of the Aegean were transported both within the region, and outside it, even as far as Britain and the upper Danube."[6] This prosperity represented not just the late flowering of a decaying and doomed society; it represented, rather, in many ways, the very apex of Graeco-Roman civilization. "If we measure 'Golden Ages'," he says, "in terms of material remains, the fifth and sixth centuries were certainly golden for most of the eastern Mediterranean, in many areas leaving archaeological traces that are more numerous and more impressive than those of the earlier Roman

---

4 Hodges and Whitehouse, op cit., p. 61

5 Ibid., p. 62

6 Ward-Perkins, op cit., p. 124

empire."[7]

Before moving on, it is important to note that the wealth and populousness of the East at this time is precisely what we would expect from the point of view of Rodney Stark and others, who see Christianity as a revitalizing force in the Roman world. The eastern provinces were of course Christianized long before those of the West and so would earlier have benefited from a natural increase in population. This of course is precisely what the archaeology shows.

None of this then sounds like the final days of a civilization that had essentially run its course and was waiting to expire. And it is worth pointing out that Ward-Perkins included North Africa within the sphere of this late Golden Age of Byzantine culture, thus standing in stark contrast to the elaborately constructed arguments of Hodges and Whitehouse, who sought to portray North Africa as an economic and cultural wasteland after 600.

The cities of the time were sustained by a vast and thriving agriculture. Evidence of this has been found everywhere. Archaeological exploration of the Limestone Massif in northern Syria, for example, has revealed that during the sixth century the region attained great prosperity thanks to the cultivation of the olive tree.[8] Studies here have revealed the co-existence of large and small holdings, but also a general trend, in the years extending from the fourth to the sixth century, towards the break-up of the bigger estates and the growth of villages composed of relatively well-to-do independent farmers.[9] During this time an enormous system of cultivation and terracing made great expanses of the Middle East and North Africa fertile and productive. It was the existence of this agricultural infrastructure that permitted the existence of the late classical cities.

The end came dramatically: In Ephesus, for example, we are told that, "suddenly, in about 614, to judge by the coin evidence, ... [the] residential complexes were destroyed by fire. There has been much debate about the cataclysmic end of these quarters: was there an earthquake, or were the houses sacked by the Persian army in 616, or was there a major fire which began by accident?"[10]

Hodges and Whitehouse answer their own question as they continue: "... the picture [in Ephesus] changed after the Persian sack in

7 Ibid.

8 G. Tchalenko, *Villages antiques de la Syrie du nord* Vol. 1 (Paris, 1953), pp. 377ff.

9 Ibid.

10 Hodges and Whitehouse, op cit., pp. 61-2

616. A new city was constructed, enclosing less than a square kilometre, while a citadel was established on the hill of Ayasuluk overlooking Ephesus. The city wall defended a little of the harbour, which was evidently silting up by this time."[11]

It was the Persian war then, in the reign of Heraclius, which began the economic destruction of the Eastern Empire. In the words of Clive Foss, whom Hodges and Whitehouse quote: "The Persian war may ... be seen as the first stage in the process which marked the end of Antiquity in Asia Minor. The Arabs continued the work."[12]

It was thus from the 620s that the great cities of the East, particularly in Asia Minor and Syria, fall into ruin. In the years after that date, to quote Clive Foss again: "Almost all the cities [of Asia Minor] suffered a substantial decline; Smyrna alone may have formed an exception. In some instances, the reduction was drastic. Sardis, Pergamum, Miletus, Priene and Magnesia became small fortresses; Colossae disappeared, to be replaced by a fort high above the ancient site. ... The cities reached their lowest point in the seventh and eighth centuries ... urban life, upon which the classical Mediterranean culture had been based, was virtually at an end; one of the richest lands of classical civilisation was now dominated by villages and fortresses."[13]

Fig. 19. Mosaic of Saint Demetrius. One of the few Byzantine mosaics to survive the destruction by the iconoclasts in the eighth century.

Thus the words of Clive Foss. Cyril Mango, one of the most important contemporary authorities on Byzantine civilization, is much more forthright: "One can hardly overestimate the catastrophic break that occurred in the seventh century. Anyone who reads the narrative of events will not fail to be struck by the calamities that befell the Empire, starting with the Persian invasion at the very beginning of the

11 Ibid., p. 62
12 Ibid., p. 61
13 Ibid., pp. 62-3

century and going on to the Arab expansion some thirty years later – a series of reverses that deprived the Empire of some of its most prosperous provinces, namely, Syria, Palestine, Egypt and, later, North Africa – and so reduced it to less than half its former size both in area and in population. But a reading of the narrative sources gives only a faint idea of the profound transformation that accompanied these events. ... It marked for the Byzantine lands the end of a way of life – the urban civilization of Antiquity – and the beginning of a very different and distinctly medieval world."[14] Like Foss, Mango remarked on the virtual abandonment of the Byzantine cities after the mid-seventh century, and the archaeology of these settlements usually reveals "a dramatic rupture in the seventh century, sometimes in the form of virtual abandonment."[15] With the cities and with the papyrus supply from Egypt went the intellectual class, who after the seventh century were reduced to a "small clique."[16] The evidence, as Mango sees it, is unmistakable: the "catastrophe" (as he names it) of the seventh century, "is the central event of Byzantine history."[17]

The "dramatic rupture" of the seventh century is therefore not simply another chapter of the Eastern Empire's past; it is the central event of her history.

Constantinople herself, the mighty million-strong capital of the East, was reduced, by the middle of the eighth century, to something resembling a ghost town. Mango quotes a document of the period which evokes a picture of "abandonment and ruination. Time and again we are told that various monuments – statues, palaces, baths – had once existed but were destroyed. What is more, the remaining monuments, many of which must have dated from the fourth and fifth centuries, were no longer understood for what they were. They had acquired a magical and generally ominous connotation."[18]

So great was the destruction that even bronze coinage, the everyday lubricant of commercial life, disappeared. According to Mango, "In sites that have been systematically excavated, such as Athens, Corinth, Sardis and others, it has been ascertained that bronze coinage, the small change used for everyday transactions, was plentiful throughout the sixth century and (depending on local circumstances)

14 Cyril Mango, op cit., p. 4
15 Ibid., p. 8
16 Ibid., p. 9
17 Ibid.
18 Ibid., p. 80

until some time in the seventh, after which it almost disappeared, then showed a slight increase in the ninth, and did not become abundant again until the latter part of the tenth."[19] Yet even the statement that some coins appeared in the ninth century has to be treated with caution. Mango notes that at Sardis the period between 491 and 616 is represented by 1,011 bronze coins, the rest of the seventh century by about 90, "and the eighth and ninth centuries combined by no more than 9."[20] And, "similar results have been obtained from nearly all provincial Byzantine cities." Even such paltry samples as have survived from the eighth and ninth centuries (nine) are usually of questionable provenance, a fact noted by Mango himself, who remarked that often, upon closer inspection, these turn out to originate either from before the dark age, or after it.

When substantial archaeology again appears, in the middle of the tenth century, the civilization it reveals has been radically altered: The old Byzantium of late antiquity is gone, and we find an impoverished and semi-literate rump; a medieval Byzantium strikingly like the medieval France, Germany and Italy with which it was contemporary. Here we find too a barter or semi-barter economy; a decline in population and literacy; and a general reduction in urban life. And the break-off point in Byzantium, as in the West, is the first half of the seventh century.

* * *

From this, it becomes clear that classical civilization, in the East as well as in the West, did not just wither away and die: it was killed. The signs of violent destruction are everywhere from around 615 onwards. But who killed it?

As might be expected, Hodges and Whitehouse, as well as Mango, attempt to exonerate the Arabs and pin the blame on the Persians – as well as on an inherent decadence on the part of classical civilization itself. They stress that, in Ephesus, "Urban life clearly was waning quite dramatically when the first Arab attack took place in 654-5."[21] Fine, but there had been wars between Persians and Romans before. Indeed, war between these two had been almost part of normal life for seven centuries. How is it then that this war led to the end of classical

19 Ibid., pp. 72-3
20 Ibid., p. 73
21 Ibid., p. 62

civilization? What was different about this conflict? Wars, no matter how destructive, are normally followed by treaties of peace; and when these are signed economic activity and prosperity recovers. It had happened before many times between Romans and Persians. It did not happen this time. Why?

It is evident that the Byzantines did not begin rebuilding in the ruined eastern provinces after the ending of the Persian war. And the fact that they did not rebuild can only mean they did not have time to rebuild before the Arabs came to waste the area permanently. Yet this statement implies two further and crucial questions: (a) Could we be mistaken about the number of years that elapsed between the Persian war and the arrival of the Arabs? And (b) What was it about the Arabs that would have caused them to bring about such lasting destruction? After all, even if the Arabs had arrived in Syria, Egypt and Asia Minor at the same time as the Persians, we might expect classical systems of agriculture and trade to have then reasserted themselves. This in fact did not happen, and even Hodges and Whitehouse admit that the Arab conquest of North Africa brought a "dark age" to the region lasting two to three centuries.[22]

The question of the chronology of Islam's expansion beyond Arabia shall be revisited near the end of the present volume, whilst the nature of Islam as a religious and political philosophy will be examined in Chapter 13. In the meantime, we should note that the Arabs themselves hinted that it was they who had wasted the cities of Anatolia. Speaking of that region, a ninth century Arab geographer noted:

> In days of old cities were numerous in Rum [Anatolia] but now they have become few. Most of the districts are prosperous and pleasant and have each an extremely strong fortress, on account of the frequency of the raids which the fighters of the faith [Muslims] direct upon them. To each village appertains a castle where in time of flight they may take shelter.[23]

These raids, as we shall see, were a perpetual feature of life along the borderlines of the Arab-controlled world, and they had an immense impact upon the entire Mediterranean region – an impact that was felt

---

22 Ibid., p. 71

23 Hodges and Whitehouse, op cit., p. 63; from M. F. Hendy, "Byzantium, 1081-1204: an economic reappraisal," *Transactions of the Royal Historical Society*, 5th series, 20 (1970), 36

even into the early years of the nineteenth century.

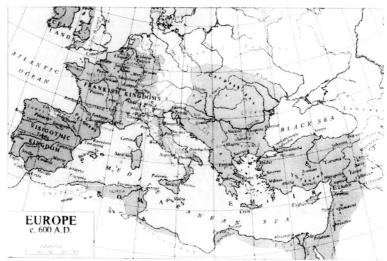

Fig. 20. Map of Europe and the Middle East around 600, just before the Arab Conquests.

In contrast to the claims of Pirenne's critics, the beginning of the seventh century was a period of rapid expansion and new development in many parts of Europe and the Middle East. The Byzantine Empire was experiencing an era of unparalleled prosperity, as cities grew larger than under the old Roman Empire. In the same way, Visigothic Spain was prosperous and highly developed, with every indication of an expanding population. The Visigoth kings had begun to found new cities. Italy under the Lombards also registered growth, after centuries of decline, with much building activity under Queen Theodelinda. The same was true of Frankish Gaul which, united again under Chlothar II, enjoyed a period of great prosperity and expansion. In the previously barbarian Celtic lands of Ireland and Scotland (Caledonia) there flourished a unique Christian civilization, and Anglo-Saxon England stood on the verge of being reincorporated into the civilized world of Latin Christianity. Even the barbarian kingdom of the Avars, centered on the Hungarian Plain, showed some continuity with Roman civilization, and there is much evidence of occupation of the towns along the Danube and parts of Transylvania.

Notwithstanding the claims of senior academics, then, the evidence of archaeology suggests a dramatic and sudden end to Byzantine civilization sometime near the first quarter of the seventh century. There was no "gradual decline" or "period of decadence." And yet, as we have seen, over the past thirty years the great majority of academics working in this area have postulated just that. How else to account for the complete disintegration of urban life and the economy in the mid-seventh century? The only alternative would be to pin the blame on the Arabs; and this is something they have, for a number of reasons, recoiled from doing. Quite apart from a now almost default habit of seeing the Arabs as a cultured and civilizing force – and therefore incapable of reducing an entire civilization to dust – there is the problem of how to account for the speed and ease with which the Arab armies swept over the provinces of the East. And the very speed of the Arab conquests has now become in itself a major proof of the inherent weakness and "decadence" of Byzantine civilization. Indeed, the notion that it was a terminal decline in late classical civilization that called forth the Arab conquests is received wisdom among many academics, and has generated a whole genre of writing.

Yet this idea, now so prevalent, ignores a glaring fact: the parts of the Roman and Byzantine worlds conquered by the Arabs were not the barbarous and uncivilized ones: It was, without exception, the civilized and prosperous provinces that fell to them. All the regions overrun by the Saracens, Anatolia, Syria, Egypt, North Africa, and Spain, were invariably the most urbanized, prosperous, and centralized parts of the late classical world. It was only indeed when they reached the more barbarous and less Romanized parts of Europe, such as northern Spain and Gaul, that they began to encounter effective resistance.

This is a topic to which we shall return in due course, for it is of central importance to the whole debate.

THE GREAT TRANSFORMATION OF THE SEVENTH CENTURY

S cholars may argue about the fine details of chronology, but on one thing at least all (including Hodges and Whitehouse and Pirenne's opponents in general) can agree: archaeology shows that the great transition from classical to medieval occurred in the first few decades of the seventh century. By the 640s virtually all trade between Europe and the Near East (and North Africa) had come to a definitive end. Luxuries which had been common in the West until that time, such as spices and various forms of high-quality ceramics, disappear never to come back. The supply of papyrus comes to an end, and Europeans are compelled to employ parchment for even basic day to day record-keeping. The great cities built by the Romans fall into decay, and in the countryside the scattered and undefended lowland farming settlements that were characteristic of the Roman epoch begin to disappear; to be replaced by secure and easily-defended hill-top settlements – the first medieval castles. Accompanying the abandonment of the lowland settlements, many previously productive regions revert to wasteland: Drained wetlands revert to marsh, and agricultural terraces and ditches are washed away. Harbors begin to silt up and a layer of subsoil forms in valley floors, covering many of the Roman age towns and villages.

One of the most striking of the above developments is the retreat to defended hill-tops. This process, known in Italy as *incastellamento* ("encastling"), marks perhaps the most visible and easily-recognized manifestation of the new and medieval civilization. The Middle Ages was, above all, the age of feudalism and castles. Hodges and Whitehouse mention the movement towards castle-building but offer no convincing explanation of it. "The reason for this shift," they note, "are many and may never be accurately determined."[1] They point out that in Italy at least, "the shift from open dispersed sites to fortified upland settlements is only explained as a defense against Lombardic invaders [late sixth century]."[2] However, "this may be a satisfactory explanation for the change on the edge of the Roman Campagna, but

---

1 Hodges and Whitehouse, op cit., p. 46
2 Ibid., p. 45

its wider implications have to be assessed."[3] In other words, a process that is observed throughout the whole of southern Europe can hardly be satisfactorily explained by the settlement in northern Italy of a single barbarian tribe. Hodges and Whitehouse suggest that, "Increased taxation by the Byzantine government after Justinian's reconquest of Italy might account for a phase of rural depopulation in the sixth century. Similarly, we cannot ignore the impact of the Great Plague of 542 which ravaged Byzantium and Europe."[4]

But there had been plagues before, and devastating wars. None of these caused the total and permanent abandonment of the lowlands and the retreat of populations to defended hilltop settlements – essentially a return to Iron Age conditions. And whilst castle-building might be explained in Italy by Lombard raids (there is in fact good evidence that the Byzantine and Lombard invasions in the mid-sixth century caused much devastation in Italy), what is the explanation elsewhere, where castle-building also appears in the early seventh century?

Interestingly, in the 1930s Alfons Dopsch had used castle-building as an argument against Pirenne. Without mentioning southern Europe – from which at that time little archaeological data was available – Dopsch noted that since castle-building (in the north) commenced in the middle of the tenth century, medievalization probably had more to do with the Viking onslaught than the Muslim. It is in fact true that castle-building commences in northern Europe in the tenth century – almost precisely three centuries after it begins in southern Europe. Indeed, the three centuries' discrepancy appears as soon as we leave the Mediterranean coastlands. Thus for example the castles which guard the Pyrenean passes, such as those at Montségur and Lourdes, only a short distance from the Mediterranean, were built in the tenth century, apparently to guard against Muslim incursions from Spain. So, on the Mediterranean shoreline, castles are built in the mid-seventh century to guard against Arab raids, whilst less than 150 kilometers away castles do not appear for another three centuries – and when they do appear they are again to guard against Arab raids. We are therefore presented with a strange dichotomy: In Europe castle-building appears to begin in the seventh century, but then goes into a kind of suspension for three centuries, when it again appears in the tenth century. Furthermore, the defended hilltop settlements, which in Mediterranean Europe form the basis of the seventh-century cas-

3 Ibid.

4 Ibid., p. 46

tles, are precisely the locations of the tenth/eleventh century castles, which appear, for all the world, to be normal and continuous developments from the seventh century fortified settlements.

Here we have yet another instance of that puzzling three-century gap in Dark Age history and archaeology.

Leaving aside the Dark Age hiatus for a moment and returning to the question of the seventh century castle-building, we should note that for Pirenne and his modern acolytes the abandonment of the classical lowland villages and villas and the retreat to defended hilltops has a simple and straightforward explanation: the appearance along the Mediterranean coastlands of Spain, southern France, Italy, and Greece, of fleets of Saracen pirates and slave-traders.

* * *

Clearly related to the phenomenon of castle-building is the appearance, throughout the Mediterranean world, of a layer of subsoil which overlies late Roman sites. This is the stratum referred to by Thomas F. Glick in Spain, who however seemed to be unaware of its occurrence throughout the Mediterranean. According to Claudio Vita-Finzi, who named it the Younger Fill, this deposit is an almost universal feature of the river valleys of the Mediterranean basin in the period roughly corresponding to the final decline of classical cultures, around the sixth to eighth centuries.[5] The origin of the Younger Fill "is the subject of considerable debate, and some scholars argue that it is simply the last stage in an intermittent process which began some two thousand years earlier in the Middle Bronze Age." However, "Vita-Finzi demonstrated that a dramatic geomorphological change took place at the end of classical antiquity."[6]

There are two main theories about the formation of the Younger Fill. "The first, proposed by Vita-Finzi, is that it was formed as a result of climatic deterioration, and that it provides us therefore with information on a major, but hitherto unsuspected, cause of the collapse of the Roman Empire."[7] However, "no contemporary chroniclers reported marked changes in climate, and consequently it is difficult to accept this explanation without further evidence."[8] And since weather

---

5 Claudio Vita-Finzi, *The Mediterranean Valleys* (Cambridge, 1969)

6 Hodges and Whitehouse, op cit., p. 57

7 Ibid.

8 Ibid.

conditions in the Mediterranean, as well as the crops the region produces, seem to be identical to those of ancient times, this too would apparently rule out the possibility of any dramatic climate change in the centuries since the end of the Roman Empire. The alternative theory, the one which Hodges and Whitehouse subscribe to, "is that the Younger Fill was formed as a direct result of the collapse of the classical agricultural system." "Failure to repair terraces as the mass-market for olive oil and wine declined," they say, "led to erosion as previously revetted soils were washed away. It is a familiar process; one sees it in many parts of the Mediterranean today, as farmers plough deeply into terraced hillsides, creating furrows at right angles to valley bottoms, down which the torrential winter rains carry soil at an alarming rate. The implications of this process in Late Antiquity are considerable. It would have led to the degradation of the hill slopes and to marked morphological changes in valleys and estuaries, with implications not only for farming but also for road networks, harbours and towns."[9]

Clearly the date assigned to the formation of the Younger Fill is crucial to the whole debate about classical civilization's fate. The Younger Fill is plainly the geological signature of the end of the classical system of agriculture. Perhaps predictably, Hodges and Whitehouse would like to place its formation in the latter sixth century, several decades before the rise of Islam. They consider the possibility that it may have something to do with the great plague of 542, but they note that at Olympia in Greece, which was covered by the Fill, coins of 565 and 575 were found, "indicating that the city's demise happened a little later."[10]

It should be noted at this point that the plague of Justinian's time is frequently cited as a suspect in the demise of Graeco-Roman civilization – especially by those who reject the idea that it could have been caused by the arrival of Islam. Yet the evidence from Olympia, by itself, indicates that life continued as normal after the plague, and that it must have been something of an altogether greater magnitude, in the decades after 575, that finally terminated the whole system. But what was this event, and when did it occur?

It so happens that in the East at least a very precise date can be given to the ending of classical agriculture and the formation of the Younger Fill. We have seen that the cities of Asia Minor, which have been extensively studied, show a thriving culture right up to the start

9 Ibid., pp. 57–8
10 Ibid., p. 57

of the Persian War in 614. These metropolises, with their enormous populations, could not have existed if the classical agricultural system had been in decay. Their very existence, with their numerous populations, presupposes a thriving agriculture producing very large food surpluses. The destruction of these centers in the years following 614 was final, and none of them recovered. It was then too, in the immediate aftermath of these events, that the Younger Fill appears and harbors begin to silt up.

In short, in the Eastern Mediterranean, which formed the very epicenter of antique civilization, the Younger Fill, and with it the abandonment of the classical system of agriculture, occurred in the years after 614, probably the two or three decades after. And if that is the date in the East, we may be fairly sure that it was the same in the West. Thus it hardly seems open to question that throughout the Mediterranean the retreat to defended hilltops and the breakdown of Roman agriculture occurred in the disturbed years which commenced in the second or perhaps third decade of the seventh century. But this then prompts the question: Who or what caused these momentous changes in the West? In the East, we might suppose they were precipitated by the Persian war; but what about the regions never touched by the Persians – everything west of Egypt? Who caused the destruction of Roman agriculture and the retreat to the hilltops in those lands?

Almost immediately after the conquest of Egypt, Arab raiders and pirates began to scour the Mediterranean. We know for certain that they quickly took to the sea, for they sent a vast fleet to besiege Constantinople in 674. Such large-scale operations were supplemented by hundreds, indeed thousands, of smaller attacks. These unleashed a wave of banditry and lawlessness which may well have been without precedent in the history of the Middle Sea. It is true that in recent years writers such Hodges and Whitehouse have tried to suggest that Arab piracy in the region did not begin until the middle of the ninth century; but their grounds for doing so are spurious.[11] As shall be demonstrated in Chapter 13, piracy and slave-raiding were activities fully sanctioned by Islamic law, and have always formed a central feature

---

11 "At the very time the Vikings were raiding Christian communities around the North Sea, Moslems from North Africa and Spain were also attacking Crete, Sicily, southern Italy, Provence and southern Anatolia. The raids began when the western Islamic kingdoms broke with the Abbasids in the 820s. The loss of wealth affected the political stability of the Maghreb and Umayyed Spain just as it had in the Baltic countries. Raids and invasions aimed at the vulnerable Christian communities were the result." Hodges and Whitehouse, op cit., p. 167

of Muslim interaction with the non-Islamic world. Pirate raids, often carried out in conjunction with large scale military operations, are recorded from the middle of the seventh century; and continued to cause immense problems in the Mediterranean *until the start of the nineteenth century.* We know that by the fifth decade of the seventh century Arab attacks on Sicily and southern Italy were incessant. A series of assaults on Sicily in 652, 667 and 720 are recorded; whilst Syracuse was conquered for the first time temporarily in 708. Sardinia was Islamicized in several stages beginning in 711, the very year of the Islamic conquest of Spain. The Italian island of Pantelleria was conquered by the Arabs in 700, and was attacked again a century later, when the Arabs sold the monks they captured into slavery in Spain.[12]

As we might expect, further to the east the Arabs were even more active and at an earlier date. The whole of the Levant was scoured by Arab fleets from the 640s onwards, and the very centre of the Eastern Empire, Constantinople, was not immune from attack. An Arab army, led by Muawiyah I, laid siege to the city between 674-678. Unable to breach the Theodosian Walls, the Muslims blockaded the metropolis along the Bosporus, but their fleet was eventually destroyed by the famous "Greek Fire" of Kallinikos (Callinicus) the Syrian. Although this was a decisive defeat, within just over half a century the Arabs were back. In 718 an 80,000-strong army led by Maslama, the brother of Caliph Suleiman, crossed the Bosporus from Anatolia to besiege the capital of the Eastern Empire by land, while a massive fleet of Arab war galleys commanded by another Suleiman, estimated to initially number 1,800 ships, sailed into the Sea of Marmara to the south of the city. After some desperate fighting, and the use once again by the defenders of "Greek Fire," this onslaught was also repulsed.

It has to be remembered that, from the years following the decline and abandonment of Europe's cities – from the 620s and 630s onwards – only a very fragmentary record of events has survived; and the incidents recounted above can only have represented a tiny fraction of the true total: they were recorded precisely because of their scale and importance. Lesser raids, almost certainly at even earlier dates, involving shiploads of pirates and slavers, must have occurred in their thousands. This is certainly the impression gained by contemporary accounts.

The threat posed by Saracen pirates, who often raided far inland, fully explains the abandonment of the Roman fields with their terraces

12 Pirenne, op cit., p. 159

and irrigation ditches, and the retreat of whole populations to hilltop strongholds. Populations along the Mediterranean coasts of Spain, France, Italy, and Greece, were to become all too familiar with these dangers over the centuries, and with time large areas of the coastlands became uninhabited and uninhabitable. The impact of Islamic piracy on the Mediterranean is a question that has never been fully understood or appreciated, in the English-speaking world at least. For a thousand years the Middle Sea, previously one of the world's great economic highways, was reduced to a hunting-ground for slavers. The cultures of all these regions were profoundly affected by this phenomenon, as were the policies and actions of kings and popes.

THE FATE OF CLASSICAL
CIVILIZATION IN ISLAMIC LANDS

Whatever arguments may be presented about Islam's impact up-on classical civilization in Europe, there is no question at all that in the East, in those regions which came under the domination of Islam, the effect was to terminate classical civilization, and to termi-nate it very quickly. Indeed, Islam eliminated the civilization of classi-cal antiquity far more completely in Syria, in Anatolia, in Egypt and in North Africa than it ever did in Europe. This is obvious enough, but it needs to be said, for it is a fact that is often overlooked.

In Europe, whatever we may say of the collapse of the economy and the dwindling of cities, some aspects of Graeco-Roman civiliza-tion survived, even at the height (or depths?) of the Middle Ages. Here Latin continued to be the language of learning and culture, and it survived too, in a moderated form, in the everyday speech of Italy, Spain, and Gaul. Christianity, the religion of Rome, continued to be the faith espoused by the populace, and we should note that in the Church, particularly in the monasteries, there existed an institution which made real efforts to preserve the learning and literature of the classical world.

It goes without saying that none of these things pertained in the territories which came under Islam. These regions, on the whole, belonged to the Greek-speaking rather than the Latin-speaking parts of the Roman Empire; but they contained by far the most important centers of classical civilization at the start of the seventh century. In Egypt, in Syria, in North Africa, and in Anatolia, Islam gained control of lands containing enormous urban centers, beside which the "cities" of the West looked like mere villages. The Levantine provinces were the cultural and economic powerhouses of the Roman world. We know that the cities of Egypt, Syria and Anatolia held great academies, in-variably equipped with well-stocked libraries; and that these remained vigorous and growing institutions into the first decades of the seventh century. The student of the time could study a wide variety of subjects in institutions throughout the Empire: "Philosophy (including in prin-ciple what we understand today by science) flourished at Athens and Alexandria; medicine also at Alexandria, at Pergamum and elsewhere;

law at Beirut."[1] Although there was nothing corresponding precisely with what we understand as a university, with a multiplicity of disciplines available at one location, nevertheless, by travelling the student could become acquainted with all kinds of knowledge: "The School of Alexandria and that of Constantinople ... came closest to our concept of a university ..."[2] "After completing his secondary schooling in a local town, he [the budding scholar] would go to a larger centre, say Antioch or Smyrna or Gaza, to study with a prominent rhetor; but if he was attracted to philosophy, he would have to travel to Alexandria or Athens. The quest for learning was synonymous with travel. ... The mobility of students was paralleled by that of professors: Libanus, for example, had taught at Nicomedia, Nicaea and Constantinople before he settled down in his native Antioch."[3]

This epoch saw extremely important advances in science and technology. We know, for example, that Aetius of Amida (mid-fifth to mid-sixth century), Paulus of Aegina (c. 625 – c. 690) and Alexander of Tralles (c. 525 – c. 605), three noted physicians, all made contributions to the study of medicine as well as other disciplines: they investigated, for example, the principles of conics and built ingenious machinery, including highly advanced astrolabes, the computers of their time.[4] According to science historian Samuel Sambursky, the researches of the Byzantine scholars of the sixth century were anticipating, in many ways, the discoveries of the Renaissance and the Enlightenment. By the sixth century, he shows, Neo-Platonic philosophers were constructing complex machines using cog-wheel technology, as well as making important discoveries about the natural world.[5] And this innovation did not end with the reign of Justinian, or with the sixth century. Thus, as we saw, "Greek Fire," a form of primitive flame-thrower devised by a Syrian architect, was used to devastating effect by the Byzantines against Muslim invaders in 677.[6]

---

1 Mango, op cit., p. 128

2 Ibid.

3 Ibid.

4 Margaret Deanesley, *A History of Early Medieval Europe, 476 to 911* (Methuen, London, 1965), p. 207

5 Samuel Sambursky, *The Physical World of Late Antiquity* (Routledge and Kegan Paul, 1962)

6 It should be noted that even in an art such as music, important developments occurred at this time. Thus the violin, which overcame the problem of tonal discontinuity through the bow, was invented in the Eastern Empire sometime between the seventh and ninth centuries. Similarly, the bagpipe, which solved the same problem in

As might be imagined, literacy rates in this late classical world were high; and there existed, as well as the great libraries attached to the academies, innumerable private ones in the possession of wealthy citizens. Industry and commerce of all kinds flourished in the ports, and merchants plied a vigorous trade with lands in the Far West and in the Far East. The process by which the great discoveries and technical innovations of China and India would reach the West had already commenced; in the time of Justinian the secrets of silk-making reached the West, prompting the growth of a silk-producing industry in the Levant and in Spain.[7]

Fig. 21. Palmyra, one of the great classical cities of the Middle East destroyed during the Arab conquests in the mid-seventh century. The settlement survived the Arab invasion, but went into an irreversible decline in the years that followed, as its hinterland became a desert.

And it is here that we must refute a hypothesis widely circulated and widely credited in academic circles over the past half century. The conquests of Islam, it is said, and the apparent ease with which they were carried out, are proof in themselves of the decadence and decline of Byzantine society in the late sixth and early seventh centuries. This, after all, is the very core of the argument present in Hodges' and Whitehouse's book. Yet it is an argument that has little to recommend it. We have seen that the regions conquered by the Arabs were without exception the most civilized and economically developed of the Ro-

wind instruments, appeared in Europe during the same epoch.
7 See eg. Bertrand, op cit.

man and Byzantine worlds. These territories seem to have fallen not because they were uncivilized and backward, but because they were in a sense too civilized. The spirit of barbarism had long disappeared from the Eastern Provinces. Under the protective shield of Rome, the farmers, artisans, and intellectuals of the eastern and southern Mediterranean had grown to despise the calling of the soldier, and to see the defense of the country as someone else's business. At the time of the Persian invasion in 619, Egypt had not experienced war for six and a half centuries. And whilst North Africa had suffered the Vandal invasion and the subsequent reconquest of the province under Justinian, these events had little direct effect upon the civilian population, which continued with its normal everyday business as before. And it is significant that the only part of mainland Europe to be conquered was Spain, by far the most prosperous and, as we would say, settled and civilized part of the continent. (Italy had forfeited that position long before in the savage wars which rent the Peninsula during the reconquest by Justinian and the subsequent Lombard invasion). The weakness of Spain, whose defense was entirely in the hands of a numerically tiny aristocratic – Visigoth – elite, may be regarded as a microcosm of the weakness of the Byzantine world. Here there existed a highly centralized society with a professional army, and an extremely rigid system of law-enforcement. The civilian populations of Anatolia, of Syria, of Egypt, and of North Africa, were vast; but they were completely unused to war. After the defeats of the Imperial forces, there existed no tradition of military training or activity which could have facilitated independent local action against the invaders. Nor was there any mechanism by which they could be recruited into the Imperial Army and rapidly trained as soldiers.

It is significant, and worth stressing, that the only part of North Africa which offered any sustained resistance to the Arabs was the relatively "uncivilized" part in the far west, which had earlier thrown off the yoke of Rome and reverted to its native tribalism and incessant internecine war. Again, as we saw in an earlier chapter, it was only when the Arabs reached the semi-tribal lands in the mountains of northern Spain that they began to meet effective resistance there

So, the prosperity of the Eastern Empire in the late sixth and early seventh centuries is not to be doubted. The archaeology, we have seen, proves it again and again, as even Hodges and Whitehouse concede. Yet all this ended with the Arab conquests. It is true, of course, that some commerce and learning continued for a while under the newcomers; and this is a topic which we shall return to in due course, for it is one upon which there has emerged a whole mythology.[8] Yet it is equally true that the process which saw the economic and cultural decline of Egypt, Syria and Anatolia began almost immediately after the Arab invasions. From Syria and Anatolia in the East to Morocco in the West, the southern shores of the Mediterranean are dotted with the ruins of abandoned Roman cities. These metropolises (and there are literally thousands of them), which were invariably in fertile and cultivated territories, now stand as mute witnesses to the reality of what Arab conquest meant: For it was only in the seventh century that these cities were abandoned and the countryside on which they stood transformed into barren wasteland.[9] These ruins are what Kenneth Clarke described as the "bleached bones" of the classical world which the Arabs left in their wake.[10] The Younger Fill silt layer occurs here too, and with the desertification of the countryside came the silting up of river valleys and harbors, as invaluable topsoil was washed away.

That so many of the Roman cities in the Middle East and North Africa were abandoned is striking and in complete contrast to what happened in Europe. In the latter region the Roman towns were continuously occupied throughout the fifth and sixth centuries and into the Middle Ages. Thus Roman Londinium became Anglo-Saxon Lundenwic and then medieval London. The Roman town of Paris became the center of Merovingian power during the sixth century and remained the capital of France thereafter. It was precisely because of the continuous occupation of Europe's Roman cities that so little of the original architecture has remained – above ground, at least. The stone and marble of the great Roman buildings of London, for example, have long since disappeared because they were recycled many times in new structures erected throughout late antiquity and the Middle Ages.

The Roman centers of the Middle East and North Africa, by contrast, were (with a handful of exceptions) completely abandoned,

---

8 Some features of classical culture survived for a short while – and in a few sites – after the Arab Conquests. Thus for example a few centers continued to erect buildings decorated with classical-style mosaics. This however only emphasizes the fact that classical culture was alive and well up until the Arab invasions, and was not terminated before that.

9 The abandoned cities of the Middle East include some of the most iconic and well-known settlements of the region, including Petra, Palmyra, Caesarea Maritima and many many more. The destruction of the latter of these by the Arabs was described in detail by the Egyptian writer John of Nikiu.

10 Kenneth Clark, op cit., p. 7

and the surrounding countryside transformed into an arid or semi-arid wasteland; with the result that very many of the great monuments of these areas have survived to become important tourist attractions.

Fig. 22. Scene from Caesarea Maritima, one of the great cities of the Middle East destroyed in the seventh century.

That these settlements were abandoned in the early to mid-seventh century admits of only two possible explanations. Either they were abandoned immediately before the arrival of the Arabs, and their demise elicited by some form of climate catastrophe or other natural disaster such as a plague; or the Arabs themselves were responsible for their demise and for the destruction of the region's agricultural base. It has to be admitted that all the literary sources point to the second solution as the correct one. Documents from the period speak unanimously of flourishing settlements and active economies brought to an end by the Arab invaders. And the archaeology too, as even Hodges and Whitehouse have admitted, has tended to confirm this picture, with clear evidence of massive destruction at the terminating point of virtually all the late Byzantine cities of the area.

Admitting then that the Arabs did immense damage to the actual buildings, how does this explain the desertification of the territories in which these cities stood? That at least, we might feel, surely cannot have been the work of the Arabs. Surely for that at least Mother Nature must take the blame!

The above question is one that has prompted a great deal of study and debate, both among scientists and historians. The definitive work however was published in 1951 by Rhoads Murphey, Professor Emeritus of History at Harvard. In an article entitled "The Decline of North Africa since the Roman Occupation: Climatic or Human?", he provides a detailed outline of the problem. I shall quote him at some length, as what he says is most instructive:

> "The Romans were an agricultural people who expanded into their Mediterranean empire from a relatively humid base in Italy. It was natural that they should extend this approach to the natural environment into the African provinces. The Arabs were on the contrary a nomadic people, nurtured in the true desert of Arabia, and totally unused to an agricultural economy. Their technique was unequal to understanding or managing the highly-developed irrigation works of North Africa bequeathed to them by the Romans, and they had no need for dependence on the agriculture which these works had supported. Their different use of the land does not need to be explained by a change in climate. No military conquest is conducive to the maintenance of civil order nor the administration and technical organization which an intricate irrigation economy requires, especially when the conquerors are nomads. The Arab conquest destroyed the Roman irrigation works, or allowed them to deteriorate, and established in their stead a nomadic pastoral economy over most of North Africa."[11]

Murphey goes on to note that "Similar well-documented cases, for example, the Masai, are recorded from east and West Africa, where Hamitic or semi-Hamitic peoples in later ripples of the Islamic invasion displaced and overlaid sedentary Negro agriculturalists and substituted nomadic herding in areas where the only change was in social and economic custom rather than in the natural environment."[12]

He continues: "Nevertheless, it is possible that the changed land use which the Arabs brought with them did in time affect the natural environment in a critical way. By the end of the eighth century

11 Rhoads Murphey, "The Decline of North Africa since the Roman Occupation: Climatic or Human?", *ANNALS, Association of American Geographers*, Vol. XLI, no. 2, (June 1951).

12 Ibid., p. 124

AD there were approximately one million Arabs in North Africa. Each Arab family kept a large flock of sheep and goats, variously estimated at between fifteen and fifty per family. Goats are notoriously close croppers, and their unrestricted grazing in the Mediterranean area has had a virtually irreparable effect. In North Africa too, the added presence of several million goats undoubtedly destroyed large areas of grass, scrub, and trees, increasing the run-off, decreasing precious supplies of groundwater and lowering the water table perhaps critically, adding to the erosion of water courses, and disrupting the optimum distribution of surface water ..."[13] Furthermore, "Contemporary Arab disrespect for trees (notorious in both Arabia and North Africa) except as lumber or firewood, and lack of understanding of the long-term value to themselves of tree-cover may suggest a further deteriorating effect of Arab land use on the productivity of North Africa. Indeed, one student of the problem, while agreeing that the North African climate has not changed significantly in the last 2000 years, states that the primary cause of the economic decline during that period has been deforestation, for which he lays the blame at the door of the Arabs."[14]

We should note that even Hodges and Whitehouse admit to the great destruction wrought by the Arabs in North Africa. They refer specifically to several locations in modern Libya, where there is evidence of deliberate and systematic devastation. The enormous palace at Apollonia in Cyrene, excavated by Richard Goodchild, was razed by the Arabs, who seem then to have squatted in the ruins for a while. Nearby churches were demolished at the same time. There are similar signs of violent overthrow in the great church at Berenice, modern Benghazi.[15] The opulence and size of these structures, incidentally, give the lie to the picture which Hodges and Whitehouse earlier attempted to paint of a decrepit and crumbling Graeco-Roman society in the region. They note that Goodchild was mystified by the overthrow of the "extraordinarily impressive" Byzantine defenses in the Cyrenaean Jebel; and he reached the conclusion that the Arabs could only have breached these fortifications with the assistance of local Coptic Christians, who were at loggerheads with the Orthodox Church in Constantinople. This is in line with the theory that the Arab conquest of Egypt was also assisted by the Coptic Christians. However, there is no documentary evidence, either in Libya or in Egypt, of Cop-

---

13 Ibid.

14 Ibid., pp. 124-5

15 Hodges and Whitehouse, op cit., p. 69

tic collusion with the invaders, and such collusion is only surmised to account for the otherwise inexplicable fact of a few Arabs on camels conquering such a vast and densely population region.

Indeed, as we saw above, it was the very rapidity and apparent ease of the Arab conquests that has, perhaps more than any other single factor, induced scholars to assume that the late classical world was somehow in terminal decline.

Fig. 23. One of the Byzantine churches at Petra, another classical city which came to an end in the mid-seventh century.

We should note, at this point, that similar destruction of churches and monumental buildings is observed throughout Syria/Palestine and Anatolia at this time; though in Anatolia the initial destruction is more commonly attributed to the Persians a couple of decades before the arrival of the Arabs.

So great was the damage wrought by the Arabs in North Africa that Hodges and Whitehouse actually speak of a "Dark Age" in the region from the late seventh century onwards: "Unlike the Vandals," they say, "who prized the classical cities of North Africa, the Arabs simply abandoned them. As a result North Africa experienced a Dark Age which lasted until the tenth century, when the Mediterranean and trans-Saharan trade revived and many new towns were developed."[16]

Hodges and Whitehouse thus hold that the Arabs simultaneously

---

16 Ibid., p. 71

initiated a Dark Age and a Golden Age! The inherent contradiction here never seemed to have troubled them.

At this point I feel I must digress: Although I agree that the Arabs brought immense destruction to North Africa and indeed to Egypt, Syria and Anatolia, any reader of these reports must none-theless find it strange that virtually all archaeology should disappear from these areas for three centuries. For disappear it did. We are told, after all, that Islam did not have a Dark Age – this was something only Europe is supposed to have experienced. Yet archaeology of all kinds disappears from the regions controlled by Islam as surely as it does from Europe. Take for example Byblos, a site excavated by a French team under M. Dunand during the 1930s. The excavators found rich strata for virtually every period of the city's history, with one excep-tion: the four centuries between 636 (the Arab conquest) and the ad-vent of the Crusaders (1098) produced *no material remains whatsoever.*[17]

Stratigraphy of Byblos since Hellenism

21st period	Ottomans	+1516 to +1918	rich finds
20th period	Mamelukes	+1291 to +1516	rich finds
19th period	Crusaders	+1098 to +1291	rich finds
Crusaders of 1110 build right on Byzantine foundations of 600			
18th period	Umayyads + Abassids	+636 to +1098	<u>no finds</u>
enigmatic hiatus			
17th period	Byzantines	+330 to +636	rich finds
16th period	Romans	-63 to +330	rich finds
15th period	Hellenism	-332 to -63	rich finds

Were Byblos the only site to display this mysterious three to four century hiatus, then there would be little problem. The difficulty is

---

17 M. Dunand, *Fouilles de Byblos I*, (Paul Geuthner, Paris, 1939); and N. Jidejian. *Byblos through the Ages*, (Beyrouth, 1971)

that it is found throughout the Islamic world. As Gunnar Heinsohn, who brought my attention to the Byblos excavations, the same hiatus is encountered in the Fars region of Nubia, where the Polish excavators discovered Christian friezes and oil lamps dated to the "6th – 7th century," after which came a hiatus of more than 300 years, when more or less the same types of friezes and lamps reappear in the 11th – 12th century.[18] The same phenomenon is found in the great majority of the excavated sites in the Middle East.

* * *

The archaeological non-appearance of the Islamic Golden Age is surely one of the most remarkable discoveries to come to light in the past century. It has not achieved the sensational headlines we might expect, for the simple reason that a non-discovery is of much less interest to the public than a discovery. Then again, as archaeologists searched in vain through site after site, they imagined they had just been unlucky; that with the next day's dig the fabulous mosques, palaces and baths would be uncovered. And this has been the pattern now for a hundred years. In fact, the entire Islamic world is a virtual blank for roughly three centuries. Normally, we find one or two finds attributed to the seventh century (or occasionally to the eighth century), then nothing for three centuries, then a resumption of archaeological material in the mid- or late-tenth century. Take for example Egypt. Egypt was the largest and most populous Islamic territory during the Early Middle Ages. The Muslim conquest of the country occurred between 638 and 639, and we should expect the invaders to have begun, almost immediately, using the wealth of the land to begin building numerous and splendid places of worship – but apparently they didn't. Only two mosques in the whole of Egypt, both in Cairo, are said to date from before the eleventh century: the Amr ibn al-As, AD 641 and the Ahmad ibn Tulun, AD 878. However, the latter building has many features found only in mosques of the eleventh century, so its date of 878 is disputed. Thus, in Egypt, we have a single place of worship, the mosque of Amr ibn al-As, dating from the mid-seventh century, then nothing for another three-and-a-half centuries. Why, in an enormous country with up to perhaps five million inhabitants, should the Muslims wait over 300 years before building themselves places of worship?

---

18 Gunnar Heinsohn, "The Gaonic Period in the Land of Israel/Palestine," *Society for Interdisciplinary Studies; Chronology and Catastrophism Review*, No. 2 (2002)

And it is the same throughout the Islamic world. The city of Baghdad, supposedly a metropolis of a million souls under the fabulous Abbasid Caliph Harun al-Rashid (763-809), has left virtually not a trace. The normal explanation is that since the Abbasid capital lies under the modern Baghdad, its treasures must remain hidden.[19] Yet Roman London, also beneath a modern metropolis, a tiny settlement compared to the legendary Abbasid capital, has revealed a wealth of archaeological finds.

Fig. 24. Carthage, one of the north African cities destroyed in the seventh century.

No matter where we go, from Spain to northern Syria, there is virtually nothing between circa 650 and 950. The only notable exceptions to the rule, apparently, are the Islamic settlements of Mesopotamia and Iran. The textbooks declare that eastern cities such as Samarra, Susa and Siraf (in Iran), have produced copious archaeology from the mid-seventh to mid-tenth centuries. The visitor to Samarra, for example, said to have been built by Harun al-Rashid's successors in the ninth century, is shown the largely mud-brick ruins of an enormous metropolis, a city excavated and mapped between 1911 and

---

19 In the words of Hodges and Whitehouse, "Abbasid Baghdad is buried beneath the modern city for, as Guy LeStrange remarked, so wise was the choice of site that it has served as the capital of Mesopotamia almost without interruption. Our knowledge of the city of al-Mansur, therefore, comes from written sources ..." op cit., p. 128

1914 by a German team under Ernst Herzfeld. The Great Mosque of Samarra, with its unique spiraling minaret, is widely advertised as a still visible representation of the flourishing Abbasid world of the ninth century. The case of Samarra is one we shall return to at a later stage (in Chapter 14). Suffice for the moment to state that the evidence indicates, notwithstanding the assertions of the textbooks, that the great metropolis dates from the late tenth century. That, at least, is the date normally assigned to the pottery and other artifacts associated with the ruins when they occur outside of Mesopotamia. Herzfeld and others attempted to stretch the range of these artifacts backwards to include the ninth century and (in places) the eighth, in order to give the supposedly thriving Abbasid Caliphate of the ninth and eighth centuries something in the range of material goods.

Thus the fabulous epoch of the Caliphs of the eighth and ninth centuries remains as elusive as ever. If we were to judge by the archaeology of Samarra, Susa and Siraf, and ignore the written sources, we would have to say that the Islamic cities were established by the Sassanids in the seventh century, then abandoned by the start of the eighth, and reoccupied in the second half of the tenth century; at which point they experienced their greatest prosperity.

No matter where we go, it is the same story. Spain, as we have seen, is supposed to have witnessed a flowering of Islamic culture and civilization in the two centuries after the Arab conquest of 711; and the city of Cordoba is said to have grown to a sophisticated metropolis of half-a-million people or more. We recall the description of a flourishing and vastly opulent metropolis painted by the medieval Arab chroniclers. Yet it is admitted that "Little remains of the architecture of this period."[20] Little indeed! As a matter of fact, the only standing Muslim structure in the whole of Spain dating from before the eleventh century is the so-called Mosque of Cordoba; yet even this, strictly-speaking, is not an Islamic construction: It was originally the Visigothic Cathedral of Saint Vincent, which was converted, supposedly in the days of Abd er-Rahman I, to a mosque. Yet the Islamic features that exist could equally belong to the time of Abd er-Rahman III (latter tenth century) whom we know did conversion work on the Cathedral, adding a minaret and a new façade.[21] Most of the Islamic features in the building actually come after Abd er-Rahman III, and there is no secure way of dating anything in it to the eighth century.

20 H. St. L. B. Moss, op cit., p. 172

21 See eg Bertrand, op cit., p. 54

The poverty of visible Islamic remains is normally explained by the proposition that the Christians destroyed the Muslim monuments after the city's re-conquest. But this solution is inherently suspect. Granted the Christians might have destroyed all the mosques – though even that seems unlikely – but they certainly would not have destroyed opulent palaces, baths, fortifications, etc. Yet none of these – none at least ascribed to the eighth, ninth or early tenth centuries – has survived. And even granting that such a universal and pointless destruction did take place, we have to assume that at least under the ground we would find an abundance of Arab foundations, as well as artifacts, tools, pottery etc. Indeed, in a city of half a million people, as Cordoba of the eight, ninth and early tenth centuries is said to have been, the archaeologist would expect to find a superabundance of such things. They should be popping out of the ground with almost every shovel-full of dirt; and yet, as we saw in Chapter 8, almost nothing in the city can be confidently assigned to the eighth or ninth centuries.

The sheer poverty of these remains makes it clear that the fabulously wealthy Cordoba of the eighth, ninth and early tenth centuries is a myth; and the elusive nature of all material from these three centuries, in every part of the Islamic world, makes us wonder whether the rise of Islam has been somehow misdated: For the first real mark left (in archaeological terms) by Islam in Spain is dated to the mid-tenth century, to the time of Abd er-Rahman III, whose life bears many striking comparisons with his namesake and supposed ancestor Abd er-Rahman I, of the eighth century. Again, there are strange and striking parallels between the major events of Islamic history of the seventh and eighth centuries on the one hand and of the tenth and eleventh centuries on the other. Thus for example the Christian Reconquista in Spain is supposed to have commenced around 720, with the victory of Don Pelayo at Covadonga; but the real Reconquista began three hundred years later with the victories of Sancho of Navarre around 1020. Similarly, the Islamic invasion of northern India supposedly commenced around 710-720 with the victories of Muhammad bin Qasim, though the "real" Islamic conquest of the region began with the victories of Mahmud of Ghazni, roughly between 1010 and 1020. Yet again, the cultural impact of Islam on Europe seems not have been felt until the late tenth and eleventh centuries, though commonsense would suggest that it should have been felt three hundred years earlier. Pirenne, for example, was criticized by Dopsch for suggesting that Islam terminated classical civilization in Europe in the seventh century by its blockade of the Mediterranean. If that were the case, said Dopsch, Europe should have become "medieval" by the late seventh century. Yet many of the characteristics of medieval society, such as the rise of feudalism and castle-building, only appear in the late tenth century. And obviously Islamic ideas, such as Holy War, were only copied by the Europeans in the eleventh century.

What then does all this mean?

The lack of substantial Muslim archaeology from before the tenth and eleventh centuries (with the exception of two or three monuments such as the Dome of the Rock in Jerusalem and the Amr ibn al-As mosque in Cairo, usually of the mid-seventh century), would seem to leave only three possible explanations. Either (1), the Arab conquests and the regime that followed were so destructive that they extinguished almost all settled life in the Middle East and North Africa for three centuries, or (2), some form of catastrophe, of a natural order, in the form of a plague or climatic disturbance, destroyed a great percentage of the populations of the Near East and North Africa sometime in the mid-seventh century, or (3) the rise of Islam has been misdated, and that some form of error, of a fundamental nature, has crept into the chronology. None of these options, so radical in their implications, have endeared themselves to the scholarly community, which naturally abhors such dramatic and revolutionary paradigm-shifts. Yet though such talk may be shunned in academia, the fundamental fact of the extreme poverty of all archaeology from the mid-seventh to mid-tenth centuries will not go away. And the circumstance that virtually nothing from before the mid-tenth century has been found means that Islam was not a flourishing, opulent and cultured civilization whilst Europe was mired in the Dark Ages. By the late tenth century Europe was experiencing her own "renaissance", with a flowering of "Romanesque" art and architecture, much of it strongly reminiscent of the late classical work of the Merovingian and Visigothic period.

The meaning of this archaeological "dark age" is then of central importance to our understanding of European and Islamic history; and it is a feature to which we are drawn repeatedly as soon as we look at the history of these obscure and enigmatic centuries. We should note that, of the above three explanations, it is likely that the answer may not reside in one alone, and we may be compelled to consider a combination of more than one. Having said that, it seems beyond question that proposition (1) will have to form a major part of the solution: For, whatever we might say about faulty chronologies or natural disasters, the destructiveness of the Arab conquests is not to be doubted; and the coming of the Arabs was a catastrophe of unprecedented proportions for the settled peoples of the Mediterranean world. It is worth remarking that even when substantial archaeology does again appear in the Middle East and North Africa, from the middle of the tenth century, the world they reveal – Islam at its most flowering and opulent – is little more than a pale shadow of the classical civilization which disappeared in the seventh century. The urban centers of the time, Cordoba, Alexandria, and Antioch, are tiny (and few and far between) compared to the great metropolises of the Byzantines, and not to be compared with them in any meaningful way.[22]

---

22 Again, the exceptions to this rule are said to be in Mesopotamia, where Baghdad and Samarra are held to have been great metropolises in the tenth and eleventh centuries. However, as we have seen, Abbasid Baghdad is notable by its non-appearance in the archaeology, whilst Samarra survived as a great center for no more than a few decades. The city seems to have experienced its first prosperity under the late Sassanids, and continued to be occupied by the early Arabs, though the latter appear to have been abandoned it at the end of the seventh century. It was reoccupied by the later Abbasids in the tenth century, and completely abandoned in the early eleventh century.

ISLAM'S VIEW OF THE WORLD

E   mpires had come and gone before in the Mediterranean. Wars
      of conquest had been waged. Barbarian peoples had occupied
territories from Asia Minor to Spain. Yet none of them had destroyed
trade and agriculture in the way these things were destroyed in the
seventh century. What was it about the Muslim empire which produced such disruption?

It has to be understood that with the coming of Islam there
appeared on the world stage an ideology like none that had existed
before. One of the fundamentals of the Islamic faith was the accept-
ability, even the duty, of Muslims to wage war against the infidel. Muhammad himself preached the necessity of war and participated in
violent conflict. Indeed, he is said to have ordered at least sixty raids
and wars and personally participated in twenty-seven of them. Gibbon, as unbiased an authority as may be found, attributed the spectacular success of Muhammad's faith to the promise of plunder. "From all
sides the roving Arabs were allured to the standard of religion and
plunder; and the apostle sanctified the licence of embracing female
captives as their wives and concubines; and the enjoyment of wealth
and beauty was a feeble type of the joys of paradise prepared for the
valiant martyrs of the faith. 'The sword,' says Mahomet, 'is the key of
heaven and of hell: a drop of blood shed in the cause of God, a night
spent in arms, is of more avail than two months of fasting or prayer:
whosoever falls in battle, his sins are forgiven ...'" (*Decline and Fall*, Ch.
50) And it cannot be stressed too strongly that all of the early spread
of Islam involved the sword. Contrast this with the growth of Christianity, or Buddhism, for that matter. In fact, Islam is virtually unique
among world religions in that its primary scriptures advocate the use
of military force and its early expansion – indeed its expansion during
the first six or seven centuries of its existence – invariably involved
military conquest and the use of force.

In 1993 Samuel P. Huntington famously noted that "Islam has
bloody borders."[1] He might have added that Islam has always had
bloody borders. Before he died, Mohammed told his followers that he
had been ordered to "fight with the people till they say, none has the

---

1 Samuel P. Huntington, "The Clash of Civilizations?" *Foreign Affairs*, (Summer,
1993)

right to be worshipped but Allah." (*Hadith*, Vol. 4:196) In this spirit, Islamic theology divides the world into two parts: the Dar al-Islam, "House of Islam" and the Dar al-Harb, "House of War." In short, a state of perpetual conflict exists between Islam and the rest of the world. There can thus never be a real and genuine peace between Islam and the Dar al-Harb. At best, there can be a temporary truce, to allow Muslims to recuperate and regroup. In the words of Bat Ye'or, "the jihad is a state of permanent war [which] excludes the possibility of true peace." All that is allowed are "provisional truces in accordance with the requirements of the political situation."[2] According to medieval historian Robert Irwin, "Since the jihad [was] ... a state of permanent war, it [excluded] ... the possibility of true peace, but it [did] ... allow for provisional truces in accordance with the requirements of the political situation."[3] Also, "Muslim religious law could not countenance the formal conclusion of any sort of permanent peace with the infidel."[4] In such circumstances, it is evident that, when the Islamic forces were in a position of strength, almost all contact between them and the outside world was warlike. And this was not war as is waged between two kingdoms, empires, or dynasties: this was total war, war that did not distinguish between combatants and non-combatants, and war that did not end. In this spirit, Islamic generals launched attack after attack against the southern shores of Europe during the seventh and eighth centuries; and these "official" actions were supplemented by hundreds, even thousands, of lesser raids, carried out by minor Muslim commanders and even by private individuals. For it was considered legitimate that the Muslim faithful should live off the infidel world. Whatever spoils could be taken, were divinely sanctioned.

The coming of Islam therefore signaled a wave of banditry and piracy in the Mediterranean such as had not been seen since before the second century BC, when such activities were severely curtailed by Roman naval power. Indeed, it seems that this new Islamic piracy surpassed in scope and destructiveness anything that had gone before.[5]

---

2 Bat Ye'or, *The Dhimmi: Jews and Christians Under Islam* (Fairleigh Dickinson University Press, 1985), p. 46

3 Robert Irwin, "Islam and the Crusades: 1096-1699," in Jonathan Riley-Smith (ed.) *The Oxford History of the Crusades* (Oxford, 1995), pp. 237

4 Ibid.

5 The sheer scope and immense impact of this Islamic piracy has been dealt with in some detail by Michael McCormick in his, *Origins of the European Economy: Communications and Commerce, AD 300 – 900* (Cambridge, 2002).

Ordinary pirates might be deterred by powerful navies which threatened them with an early death: Muslim pirates would be less put off by such dangers since, in their minds, they were executing a divine ordnance, and to die in such activity was considered a sure to way paradise.[6]

In the long stretch of time since the life of Muhammad, it is doubtful if there has been a single year in which Muslims, in some part of the world, have not been fighting against Infidels. In the history of relations between Europe and the House of Islam alone, there was continual and almost uninterrupted war between Muslims and Christians since the first attack on Sicily in 652 and on Constantinople in 674. In the great majority of these wars, the Muslims were the aggressors. And even the short periods of official peace were disturbed by the "unofficial" activities of privateers and slave-traders. For centuries, Muslim pirates based in North Africa made large parts of the Mediterranean shore-line uninhabitable, and it is estimated that between the sixteenth and nineteenth centuries alone they captured and enslaved something in excess of a million Europeans.

The centrality of war in Islamic theology is expressed succinctly by Ibn Abi Zayd al Qayrawani, who died in 966:

> Jihad is a precept of Divine institution. Its performance by certain individuals may dispense others from it. We Malikis [one of the four schools of Muslim jurisprudence] maintain that it is preferable not to begin hostilities with the enemy before having invited the latter to embrace the religion of Allah except where the enemy attacks first. They have the alternative of either converting to Islam or paying the poll tax (jizya), short of which war will be declared against them. The jizya can only be accepted from them if they occupy a territory where our laws can be enforced. If they are out of our reach, the jizya cannot be accepted from them unless they come with-

---

6 That piracy was seen by Muslims as a legitimate part of jihad against unbelievers is seen is quite literally thousands of pronouncements from Islamic sources over the centuries. As an example, we might quote the reply of the Barbary ambassador to Thomas Jefferson when he enquired why they attacked American ships, vessels from a land with whom they were not at war: "…it was written in the Koran, that all Nations who should not have acknowledged their authority were sinners, that it was their right and duty to make war upon whoever they could find and to make Slaves of all they could take as prisoners, and that every Mussulman who should be slain in battle was sure to go to Paradise."

in our territory. Otherwise we will make war against them ...

It is incumbent upon us to fight the enemy without inquiring as to whether we shall be under the command of a pious or depraved leader.

It is not prohibited to kill white non-Arabs who have been taken prisoner. But no one can be executed after having been granted the aman (protection). The promises made to them must not be broken. Women and children must not be executed and the killing of monks and rabbis must be avoided unless they have taken part in battle. Women also may be executed if they have participated in the fighting. The aman granted by the humblest Muslim must be recognized by other [Muslims]. Women and young children can also grant the aman when they are aware of its significance. However, according to another opinion, it is only valid if confirmed by the imam (spiritual leader). The imam will retain a fifth of the booty captured by the Muslims in the course of warfare and he will share the remaining four fifths among the soldiers of the army. Preferably, the apportioning will take place on enemy ground.[7]

The long-term consequences of this attitude are plain to be seen in any of the societies that came under the dominion of Islam. Early in the 20th century historian Louis Bertrand wrote extensively of Islam's impact upon Spain; and what he says is devastating. In his words, "...the first part of this period [of Islam's rule], that of the Emirs dependent upon the Caliphate of Damascus ... is nothing but a long series of intestinal struggles, slaughterings, massacres, and assassinations. It was anarchy in all its horror, fed by family hatreds and the rivalry of tribe against tribe – Arabs of the North against Arabs of the South, Yemenites against Kaishites, Syrians against Medinites. All these Asiatics had a common enemy in the nomad African, the Berber, the eternal spoiler of cities and the auxiliary of all invaders."[8]

Executions, normally following torture, were most often by crucifixion. This was the fate even of the ninety year-old Abd el-Malik,

---

7 Ibn Khaldun, *The Muqaddimah: An Introduction to History* Vol. 1 (Trans. Franz Rosenthal, Bollingen Series 43: Princeton University Press, 1958), p. 163. Cited from Bat Ye'or, op cit., p. 161

8 Bertrand, op cit., p. 36

who was beaten, slashed with swords and then crucified between a pig and a dog. "After that, Bertrand continues, "Yemenites and Kaishites ... came to blows among themselves. The Kaishites, under the leadership of their chief, Somail, routed their adversaries in the plain of Secunda, the Roman town on the other side of the Guadalquiver opposite Cordova. The victorious Somail had the Yemenite chiefs beheaded in the square in front of the Cathedral of Saint Vincent, which as yet was only half turned into a mosque. "Seventy heads had already fallen when one of the chiefs in alliance with Somail protested against this horrible butchery, not in the name of humanity, but in the name of Musulman solidarity. Somail, nevertheless, went on with his executions until his ally, indignant at his excessive cruelty, threatened to turn against him."[9]

Again, "Nothing emerges from this perpetual killing but the savagery, the brutality, and the cruelty of the new-comers. Under their domination ... Spain got used to being ridden over and devastated periodically, in a way that soon became as regular as the alteration of the seasons."[10] This pattern, set at the beginning, continued throughout the Muslim period. The savagery inflicted upon fellow Muslims was but a pale reflection of the atrocities committed against the Christian unbelievers in the North, whose territory was raided twice a year by every Muslim ruler.[11] And to top all of this, Islamic Spain became the hub of a vast new slave-trade. Hundreds of thousands of European slaves, both from Christian territories and from the lands of the pagan Slavs, were imported into the Caliphate, there to be used (if female) as concubines or to be castrated (if male) and made into harem guards or the personal body-guards of the Caliph. According to Bertrand, "This army of Slavs [eunuchs] ... was the main instrument of the Caliph's authority. His power was a military dictatorship. He maintained himself only thanks to these foreigners."[12]

It is evident then that the Islamic conquests, wherever they occurred, unleashed a flood of anarchic violence. This was not war as was waged by highly disciplined and strictly commanded armies such as those of the Caesars. Islamic war had far more in common with the wars waged by barbarian peoples such as the Huns or Vandals. Yet even their conquests were arguably less violent and destructive than

---

9 Ibid., pp. 37–8
10 Ibid., p. 37
11 Ibid., p. 45
12 Ibid.

those of the Muslims; for they lacked the religious fanaticism that motivated the latter.

* * *

So much for the Dar al-Islam's fraught relationship with the outside world: But even after the conquest of a territory and the submission of its inhabitants, the dictates of Islamic law meant that the non-Muslim inhabitants could never again enjoy lasting peace and security. In theory, the "religions of the Book" (ie. Christianity and Judaism), enjoyed a special "protected" (dhimmi) status under the new regime. In practice however the position of the Christian and Jewish population was anything but protected. This was because under the provisions of Islamic law (sharia), the rights of Jews and Christians were subordinate to those of Muslims. The legal testimony of a Muslim always trumped that of a Christian or Jew, no matter how many Christians or Jews testified. In practical terms, this meant that a dhimmi Jew or Christian might be insulted, robbed, or even murdered in the street, without any hope of legal redress. If such a complaint were taken to the authorities, the Muslim culprit would claim that the infidel had insulted the Prophet or the Koran. Two other male Muslim witnesses were needed to substantiate this claim, but these were invariably forthcoming, and the suit ended in the execution of the Jewish or Christian complainant.

As might be imagined, such oppressive conditions meant that Christians and Jews lived in permanent fear of the predatory attentions of Muslim neighbors, with the result that, over the centuries, the pressure to convert to Islam, or to emigrate from the Muslim-controlled territory, became almost irresistible.

A further exacerbating factor was that under Islamic law Muslims have a right to subsist off the labors and property of the infidel. This is enshrined in the concept of jizya, the tax which all infidels living in the Dar al-Islam must pay to their Muslim masters. But it was not just the Caliph and his emirs who were entitled to live off the infidels. All Muslims, irrespective of position, had this right; and Islamic law thus sanctified the plundering by individual Muslims of the local Christian and Jewish populations.

The long-term consequences of such an outlook are not too difficult to imagine. A general climate of banditry and lawlessness was fostered; and we see, for example, in a very immediate way why immigrant Arab goat-herders in the Middle East and North Africa felt free to allow their flocks to graze on the cultivated lands of their Christian and Jewish neighbors, thus destroying the agricultural viability of these territories and reducing them, within a very short time, to arid semi-desert. One of the most immediate consequences was a dramatic decline in the population. Although precise figures are unavailable, we know that the medieval populations of Anatolia, Syria, Egypt, and North Africa were much smaller than those under the last Byzantine administration. Estimates put the decline at anything from threefold to tenfold; and the result was that by the later Middle Ages large parts of the Middle East and North Africa comprised sparsely populated wasteland, housing economically oppressed and largely impoverished populations. In the fourteenth century, for example, the Islamic scholar Ibn Khaldun, writing in the squalor of what is now Tunisia, marveled at the wealth of a visiting delegation of Italian merchants. And the same attitudes continued to produce the same results well into the nineteenth and even twentieth centuries.

We possess, from the early Middle Ages onwards, accounts of these regions from European travelers (often pilgrims), who were generally appalled by what they saw. Thus for example in the late eighteenth century C. F. Volney, "probably the most perceptive European traveler to visit the Middle East before the nineteenth century" described in detail conditions in Syria and Egypt under the then Ottoman administration. The main problems identified by Volney were extortionate taxation, the lawlessness of the soldiery, the depredation of Bedouin Arabs, usurious interest rates, and the primitive state of agricultural methods and implements. After describing the routine pillaging of the Ottoman troops, Volney goes on to note that, "These burthens are more especially oppressive in the countries bestowed as an appendage, and in those which are exposed to the Arabs [ie. Bedouins]. ... With respect to the Bedouins, if they are at war, they pillage as enemies; and if they are at peace, devour every thing they can find as guests; hence the proverb, Avoid the Bedouin, whether friend or enemy."[13] The latter is a clear reference to the Bedouin custom of permitting their herds to graze on crop-land.

Volney also remarked on the almost total lack of security while travelling: "...nobody travels alone, from the insecurity of the roads.

---

13 C. F. Volney, *Travels through Syria and Egypt* (London, 1787), Vol. 2, pp. 406-31; in Charles Issawi, ed. *The Economic History of the Middle East, 1800-1914* (University of Chicago Press, 1966), p. 215

One must wait for several travellers who are going to the same place, or take advantage of the passage of some great man, who assumed the office of protector, but is more frequently the oppressor of the caravan. These precautions are, above all, necessary in the countries exposed to the Arabs, such as Palestine, and the whole frontier of the desert, and even on the road from Aleppo to Skandaroon, on account of the Curd robbers."[14]

One does not have to be a genius to imagine the impact of such conditions on trade and commerce.

About eighty years later Mark Twain visited the region and described it pretty much as had Volney, though using slightly more colorful language. Palestine, he says, is "A desolate country whose soil is rich enough, but is given over wholly to weeds ... a silent mournful expanse ... a desolation ... we never saw a human being on the whole route.... hardly a tree or shrub anywhere. Even the olive tree and the cactus, those fast friends of a worthless soil, had almost deserted the country."[15]

The above writers also noted a striking feature remarked upon by many other travelers: the almost complete absence of wheeled vehicles. The same feature was mentioned by Bernard Lewis, the doyen of Middle Eastern studies at Princeton. In his 2001 book *What Went Wrong?* Lewis asked the question: What went wrong with a civilization which – he believes – showed such promise at the start, only to be mired in poverty and backwardness from the 12th-13th century onwards? Lewis concludes his volume without arriving at an answer. Yet at one point he makes a telling observation: Wheeled vehicles, he notes, were virtually unknown, up until modern times, throughout the Muslim lands. This was all the more strange given the fact that the wheel was invented in the Middle East (in Babylonia) and had been commonly used in earlier ages. The conclusion he comes to, in line with that of Volney and many others, is that: "A cart is large and, for a peasant, relatively costly. It is difficult to conceal and easy for requisition. At a time and place where neither law nor custom restricted the powers of even local authorities, visible and mobile assets were a poor investment. The same fear of predatory authority – or neighbors – may be seen in the structure of traditional houses and quarters: the high, windowless walls, the almost hidden entrances in narrow alley-

---

14 Ibid., p. 217

15 Mark Twain, *The Innocents Abroad*, (New York, 1869), pp. 361-2

ways, the careful avoidance of any visible sign of wealth."[16] In the kleptocracy that was the Caliphate, it seems, not even Muslims – far less Christians and Jews – were free to prosper.

---

16 Bernard Lewis, *What Went Wrong? The Clash between Islam and Modernity in the Middle East* (New York, 2002), p. 158

INTERNATIONAL TRADE AND THE CALIPHATE

W e have argued that the advent of Islam did indeed terminate all normal trading relations between Europe and the Near East, precisely as Pirenne claimed. This of course stands in striking contrast to the position of Hodges, Whitehouse, and a host of others, who found evidence of extensive trade between Islam and the outside world during the seventh to eleventh centuries. More recently, Michael McCormick has reiterated this criticism of Pirenne,[1] and the same has been forcefully restated by Thomas Glick. "In fact," says Glick, "the Islamic conquest had more nearly the opposite effect than that posited by Pirenne: it opened the Mediterranean, previously a Roman lake, and, by connecting it with the Indian Ocean, converted it into a route of world trade."[2]

The evidence garnered over the past century by innumerable archaeologists working throughout the Middle East, has confirmed that, during the seventh to eleventh centuries there was indeed a vibrant trade conducted in the Indian Ocean between the Arabian Peninsula and India and South-East Asia. Of the existence of this trade, and its economic importance, there can be no doubt. This does not, however, I will suggest, present a problem for the Pirenne thesis. The thriving Indian Ocean trade can be explained quite easily if we remember some basic facts: First of all, those conducting this trade were native Arabs and Muslims, based mainly in the Persian Gulf and Yemen, and it was essential to the prosperity of the entire Arabian Peninsula. The Arabs of southern and eastern Arabia had lived off the Indian Ocean trade for centuries, and many had grown prosperous on it. They imported from southern and eastern Asia highly sought-after luxuries, which all the peoples of the Arabian Peninsula had become used to. If this commerce had been disrupted through piracy, the main sufferers would have been the Arabs themselves.

The Mediterranean trade, by contrast, was mainly in the hands of Christian Syrians and Jews. These peoples were not Arabs and very definitely not Muslims. They were inimical to Islam, and therefore of no concern to the Caliph and his ministers. Furthermore, what they

---

1 Michael McCormick, op cit.

2 Thomas Glick, op cit., p. 19

imported from Europe and the West was of little interest to the Arabs. It is true that in antiquity Syrian (Phoenician) traders had brought much of great value from western Europe. Britain and, to some degree, Spain, were important sources of tin; and it seems that for a large part of the Bronze Age these regions, as well as central Europe, exported large quantities of ore, as well as finished products of bronze (such as swords) to the Middle East. By late antiquity however other sources of tin had been discovered, and western Europe thus lost much of her importance in this context. One "product" of Europe however did remain of interest to the Arabs, and that was the bodies of the Europeans themselves. White-skinned slaves, both male and female, were highly sought after in the Caliphate. The males were generally castrated and employed in the various offices of eunuchs. The females, as might be imagined, were placed in harems.

Such slaves, however, were not, in the initial stages at least, acquired by trade. The Europeans that the Arabs first came into contact with were all Christians from the southern reaches of the continent. Christian Europeans were not likely to sell their co-religionists into bondage in the Caliphate. But the Muslims had other, more direct ways, of procuring slaves: war and piracy. And, as we have seen, both these were waged against southern Europe with great intensity during the first century of the Islamic expansion.

At this point we recall another facet of the argument against Pirenne, one which we have already briefly alluded to throughout the present work. McCormick and various others have suggested that the slave trade, which the Vikings of northern Europe indubitably conducted with the Muslim world from the late ninth century onwards, must have been a source of wealth for Europe as a whole. Far from terminating trade between Europe and the East, say these writers, the Muslims might actually have increased it.[3]

Hodges and Whitehouse too emphasize the economic importance of the slave trade (though they demure from calling it a "slave trade"), and point to the rich finds of gold and luxury items of oriental origin recovered over the past century from various parts of Scandinavia. They also emphasize the part played by European ports on the Mediterranean. Venice, we know, was involved, as was – for a while – Marseilles; and so too was Constantinople; though Hodges and Whitehouse admit that a great degree of this commerce was conducted entirely outside the boundaries of Christian Europe: one of the most

---

3 McCormick, op cit.

important of all slave-trading depots was located at Astrakhan, at the mouth of the Volga on the Caspian Sea, where the commerce was entirely with Scandinavians.[4] Having said that, there is no doubt that, at certain periods, the above-mentioned Christian cities did take part in the traffic; and not a few authors have waxed lyrical about the mighty benefits that must have accrued from it. In the words of Glick: "By the tenth century, when the Muslims had taken control of strategically important islands (Crete, Sicily, the Balearics) Islam effectively controlled the Mediterranean, which did not constitute a barrier to trade, but rather a medium whereby all bordering states could participate in a world economy, fertilized by healthy injections of Sudanese gold."[5]

Why, the objective reader might ask at this stage, does Glick fail to mention the ravaging of the coastlands of northern Spain, southern France, Italy, and Greece by Muslim pirates at this time; a ravaging so intense that large areas became uninhabitable? And whilst it is true, as we have seen, that some Christian states in the region did become involved, these were the exception. Also, Glick must surely be aware that most of the "Sudanese gold" arriving in Europe ended up Scandinavia; which destination it reached by way of the Volga or Dnieper Rivers, thus bypassing Christian Europe altogether.

Furthermore, we should note that the Viking raids, which devastated much of northern and western Europe for about two centuries, was intimately tied to the Muslim demand for European slaves, begging further the question of how this could be viewed as in any way beneficial to Europe and European civilization.

Again, if so much gold were now arriving in Europe, why was this not translated into gold coinage? In answer to this, Glick treats us to a large paragraph in which he speaks of the "relative value" of gold and silver, and basically tells us that in Europe during the seventh to eleventh centuries silver was more valuable than gold; hence they minted their money in silver. What he fails to tell his readers is that virtually all coinage – even bronze coinage – was extremely scarce during these centuries, apparently proving beyond question that the continent was impoverished and reduced to a barter economy, as Pirenne claimed.

We might conclude then that, whilst Muslim traders paid for their human captives in gold and silver, the amount they paid must have been small in comparison with the quantities reaching Europe

---

4 Hodges and Whitehouse, op cit., pp. 117-8

5 Glick, op cit., pp. 20-1

during the final pre-Islamic centuries. Even more importantly, we must never lose sight of the fact that this "trade" was in no way a normal one: European slaves were procured equally by purchasing them from Viking pirates or through their Christian European intermediaries – or they were taken directly from southern Europe by Arab and Muslim pirates. Indeed, the great majority of the human cargo reaching Cordoba, Damascus and Baghdad seems to have been procured in the latter way; and this was an activity which, as we argued, must have commenced at the very beginning of the Islamic period. Statements such as that of Hodges and Whitehouse, which attribute Saracen piracy and raiding to specific socio-economic conditions at certain epochs, betray a woeful misunderstanding of Islam and a willful ignorance of its history. War against the infidel was a fundamental duty of every Muslim, and a state of permanent conflict existed between the House of Islam and the outside world.

The first appearance of Saracen pirates and slave-raiders would have terminated all normal commercial intercourse in the Mediterranean; and so it is futile to talk of any "benefits" to Europe. Some time later, Scandinavian pirates became involved, and we should stress that the entire Viking phenomenon was intimately connected with the expansion of Islam. In the words of Hugh Trevor-Roper: "What were these Vikings doing? What sudden force drove these piratical Northmen to range over the seas and rivers of Europe, creating havoc? It used to be supposed that it was merely a sudden, unexplained growth of population in Scandinavia which lay behind this extraordinary outburst. No doubt this was true: so vast an expansion cannot have been sustained by a static population. But the scope and direction of the raids point also to other motives. There were opportunities abroad as well as pressures at home; and these opportunities link together the Viking raids and the Moslem conquests."[6]

Trevor-Roper goes on to describe the vast wealth accumulated by the Caliphate in its expansion across Asia and Africa, and how, with this wealth, it could purchase what it wanted from Europe. What the Muslims wanted, above all, was "eunuchs and slaves." He continues: "It was one of the functions of the Vikings to supply these goods. Half traders, half pirates, they ranged over all northern Europe, and in their ranging, or through the method of piracy, they collected furs and kidnapped human beings. For preference they dealt in heathen Slavs, since Christian States had less compunction in handling a slave-trade

---

6 Trevor-Roper, op cit., p. 90

in heathen bodies – they could always quote that useful text, Leviticus xxv, 44. So the Vikings fed both Byzantium and the rich new civilization of Islam with the goods which they demanded and for which they could pay. In doing so they penetrated all the coasts and rivers of Europe."[7]

It is generally supposedly that the Viking epoch commenced in the early ninth century. Yet we should note that the existence of a seventh century Viking trading centre at Staraja Ladoga in north-west Russia has now been confirmed, whilst a very large number of Arab dirhams, dating from the seventh century, has been found in various parts of Scandinavia.[8] The existence of these coins can only mean either of two things: (a) That the Arabs were using two or three hundred year old coins in their regular trading relations with the Vikings, or (b) that the Viking Age began in the seventh century, right at the start of the Islamic epoch. Of these, option (b) seems by far the more probable; yet the implications of such a conclusion are so far-reaching and so unsettling to the conventional view of Dark Age history that the evidence has been largely bypassed in textbooks and scholarly publications.

We should note that, here again, we have an example of a phenomenon of the seventh century apparently mirrored by one in the tenth.

* * *

Hodges and Whitehouse emphasized that the early Caliphs presided over an opulent and flourishing civilization, and they pointed to the legendary status of Baghdad during the eighth century and Samarra during the ninth as evidence of this. As we saw, Baghdad of the eighth century has provided few proofs of its wealth and size, though Samarra has indeed revealed an enormous settlement replete with gardens, palaces, mosques and baths. Other cities of Mesopotamia and Iran, such as Siraf, have also been found to have flourished at this time.

Before continuing, it needs to be emphasized that the early Islamic centers which are said to have revealed substantial archaeology

---

7 Ibid., pp. 90-1

8 See Pirenne, op cit., pp. 239-40. More recently, in 1999 a hoard found at Gotland in Sweden included "Arabic coins from the Sassanidian dynasty from the mid-7th century ..." Ola Korpås, Per Wideström and Jonas Ström, "The recently found hoards from Spillings farm on Gotland, Sweden," *Viking Heritage Magazine*, 4 (2000).

– that is, from the seventh to tenth centuries – are invariably in Mesopotamia and to the east, most especially in Iran; and it seems beyond question that the Islamicization of Mesopotamia and Persia, the former territories of the Sassanid Empire, was a far less violent affair than the Islamicization of the Byzantine lands. There is evidence of much greater cultural and economic continuity in the former than in the latter. Almost all excavated sites west of the northern Euphrates have revealed a destruction layer separating Byzantine and Islamic epochs; whilst in Mesopotamia and Iran this is lacking, with the evidence pointing to a relatively peaceful transition from Zoroastrian to Islamic civilization.

Whether or not this be the case, it is clear that the eastern regions of the Caliphate, in Mesopotamia and Iran, enjoyed a great deal more wealth and continuity from the seventh to tenth centuries than did the territories of the west, the former lands of the Eastern Roman Empire.

Yet even in the east, the continuity which Hodges and Whitehouse lay so much emphasis upon is open to question. The dates provided by excavators at the Mesopotamian sites are often based on little more than a handful of barely legible coins. These, as well as the testimony of the medieval Arab chroniclers, form the basis of early Islamic chronology. Thus about five separate occupation layers are mentioned by Hodges and Whitehouse as occurring at Siraf, a Persian Gulf port of southern Iran, between the mid-seventh and early tenth centuries, though in fact the only ruins they can actually show, of a bazaar site, of a residential quarter, and of a house courtyard, all date from the tenth century. Furthermore, the depth of strata is nowhere near what we would expect from the supposedly four centuries during which the site was occupied. This was a fact overlooked by David Whitehouse in his several published reports on the site.[9] We encounter a similar situation at Samarra, though in an even more acute form. There we find that the traditional Arab account of the city's history, which Hodges and Whitehouse seem to trust implicitly, has been thoroughly debunked by archaeology. According to the Arabs, in the year 836 Caliph Al-Mutasim decided to move his capital from Baghdad, following riots at the city. His attention was drawn to an empty site about 120 kilometers

---

9 See D. Whitehouse, *Siraf III. The Congregational Mosque* (London, British Institute of Persian Studies, 1980); also Whitehouse, "Siraf: a medieval port on the Persian coast," *World Archaeology* 2 (1970), and "Excavations at Siraf. First-Sixth Interim Reports," *Iran*, 6-12 (1968-74)

upstream on the Tigris, inhabited only by a few monks, who informed him of a former city in the area and a legend that it would be rebuilt by "a great, victorious and powerful king," at which point the Caliph began construction there of his new capital. Archaeology however has shown that Samarra was already a large and important center under the Sassanids, whose king Chosroes I (late sixth century) extended the Nahrawan canal to the locality, thus opening it for settlement. To celebrate the completion of this project, a commemorative tower (modern Burj al-Qa'im) was built at the southern inlet south of Samarra, and a palace with a "paradise" or walled hunting park was constructed at the northern inlet (modern Nahr al-Rasasi) near to al-Daur. Later Sassanid rulers added to the settlement, and Herzfeld found evidence of a large and important Sassanid metropolis, replete with palaces, gardens, etc. The city continued to be inhabited and to expand under the first Islamic rulers. We know, for example, that another irrigation canal, the Qatul al-Jund, was excavated by the Abbasid Caliph Harun Al-Rashid, who began the construction of a new planned city, though this project was supposedly abandoned unfinished in 796.

Strangely, Hodges and Whitehouse make no mention of these Sassanid and early Islamic cities.

Thus Arab tradition proved unreliable with regard to Samarra's beginnings. It proved equally unreliable with regard to its end. Judging by the testimony of Ya'qubi, archaeologists expected to find a city founded in 836 and inhabited for around fifty years before being completely abandoned at the end of the ninth century. This was not however the case. On the contrary, Herzfeld was forced to concede, on the evidence of pottery, coins, and other artifacts, the continued existence of the metropolis into the tenth and even eleventh centuries.[10]

Reflecting this, the *Encyclopaedia Iranica* admits to a "problem" regarding the traditional ceramic chronology at the site, conceding that Herzfeld's excavations were carried out without due regard for stratigraphy, and that the city, contrary to traditional notions, continued to be occupied into the late tenth century and beyond:

"The problem of traditional ceramic chronology. At Samar-

---

10 Herzfeld never published a detailed description of the site, only a series of aerial photgraphs. See Ernst Herzfeld, *Ausgrabungen von Samarra VI. Geschichte der Stadt Samarra* (Berlin, 1948). More detail is provided by K. A. C. Creswell, *Early Muslim Architecture* Vol. 2 (London, 1968), pp. 1-5, and J. M. Rogers, "Samarra: a study in medieval town planning," in A. Hourani and S. M. Stern (eds), *The Islamic City* (Oxford, 1970).

ra the finds included lustered wall tiles from the palace of
Jawsaq al-Khaqani, al-Mutasem's residence. The ornament
includes several familiar elements: half-palmettes, Sasanian
wing motifs, and leaf scrolls. Some of the tiles are painted
with birds encircled by wreaths. A second, larger group of
luster-painted tiles, set into the frame of the *mehrab* (niche)
at the Great Mosque of Qayrawan in Tunisia, has much in
common with the finds from Samarra. ... Taking these two
groups of tiles as his starting point, Ernst Kühnel proposed a
hypothetical development of luster ceramics in Iraq: The earliest pieces were ornamented in polychrome; in about 246/860
a bichrome palette composed of brown and yellow came into
use; and soon after the abandonment of Samarra as capital
monochrome luster was introduced. The tiles from the palace
of Jawsaq al-Khaqani were not found in place, however, and it
is therefore not certain that they formed part of the original
decoration. The reports about the Qayrawan tiles also leave
room for doubt about the accepted dating (Hansman, pp. 145-
46).

"The conclusion that new wares were developed in the Islamic
world in the 3rd/9th century as a result of the importation
of ceramics from China was based partly on the assumption
that Samarra was occupied for only fifty years. Yet, although
Samarra ceased to be the capital in 279/892, silver coins continued to be minted there until 341/952-53 (Miles). Furthermore, according to Ebn Hawqal, who probably visited the area
in ca. 358/969 (pp. 243-44, 247; tr. Kramers, pp. 236, 239)
and Maqdesi (Moqaddasi, pp. 122-23), who wrote in about
375/985, parts of it were still inhabited. As the excavations of
1911-13 were conducted without regard for stratigraphy, all
that can properly be said about an object from the site is that
it may date from 221-375/836-985, but it may be even later.
On the basis of the Samarra finds alone there is thus no way
of knowing whether new types were introduced all at once or
at intervals over a period of a century and a half; for further
information, it is necessary to turn to related finds from Susa,
Siraf, and other sites."[11]

11 Ceramics xiii. The Early Islamic Period, 7th-11th Centuries, in *Encyclopaedia
Iranica*, at www.iranica.com/articles/ceramics-xiii

So, although Ya'qubi and other Arab sources claimed that Samarra had been occupied for only fifty years, in the ninth century, excavation has shown that it was in fact occupied during the tenth century, and that, furthermore, the artifacts found there can date from anywhere between the mid-ninth to the late tenth century, or "even later". This last comment in fact gives the game away. The fact is, the pottery and material culture of tenth/eleventh century Mesopotamia is virtually indistinguishable from that of the eighth and ninth centuries. The blue-glazed barbotine ware, for example, so characteristic of all the early Islamic sites of the region, is in fact equally characteristic of the tenth and eleventh centuries.[12]

Let's look at this again: Arab history tells us that Samarra, a vast royal metropolis, was constructed in the second half of the ninth century, inhabited for about fifty years, and abandoned around 900 or shortly before; and this is the narrative accepted by Hodges and Whitehouse, who present the metropolis as proof of a flowering Islamic civilization during an age of depopulation and barbarism in Europe. Yet what the archaeologists have found is a city constructed by the Sassanid Persians in the latter years of the sixth and early part of the seventh century, a city that continued to be occupied into the late tenth and eleventh centuries. So, instead of a fifty year old settlement, we have a four hundred year old one! Yet here again there is a problem. In a four hundred year old settlement we would expect strata many meters in depth. Comparable epochs in the city of Babylon, for example, have produced anything from four to six meters. Yet the depth of strata at Samarra is nothing like this, and on the contrary would lead to the conclusion of a city settled only – as the Arab historians insisted – for about half a century!

What can all this mean? Here again we find that enigmatic hiatus that we have encountered again and again in the archaeology of the "dark age" irrespective of where we have looked. Was Samarra then constructed by the Sassanid Persians in the late sixth and early seventh centuries and abandoned for three hundred years, before being reoccupied by the Muslims in the tenth century?

The only evidence for a ninth century Samarra (apart from the discredited testimony of Ya'qubi), is the discovery of a rather small number of coins which appeared to concur with the latter. The numerous problems raised by early Islamic coinage would take a volume in themselves to investigate. We have already seen, for example, how

---

12 Ibid.

Islamic coins of the mid-seventh century made their way to Scandinavia – a full two centuries before they were expected. Again, we should note that these early coins look entirely Persian, showing on one side the portrait of a Sassanid monarch and on the other a Zoroastrian fire temple. The only thing that distinguishes them as Islamic is a brief Arabic religious inscription and a number, presumed to be an Age of Hegira date. Something more shall be said about this thoroughly confusing topic in the final chapter; suffice here to note that there are very good grounds for believing the numbers found on these coins do not represent Age of Hegira dates, and that, furthermore, the entire system of notation was changed on more than one occasion by the early Muslim rulers.

Whatever we might say about traditional written histories and the dating of coins, we can say that the archaeology of Samarra and the other flourishing urban centers of Mesopotamia/Iran of the early Caliphate, looks as if it could equally belong, on the one hand, in the late Sassanid epoch, and, on the other, to the tenth or eleventh centuries. Furthermore, the depth of strata and the amount of archaeology uncovered would suffice for about a century at maximum, but certainly not the four centuries which apparently separate the rise of Islam from the abandonment of Samarra and Siraf in the eleventh century.

CLASSICAL LEARNING AND THE LOSS OF ANCIENT LITERATURE

T he territories which came under the dominion of Islam during the seventh century formed by far the most advanced and prosperous regions of the Mediterranean, or classical, civilization. In Persia, Mesopotamia, Syria, and Egypt, the House of Islam came to include cultures and civilizations whose roots lay in the remotest antiquity. With the conquests of Alexander, in the fourth century BC, all these lands had come under the influence of Hellenism, an influence which acted as a spur to the cross-fertilization of ideas and led to a flowering of science and technology. Great academies and centers of learning were established, and the cities of the region supported an educated and articulate population, whose levels of literacy have perhaps only again been equaled in the twentieth century. By the sixth century AD the wealth and prosperity of these territories had reached its apogee. Persia in particular, which under the Sassanids had become a world power on a par with Rome, was a veritable hive of commercial and intellectual innovation. New ideas, travelling along the Silk Road from China, began to appear in the Iranian Plateau; and it is possible that some of the most important Chinese inventions, such as papermaking, had already reached the Sassanid territories before the arrival of Islam.

With the conquest of Mesopotamia, Syria, Egypt and Persia, the Arabs therefore came into the possession of some of the most technically and culturally advanced regions of the world. In the words of James Thompson and Edgar Johnson, "The Arabs ... incorporated as part of their new empire areas that had originally been the cradle of occidental civilization. ... To administer these areas the[y] ... could do nothing but take over what they found of the Byzantine and Persian administrations and employ as governors trained and experienced natives; they had nothing of their own to offer in this field. The same thing is true in the domain of culture. Egypt, Palestine, Syria, and Persia were provinces of Hellenistic civilization, and Sassanid Persia had also developed a civilization of its own. Moreover, in Egypt, Palestine, and Syria, under the stimulus of Christianity a new literature and art had developed. Indeed, recent cultural developments in all these countries just before the Mohammedan conquest seemed to point to a new outburst of oriental activity."[1] What then did the Caliphs do with this rich legacy? As we have seen, the opinion which has held sway now for over a century is that they enthusiastically embraced the intellectual and philosophical traditions of the above-named peoples, and that under them science and philosophy flourished as never before. We have seen how Robert Briffault waxed lyrical about "The incorruptible treasures and delights of intellectual culture" of the Caliphate, which "were accounted by the princes of Baghdad, Shiraz and Cordova, the truest and proudest pomps of their courts."[2] And similar opinions, if not quite so poetically expressed, are encountered regularly in the most up to date historical publications. But how true a picture is it? Is it really conceivable that a civilization which regarded war as a sacred duty, which looked upon the taking of slaves as a divinely-sanctioned activity, and which regarded the execution of apostates and heretics as a heavenly command could be so enthusiastic about the efforts of philosophers?

It is undeniable that, to begin with at least, some Muslim rulers did patronize universities and other seats of learning.[3] Scientific and philosophic treatises were indeed composed, and there is no doubt that Arab, or at least Arabic-speaking scholars were in possession of many classical texts not generally available in Europe. These men, it is evident, made important contributions, in various areas of scientific and scholarly endeavor. In addition, the Arabs, or rather the Arab rulers of the Near East (for the great majority of the population remained non-Arab in language and non-Muslim in religion for several centuries after the conquest), learnt the secrets of paper-making, printing, the compass, and various other crucial technologies from the Chinese between the eighth and eleventh centuries, which technologies they utilized and eventually (inadvertently) spread to Europe. Yet we also know that, in the years before the Arab conquests, Persia in particular was a conduit through which flowed new ideas and techniques from India and China; and everyone admits that most of the new technologies and methods medieval Europeans learned from the Arabs were not Arab or even Near Eastern at all, but Chinese and Indian. Europeans used the Arabic names for these things (such as "zero", from the Arabic zirr), because it was from Arab sources that they learned them.

---

1 Thompson and Johnson, op cit., p. 172

2 Briffault, op cit., p. 188

3 See A. Butler, *The Arab Conquest of Egypt* (London, 1902), who speaks of some continuity in the academic institutions of the country after the Muslim invasion.

But they were neither Arab nor Middle Eastern.

As our knowledge of early medieval history has improved, it has become ever more clear that virtually all of the learning previously attributed to "the Arabs" had little or nothing to do with them.[4] Thus for example the claim that the Arabs discovered the distillation of alcohol, which was regularly found in textbooks until the middle of the twentieth century, is quite simply false. Alcohol had been distilled in Babylonia prior to the Arab conquest.[5] Under the Arabs, distillation techniques were improved; but they did not invent distillation. Again, the claim that the Persian Al-Khwarizmi invented algebra is untrue; and it is now widely admitted that the Greek mathematician Diophantes, building on the knowledge of the Babylonians, was the first to outline the principles (in his *Arithmetica*) of what we now call algebra.[6] Al-Khwarizmi did make a number of important contributions, such as the quadratic equation and the introduction of the decenary numerical system from India, but in many other respects his work was not as advanced as that of Diophantes. Furthermore, he clearly owed much to the fifth century Indian mathematician and astronomer Aryabhata, whose 121-verse *Aryabhatiya* expostulated on astronomy, arithmetic, geometry, algebra, trigonometry, methods of determining the movements of the planets and descriptions of their movements, as well as methods of calculating the movements of the sun and moon and predicting their eclipses. And we note too that Aryabhata was manifestly the source of the astronomical ideas attributed to Al-Zarkyal and Al-Farani, which Briffault places such store in.

There is another important consideration to remember: Whilst "Arab" scientists and philosophers of this time used Arab names and wrote in Arabic, the great majority of them were not Arabs or Muslims at all, but Christians and Jews who worked under Arab regimes. The Saracen armies which conquered the Near East in the seventh century imposed their faith and their language in the corridors of power; and the subdued peoples were forced to learn it. At no time, not even at the beginning, did genuine Arabs and Muslims show much

---

4 See for example Toby E. Huff's *The Rise of Early Modern Science: Islam, China and the West* (Cambridge University Press, 1993), where the basic incompatibility of Islam with scientific and philosophical thinking is explained in detail.

5 Charles Simmonds (1919). *Alcohol: With Chapters on Methyl Alcohol, Fusel Oil, and Spirituous Beverages* (Macmillan, 1919), pp. 6ff.

6 See eg. Carl B. Boyer, *A History of Mathematics*, Second Edition (Wiley, 1991), p. 228

interest in science and scholarship. Aristotle's work was preserved in Arabic not initially by Muslims, but by Christians such as the fifth century priest Probus of Antioch, who introduced Aristotle to the Arabic-speaking world. In fact, during the eighth and ninth centuries, "the whole corpus of Greek scientific and philosophical learning was translated into Arabic, mainly by Nestorian Christians."[7] We know that "Schools, often headed by Christians, were ... established in connection with mosques."[8] The leading figure in the Baghdad school was the Christian Huneyn ibn Ishaq (809-873), who translated many works by Aristotle, Galen, Plato and Hippocrates into Syriac. His son then translated them into Arabic. The Syrian Christian Yahya ibn 'Adi (893-974) also translated works of philosophy into Arabic, and wrote one of his own, *The Reformation of Morals*. Throughout the Muslim world it was Christians and Jews (especially the latter), who did almost all the scientific research and enquiry at this time. And there is much evidence to suggest that the efforts of these scholars were often viewed by their Muslim masters with the deepest suspicion. Certainly there was not the encouragement to learning, much less to new research, that is so frequently boasted.

Even the limited number of "Arab" scholars who were not Jews and Christians were rarely Arabs. We are told that Al-Kindi was "one of the few pure Arabs to achieve intellectual distinction."[9] More often than not they were actually Persians. This was the case, as we saw, with the mathematician Al-Khwarizmi, and also with the great philosopher Avicenna, among many others. The Persian origin of so much "Arab" learning reminds us again that a great deal of what has been attributed to the Arabs was in reality Persian, and that, prior to the Islamicization of Persia in the seventh century, the country had, under the Sassanids, been a cultural and intellectual crossroads, bringing together the latest mathematics from India, the latest technology from China, and the latest philosophy from Byzantium; and making important contributions to all of these herself. This leads to the suspicion that "Al-Khwarizmi" and "Avicenna" (Ibn-Sina), were scholars of the Sassanid period, whose works were translated into Arabic and their names "Arabized" during the Abbasid period. Alternatively, at the very least, it would appear that they were representatives of the final flowering of Sassanid science and philosophy – representatives of an

7 Thompson and Johnson, op cit., p. 175
8 Ibid., p. 176
9 Ibid., p. 178

ancient tradition of learning which had nothing to do with Islam, but which survived for a while under the new Islamic regime.

Yet leaving aside for the present the question of the identity of the "Muslim" or "Arab" scholars, there is much that can be said about the Arab attitude to learning, which no one will dissent from. Everyone agrees that the classical learning which the Arabs valued was invariably that of a purely practical or utilitarian nature. The sciences (especially medicine) and mathematics were indeed patronized and encouraged by the early Caliphs at least. However, all the other learning of antiquity, most especially the liberal arts and the literature, were not valued at all. Indeed, there is very good evidence to show that the Arabs treated these parts of the classical heritage with indifference and even outright hostility. The parts of classical literature to which we refer are of course those which we perhaps now value most: the histories, the plays, and what might be called the "Literature" of the time. This type of writing of course took in the vast majority of what we now call Classical Letters; and almost all of it is lost.

Since the loss of Classical Literature is one of the great conundrums of history, it is incumbent upon us here to take a broad view of the question.

* * *

We know that in the sixth century, as before, the West was largely a cultural and economic backwater of the Mediterranean Civilization. Some reasonably large urban centers existed in Spain, but even these were small in comparison with those of the East, whilst Gaul and Britain, as well as Germany (with the exception of Trier), were devoid of real cities. Yet such urban centers as existed in the West all had libraries, both privately and publicly owned. The great majority of the volumes contained in these collections – the hundreds of thousands of books written by Greek and Latin authors over a period of ten or eleven centuries – were written on papyrus, and they needed the type of society which generated them in order to survive. They needed a literate and wealthy class of laypeople who could appreciate and patronize them. They also needed governmental support. Great public libraries and academies of the type which flourished in the territory of the Roman Empire could not survive without the economic assistance of kings and emperors. This assistance had been forthcoming and generously given until the middle of the seventh century. Any loss of tax revenue would have placed these collections in jeopardy. In times of economic recession "cultural" activities are usually first to be hit.

The closing of the Mediterranean to trade in luxuries, following the arrival of Islam, would have had such a result; but it would have dealt another and far more lethal blow. Henri Pirenne noted that one of the products of the East which disappears in the seventh century is papyrus. Until the first quarter of that century, Egyptian papyrus is ubiquitous in the records and documents of western Europe, but by the 640s or 650s it disappears more or less completely, to be replaced by parchment. Now parchment, of course, was immensely expensive in comparison with papyrus, and there can be no doubt that the loss of the papyrus supply would, on its own, have had a devastating effect upon the state of literacy and literature in Europe. Pirenne himself recognized this, and rightly saw the disappearance of papyrus from the West as a seminal event.

The great majority of works of the classical authors, of which an estimated 95% - 98% have been lost, were written on papyrus. A whole industry existed employing scribes to copy these books, which were then sold to other libraries, academies, or private collectors. Papyrus is more delicate than parchment and disintegrates after a few centuries if stored in a humid environment. But this did not matter as long as there were fresh supplies upon which to make new copies and rich patrons to pay for them. The disappearance of both these in the seventh century meant that, in Europe at least, the great majority of the classical works were doomed to disappear. It is known that even those works written on parchment were frequently lost when, in later centuries, old parchments were reused many times, after being cleaned of existing texts. The very expense of parchment made such catastrophes all too commonplace.

The one institution in Europe that could save the classical works was the Church; and we know that from the middle of the seventh century many monasteries had large collections of the "pagan" authors. Indeed, the great majority of the literature of Greece and Rome that has survived into modern times was preserved not – as is so often claimed – by the Arabs, but by European monks of the sixth and seventh centuries. Thus for example Alcuin, the polyglot theologian of Charlemagne's court, mentioned that his library in York contained works by Aristotle, Cicero, Lucan, Pliny, Statius, Trogus Pompeius, and Virgil. In his correspondences he quotes still other classical authors, including Ovid, Horace, and Terence. Abbo of Fleury (latter tenth century), who served as abbot of the monastery of Fleury, demonstrates familiarity with Horace, Sallust, Terence, and Virgil. Desiderius, described as the greatest of the abbots of Monte Cassino after Benedict himself, and who became Pope Victor III in 1086, oversaw the transcription of Horace and Seneca, as well as Cicero's *De Natura Deorum* and Ovid's *Fasti.*[10] His friend Archbishop Alfano, who had also been a monk of Monte Cassino, possessed a deep knowledge of the ancient writers, frequently quoting from Apuleius, Aristotle, Cicero, Plato, Varro, and Virgil, and imitating Ovid and Horace in his verse.

Notwithstanding the efforts of the monks, it must be understood that the Church did not see its primary role as the preservation of profane knowledge. And even if it had devoted greater effort to transcribing from papyrus to parchment the great works of the Greeks and Romans, it is doubtful if they could have saved little more than it did. The immense expense of parchment would have been prohibitive; wealth that the monasteries would no doubt have felt better expended upon the care of the poor and sick.

The one major library of antiquity to survive in the West into the High Middle Ages was that of the Vatican; but the great majority of this was lost during the removal of the papal court to Avignon in the fourteenth century.

That was the situation in the West. It was also, incidentally, the situation in Byzantium, which, as we have seen, is now known to have experienced its own "Dark Age" after the middle of the seventh century. Here too we find impoverishment, the abandonment of cities, and the growth of a feudal system. Cyril Mango, as we have seen, remarked on the virtual abandonment of the Byzantine cities after the mid-seventh century, and the archaeology of these settlements usually reveals "a dramatic rupture in the seventh century, sometimes in the form of virtual abandonment."[11] With the cities and with the papyrus supply from Egypt went the intellectual class, who after the seventh century were reduced to a "small clique."[12] The evidence, as Mango sees it, is unmistakable: the "catastrophe" (as he names it) of the seventh century, "is the central event of Byzantine history."

The final conquest of Byzantium by the Turks in 1453 saw the destruction of what libraries still existed, and we cannot doubt that

10 Charles Montalembert, op cit., p. 146

11 Mango, op cit., p. 8

12 Ibid., p. 9

the few texts which reached the West with refugees in the years that followed represented but a pitiable remnant of what once existed.

Thus we have seen that all of Christendom was devastated by the Muslim conquests. What then, we might ask, of the Islamic world itself; those regions of the Middle East and North Africa conquered and held by the Muslims in the seventh century and which were to become the core of the Muslim world as we now understand it?

As we saw, until the first quarter of the seventh century literacy was widespread in the Near East, and the works of the classical historians, as well as the philosophers, mathematicians, and physicians, were readily available and discussed in the academies and libraries located throughout the region. In Egypt, during the sixth century, renowned philosophers such as Olympiodorus (died 570) presided over the Alexandrian academy which possessed a well-stocked and funded library packed with probably thousands of volumes. The Alexandrian academy of this time was the most illustrious institute of learning in the known world; and it is beyond doubt that its library matched, if indeed it did not surpass, the original Library founded by Ptolemy II. The writings of Olympiodorus and his contemporaries demonstrate intimate familiarity with the great works of classical antiquity – very often quoting obscure philosophers and historians whose works have long since disappeared. Among the general population of the time literacy was the norm, and the appetite for reading was fed by a large class of professional writers who composed plays, poems and short stories – the latter taking the form of mini-novels. In Egypt, the works of Greek writers such as Herodotus and Diodorus were familiar and widely quoted. Both the latter, as well as native Egyptian writers such as Manetho, had composed extensive histories of Egypt of the time of the pharaohs. These works provided, for the citizens of Egypt and other parts of the Empire, a direct link with the pharaohnic past. Here the educated citizen encountered the name of the pharaoh (Kheops) who built the Great Pyramid, as well as that of his son (Khephren), who built the second pyramid at Giza, and that of his grandson Mykerinos, who raised the third and smallest structure. These Hellenized versions of the names were extremely accurate transcriptions of the actual Egyptian names (Khufu, Khafre, and Menkaure). In the history of the country written by Manetho, the educated citizen of the Empire would have had a detailed description of Egypt's past, complete with an in-depth account of the deeds of the pharaohs as well as descriptions of the various monuments and the kings who built them.

The change that came over Egypt and the other regions of the Middle East following the Arab Conquest can only be described as catastrophic. Almost all knowledge of these countries' histories disappears, and does so almost overnight. Consider the account of the Giza Pyramids and their construction written by the Arab historian Al-Masudi (regarded as the "Arab Herodotus"), apparently in the tenth century:

> Surid, Ben Shaluk, Ben Sermuni, Ben Termidun, Ben Tedresan, Ben Sal, one of the kings of Egypt before the flood, built two great pyramids; and, notwithstanding, they were subsequently named after a person called Shaddad Ben Ad ... they were not built by the Adites, who could not conquer Egypt, on account of their powers, which the Egyptians possessed by means of enchantment ... the reason for the building of the pyramids was the following dream, which happened to Surid three hundred years previous to the flood. It appeared to him that the earth was overthrown, and that the inhabitants were laid prostrate upon it, that the stars wandered confusedly from their courses, and clashed together with tremendous noise. The king though greatly affected by this vision, did not disclose it to any person, but was conscious that some great event was about to take place.[13]

This was what passed for "history" in Egypt after the Arab conquest – little more than a collection of Arab fables.[14] Egypt, effectively, had lost her history. Other Arab writers display the same ignorance. Take for example the comments of Ibn Jubayr, who worked as a secretary to the Moorish governor of Granada, and who visited Cairo in 1182. He commented on "the ancient pyramids, of miraculous construction and wonderful to look upon, [which looked] like huge pavilions rearing to the skies; two in particular shock the firmament ..." He wondered whether they might be the tombs of early prophets mention in the Koran, or whether they were granaries of the biblical patriarch Joseph, but in the end came to the conclusion, "To be short, none but

---

13 Cited from L. Cottrell, *The Mountains of Pharaoh* (London, 1956)

14 The tale may, however, have been partly influenced by oral traditions among the Copts, for the connection of pyramid-building with catastrophic events among the stars is found in ancient Egyptian tradition itself.

the Great and Glorious God can know their story."[15]

The loss of Egypt's history, particularly the effacing all knowledge about the Great Pyramid, in such a short period of time, speaks of a major episode of cultural destruction. To find a parallel we would perhaps need to refer to the Spanish conquests in Mexico and Peru in the sixteenth century – and even these were arguably less damaging. The Mexicans and Peruvians could still tell visitors the histories and traditions of the great monuments of their lands long after the Conquest, and these traditions are preserved to this day. In view of this, the story of Caliph Umar's destruction of the last library at Alexandria, often dismissed as apocryphal – especially in the more polite academic circles – needs to be fundamentally reconsidered.

The disconnection with the past experienced in Egypt was paralleled throughout all the territories that came under Islam. We find, for example, that in the tenth century the Persian poet Ferdowsi, although knowledgeable about the Sassanid period, is completely ignorant of the earlier and far more glorious epoch of the Achaemenids. His "history" of the Persian people, prior to the time of the Sassanids, is little more than a collection of orally-preserved Iranian myths and legends. We observe the same ignorance on the part of the great poet and mathematician Omar Khayyam, who imagined that the palaces of the Achaemenid Great Kings Darius I and Xerxes were built by the genie-king Jamshid.

We should not imagine that this loss of connection with the past occurred gradually. Nor can the loss of Egypt's and Persia's histories be blamed on poverty or absence of cheap writing materials such as papyrus. The Caliphate established in the Middle East was neither impoverished nor lacking in resources. Egypt, after all, was the source of papyrus, and it was right at the heart of the Caliphate. And, we must stress again, in conquering the regions of the Middle East the Arabs came to possess the most populous, the most wealthy, and the most venerable centers of civilization in the known world. For the histories of Egypt and Syria and Babylonia and Persia written or preserved by the Greek and Hellenistic authors to have disappeared they must have been destroyed deliberately; or at the very least the libraries and academies wherein they were stored must have been deprived of all funding and allowed to fall into decay. More likely, however, they were actively destroyed. How else can we explain the loss of every copy of Herodotus, Diodorus and Manetho (and every other classical author

---

15 Andrew Beattie, *Cairo: A Cultural History* (Oxford University Press, 2005), p. 50

who wrote of Egypt's pharaohnic past) in such a short period of time? And the impression of active destruction is confirmed by what we see in other areas. We know, for example, that from the very beginning the Arabs displayed indifference and contempt for the culture and history of both Egypt and the other countries of the regions they conquered. Immediately upon the invasion of Egypt, the Caliph established a commission whose purpose was to discover and plunder the pharaohnic tombs. We know that Christian churches and monasteries – many of the latter possessing well-stocked libraries – suffered the same fate. The larger monuments of Roman and pharaohnic times were similarly plundered for their cut-stone, and Saladin, the Muslim hero lionized in so much politically-correct literature and art, began the process by the exploitation of the smaller Giza monuments. From these, he constructed the citadel at Cairo (between 1193 and 1198). His son and successor, Al-Aziz Uthman, went further, and made a determined effort to demolish the Great Pyramid itself.[16] He succeeded in stripping the outer casing of smooth limestone blocks from the structure (covered with historically invaluable inscriptions), but eventually cancelled the project owing to its cost.

What then of the much-vaunted Arab respect for learning and science that we hear so much of in modern academic literature? That the Arabs did permit some of the science and learning they encountered in the great cities of Egypt, Syria, Babylonia, and Persia to survive – for a while – is beyond doubt. Yet the learning they tolerated was entirely of a practical or utilitarian nature – and this is a fact admitted even by Islamophile writers.[17] Thus, for a while, they patronized physicists, mathematicians and physicians. Yet the very fact that knowledge has to plead its usefulness in order to be permitted to survive at all speaks volumes in itself. Is not this an infallible mark of barbarism? And we should note that even the utilitarian learning which the earliest Caliphs fostered was soon to be snuffed out under the weight of an Islamic theocracy (promulgated by Al-Ghazali in the eleventh century) which regarded the very concept of scientific laws as an affront to Allah and an infringement of his freedom to act.

In this way then the vast body of classical literature disappeared from the lands of the Caliphate. Thus the Arabs undermined classical

---

16 Andrew Beattie, op cit.

17 Robert Briffault, for example, admits that, "Of the poets and historians of Greece, beyond satisfying their curiosity by a few samples, they [the Arabs] took little account." Briffault, op cit., p. 192

civilization and its literary heritage in Europe through an economic blockade, whilst in the Middle East they destroyed it deliberately and methodically.

CONCLUSION

T he entire Mediterranean world was utterly transformed in the seventh century. Everywhere, from Palestine in the East to Spain in the West, the Roman style of life disappeared. Cities were destroyed or abandoned and life rapidly became more rural. The Roman system of agriculture, which had sustained the great cities of the classical age, broke down. The dykes, irrigation ditches and terraces which had for centuries produced vast food surpluses to feed Rome and the other metropolises of the Empire, fell into disrepair. Topsoil was washed away and a layer of silt, now known as the Younger Fill, began to cover many of the towns and villages. As the scattered farming settlements and cities of the Empire were deserted, new settlements, especially in southern Europe, began to appear on defended hill-tops.

If the above transformation occurred in 600 AD or slightly earlier, as Hodges, Whitehouse, and a host of other contemporary academics maintain, then it must be regarded as one of history's greatest enigmas. Nothing that we know of the late sixth century could account for it. That the plague of Justinian's time (542) was not to blame is proved beyond question by the thriving and populous cities of the Middle East, which excavators found were destroyed violently from 614 onwards. If however the great transformation occurred in the two or three decades following 614, then it makes perfect sense. These years saw the commencement of the ruinous Persian war which damaged many of the cities of Anatolia and Syria, and which was soon followed by the appearance on the world stage of the Arabs. And it was the Arab wars of conquest, far more than the Persian war, which explains the permanence and completeness of the devastation. The damage done during the Persian conflict would have been swiftly repaired – as it had always been before – had not the latter been immediately followed by the arrival on the scene of the Arabs. The religious concept of jihad (permanent religious war) made any kind of peace between the Arabs and the outside world impossible. Since it was the duty of every able-bodied Muslim to wage jihad, it became the custom of Arab rulers to engage in raids on infidel territory on an annual (or twice-annual) basis. All regions on the borders of the Dar al-Islam were liable to be ridden over; and this is precisely what we see occurring in Anatolia and large areas of Spain, such as La Mancha. At a later stage Islamic armies created a similar wasteland in Hungary, where the once-heavily populated Hungarian Plain, the Pushta, became a dreary prairie.

Whilst the concept of jihad ensured a permanent war on Islam's borders, the provisions of sharia law meant that even in the regions controlled by the Muslims, such as Syria and North Africa, native husbandmen and traders were afforded no protection from the predatory attentions of bedouin bandits and herders, who let their flocks graze on the irrigated lands of the former, thus degrading and destroying them. The result was that within a very short time, the whole economy and lifestyle of the classical world disappeared. Once-fertile and irrigated territories were reduced to semi-desert, and the great cities which dotted these regions, from northern Syria to the Atlantic coast of North Africa, were reduced to ghost towns. The urban life which these cities had supported, with their academies, libraries, and theatres, disappeared; and with them went the great bulk of the artistic and intellectual heritage of Greece and Rome.

In Mediterranean Europe, in the meantime, Arab raiders, fired by the belief that it was legitimate and even righteous to live off the wealth and resources of the infidel, launched raid after raid against the towns and villages on the coasts, plundering both lay and ecclesiastical settlements and destroying crops in the fields. Early medieval documents are full of descriptions of these atrocities. In the same way, sea traffic was targeted by the jihadis, who confiscated cargoes and enslaved crews and passengers. Within a short time, all trade between Christian Europe and the newly Islamicized East came to an end. The supply of all the Levantine luxuries, which had hitherto provided a modicum of civilized life in the towns and villages of the West, dried up, and Europe was thrown back on its own resources. The centre of gravity in Gaul moved decisively to the North, and a distinctly medieval culture rapidly took shape.

* * *

The above describes how classical civilization was terminated. Yet there still remains a problem; and that is one of chronology. We have found that the real break-off point between classical civilization and the medieval world is 614, the year of the commencement of the Persian War. It was then, or in the years immediately after, that the great cities of Asia Minor and Syria were destroyed or abandoned, never to rise again. That there was no attempt to repair them after the end of the Persian War (627) indicates that there was insufficient time to do so before the coming of the Arabs (in 638). Yet in a decade we might expect some signs of revival or rebuilding. That there were almost none could suggest that the arrival of the Arabs and Islam on the world stage was slightly closer to the time of the Persian War than is allowed.

It is generally believed that Muslim armies did not emerge from Arabia until after Muhammad's death in 638. Yet there is evidence to suggest otherwise. A letter exists purportedly from Muhammad to the Persian king Chosroes II, inviting him to embrace Islam. Whether this communication is genuine or not (actually, it is without question a forgery), it does illustrate an important truth: The Persians had a long history of religious antagonism towards Christianity and towards Byzantium, and as such would have been natural allies of the Arabs against the latter. Indeed, the war between Chosroes II and Heraclius had all the characteristics of a religious conflict – a veritable jihad, no less. The Persians took Jerusalem in 614 and carried out a terrible massacre of the Christian population; after which they looted the churches and seized some of Christendom's most sacred relics – including the Holy Cross upon which Christ was crucified. The story told by the Byzantines of how Heraclius, against all the odds, turned the tide of war and won back the sacred relics, strikes one as fictitious. And indeed, it is just with the reign of Heraclius that the dim and little-known period we now call the Dark Ages commences.

German writer Heribert Illig (of whom more shall be said presently) has put forward the interesting suggestion that the Persians encountered Islam in Syria and, seeing the latter as a valuable ally against Byzantium, joined forces with the Arabs. It is not inconceivable that some of the Persian ruling class may have converted to Islam and gradually imposed the new faith upon the populace. This would explain why the Arabs were able to conquer – with such apparent ease – the mighty and invincible Persian Empire, an Empire that had withstood the best efforts of Rome to subdue it for seven centuries.[1] And

---

1 It should be noted that the accepted narrative of Islam's early expansion beyond Arabia strikes one as utterly fictitious. That the Arabs, a numerically tiny and backward people, should simultaneously attack and overcome both the might of Byzantium and of Sassanid Persia, is quite simply beyond belief. And it is no use to plead that these powers were "exhausted" by the war they had just recently waged against each other. Victorious armies do not tend to be "exhausted", irrespective of their losses. Witness the mighty Soviet army at the end of World War 2, compared to

it would further explain why early Islam is so thoroughly Persian in character. The earliest Islamic coins, for example, are simply Sassanid Persian, usually with the addition of an Arab phrase such as *besm Allah* – "in the name of God," and with the name of Chosroes II or his successor Yazdegerd III. But in all other particulars they are indistinguishable from Sassanid currency. According to the *Encyclopdaedia Iranica*,

> "These coins usually have a portrait of a Sasanian emperor with an honorific inscription and various ornaments. To the right of the portrait is a ruler's or governor's name written in Pahlavi script. On the reverse there is a Zoroastrian fire altar with attendants on either side. At the far left is the year of issue expressed in words, and at the right is the place of minting. In all these features, the Arab-Sasanian coinages are similar to Sasanian silver drahms. The major difference between the two series is the presence of some additional Arabic inscription on most coins issued under Muslim authority, but some coins with no Arabic can still be attributed to the Islamic period. The Arab-Sasanian coinages are not imitations, since they were surely designed and manufactured by the same people as the late Sasanian issues, illustrating the continuity of administration and economic life in the early years of Muslim rule in Iran."[2]

Importantly, the date is written in Persian Pahlavi script, and it would appear that those who minted the coins, native Persians, did not understand Arabic. We hear that under the Arabs the mints were "evidently allowed to go on as before," and that there are "a small number of coins indistinguishable from the drahms of the last emperor, Yazdegerd III, dated during his reign but after the Arab capture of the cities of issue. It was only when Yazdegerd died (A.D. 651) that some mark of Arab authority was added to the coinage."[3] Even more puzzling is the fact that the most common coins during the first decades

---

the weak and incompetent Soviet army at the beginning of the same conflict. Thus Heraclius' Byzantine army, newly victorious over the Persians, would have been no pushover.

2 "Arab-Sasanian Coins," *Encyclopdaedia Iranica*, at www.iranica.com/articles/arab-sasanian-coins

3 Ibid.

of Islamic rule were those of Chosroes II, and many of these too bear the Arabic inscription *besm Allah*. Now, it is just conceivable that invading Arabs might have issued slightly amended coins of the last Sassanid monarch, Yazdegerd III, but why continue to issue money in the name of a previous Sassanid king, one who, supposedly, had died ten years earlier? This surely stretches credulity.

Fig. 25. Early Islamic coin, with head of Sassanid monarch and, on reverse, Zoroastrian Fire Temple. Mid-seventh century.

Did then Chosroes II convert to Islam as part of Persia's ongoing Holy War against Christian Byzantium? Conventional history tells us that Yazdegerd III was the last of the pre-Islamic rulers of Iran, and that, in his time Caliph Umar conquered the country. Yet the poet Ferdowsi, who seems to have possessed a detailed knowledge of the period, mentions no Arab conquest at all. The Arabs are mentioned, but not as enemies of Yazdegerd III. The latter, who is portrayed as a villain, is killed by a miller, not by the Arabs (who are also portrayed as villains). Indeed, the events described by Ferdowsi have all the hallmarks of a Persian civil war. Is it possible that during the time of Yazdegerd III an internecine war erupted between an "Arabizing" group of extreme Islamists and a more traditional Persian faction? Later Islamic propagandists could have portrayed this conflict as an Arab "conquest" of Persia.

As we saw earlier, excavation has revealed few signs of violent overthrow at the termination of the Sassanid epoch, and all the indications are of a relatively peaceful transition from Sassanid rule to Islamic in the middle of the seventh century. Pottery and other artwork of the period continue to be thoroughly Persian in character.

If the Persians converted to Islam around 620, then the Arab conquests of Syria, Anatolia, Egypt and North Africa, which have always presented such a problem for historians (how could a few nomads on camels conquer such powerful and heavily-populated provinces?) would thus be at least partly explained as the work not of the Arabs but of Islamicized Persians.[4] Is this possible? Well, historical criticism has increasingly come to recognize the narrative of Arab expansion as, in some respects at least, an enormous fabrication. Thus for example German orientalist Günter Lüling opined that the earliest "Islam possessed an almost exclusively Abbasid [ie Persian] historiography, which Omayyad historical literature deliberately and extraordinarily successfully suppressed. ... The entire old-Arabian historiography was, for the period until circa 400 AH/1000 AD, completely reworked on dogmatic lines."[5] That the Arabs of the later Middle Ages were actively involved in falsifying history is proved by the existence of a number of forged documents purporting to treat of events of the early seventh century. In this category is the "letter from Muhammad" to Chosroes II, mentioned above. And if the invasion and conquest of Persia by the Arabs is a fiction, then the purpose of this letter is obvious: According to Islamic law, offensive action against the Infidel could take place only after the latter had been invited to accept Islam and had rejected the offer. The Muhammad letter would then have been part of the general invention of an Arab invasion of Iran, providing the event with its justification.[6]

If the arrival of Islam on the world stage were thus dated from the 620s, rather than the 640s, then we would be presented with an entirely new view of the past; and much that was previously incomprehensible would begin to make sense. The failure of the cities of Asia Minor to recover after the destruction by the Persians from 616 onwards would no longer be a mystery, whilst the precipitate decline of Carthage at the same time would be explained. And such a chron-

---

4 Art historian Kenneth Clark speaks of the "miraculously short time" which the Arabs took to conquer the Byzantine territories of the Eastern Mediterranean and North Africa. Clark, op cit., p. 7

5 Günter Lüling, *Die Wiederentdeckung des Propheten Muhammad. Eine Kritik am "christlichen" Abendland* (Erlangen, 1981) p. 411

6 Arab-Persian rivalry is alive and well to this day. Distrust of Iran remains notorious amongst the Arab states of the Middle East, whilst the last words of Saddam Hussein, who launched a murderous war of attrition against Iran in 1980, were reputed to have been "Death to the Persians."

ological realignment would have implications for Europe. Most importantly, it would mean that the termination of Mediterranean and eastern influences occurred precisely in the 620s, and that it was from this decade that there commenced the historically obscure period we now call the Dark Ages. Trying to pin down the precise point at which the latter epoch commenced is of course a notoriously difficult task and, as we have seen repeatedly in the present study, significantly differing interpretations can be derived from the same bits of evidence. Hodges and Whitehouse, we saw, were rather keen to place the break-off point at 600 or shortly beforehand, whilst the latest archaeological data seemed to place it a couple of decades later. Thus we know that African Red Slip Ware and Carthaginian amphorae were still being imported into Britain and Ireland as late as the 620s, but not after that.

With the general break-off point then in the 620s, we would need to reconsider much of the classical-looking archaeology of Britain, France and Spain which is currently dated to later decades. Thus the surviving British churches which are said to have been built into the 650s and 660s – before ceasing for three hundred years – would probably have been built rather in the 610s and 620s, and have been part of the church-building program initiated by Augustine's mission in the 590s. Thus too the Merovingian structures said to have been built after the reign of Chlothar II (584-629), such as the church of Saint Denis in Paris, probably need to be reassigned to earlier decades.

It cannot be stressed too strongly that the chronology of this obscure period is much less secure than generally imagined. Often a date is supplied by little more than guesswork or analogy, and there is a tendency to "stretch" archaeological finds into the middle or later seventh century in order to have something – anything – to show for that period. Precisely the same phenomenon is encountered at the other end of the Dark Age where, as Hodges and Whitehouse noted, there is a temptation to assign material of the tenth century into the ninth in order to have something to show for that epoch. In the Islamic world, dates are often derived from a tiny handful of often barely legible coins which apparently bear an "Age of Hegira" date. If however what we have said above holds good, and the Persians adopted Islam voluntarily, it is highly likely that the system of notation found on the early coins is not to be automatically accepted as indicating the Age of the Hegira. We remember that the first Islamic coins are basically Sassanid with the addition of the Arabic legend *besm Allah*. The date, however, or the year number, is written in Persian (Pahlavi). It does not say "Age of Hegira," and it is merely assumed that this is what is referred to. But what if that is wrong? The term Age of Hegira actually only appears on Islamic coins from the eleventh century on-wards, when it is generally written in conjunction with the *anno domini* date of the Christians. The two appear on coins side by side. Could it be then that all the so-called Age of Hegira dates found on Islamic coins between the seventh and early eleventh centuries do not refer to the Hegira of Muhammad at all, but are a reference to some event or events of Persian history? Could it be too that successive Muslim rul-ers changed the dating system arbitrarily on more than one occasion? This latter is suggested by the discovery of Islamic coins of wildly differing dates in sites and strata of the same epoch.

If such be the case, then everything we understand about early Islamic history and its progression will need to be re-examined in a fundamental way. For the moment, however, all such suggestions re-main speculative. All we can say with certainty is that with the com-mencement of the Persian and Arab Wars in the early part of the seventh century, Byzantine civilization begins its rapid and complete disappearance in Syria, most of Anatolia, Egypt, and North Africa. Since these were by far the most important centers of late classi-cal civilization, it is therefore little more than a travesty for Hodges, Whitehouse, and the rest of Pirenne's critics, to suggest that the ar-rival of the Arabs had nothing to do with the disappearance of that very civilization.

The destructive work of the Arabs was not therefore confined to Europe, as Pirenne had somehow imagined. As we have noted again and again throughout the present study, archaeology had revealed a puzzling hiatus in settlement between the mid-seventh and mid-tenth centuries all over the Middle East and North Africa. This gap mirrors the hiatus in Europe – the Dark Age gap that was always attributed there to the destructive work of "the Barbarians." Indeed, the absence of archaeology in both Europe and the Islamic world during these centuries has now become so acute and embarrassing that it has elic-ited some radical explanations.

The first of these, popular with certain academics specializing in climate history, has a long pedigree. The idea that the Dark Age was caused by a climate or other form of natural disaster was in fact first proposed as long ago as the nineteenth century. More recently, as we saw in Chapter 11, the theory was called forth to explain the abandon-ment of North Africa's late Roman cities and the desertification of much of the region. By the 1960s a similar event or series of events was invoked to explain the appearance throughout the Mediterranean basin of the Younger Fill, the layer of sediment which covers most of the late Roman sites of the region. This was the view of Claudio Vita-Finzi.[7] An even more radical version of the theory appeared in 1976 with the publication of astronomers Victor Clube's and Bill Napier's book *The Cosmic Serpent: A Catastrophist View of Earth History.* Here Clube and Napier argued that various myths and legends from ancient history, as well as the disappearance of several ancient civilizations, could be traced to a series of cosmic catastrophes triggered by the earth's encounter with an enormous comet. The last of these events, said Clube and Napier, may have occurred at the start of the seventh century and caused the Dark Age. A more recent incarnation of the same thesis appeared in 1999 with dendrochronologist Mike Baillie's *Exodus to Arthur: Catastrophic Encounters with Comets.*[8]

Whilst at first glance the cosmic catastrophe hypothesis sounds outlandish, it has to be admitted that the very completeness of the demographic collapse of the Dark Age throughout Europe and the Middle East favors it above the simple climate-change hypothesis of Vita-Finzi, or the plague thesis of various others. Nonetheless, there are several major problems with any natural disaster solution. First and foremost, were such a terrible event or series of events to have occurred, we should expect it/them to have figured very prominently in the literature of the age, or subsequent ages. It is true, of course, that chronicles and various other documents of this time do speak of plagues, floods, earthquakes, etc. But these have always been the stock-in-trade of the chronicler, and similar events, much more reliably reported, are recorded throughout the period of the Roman Republic and Roman Empire. But nothing of the type envisaged by Clube and Napier, or even by Vita-Finzi, appears in the documentary records. Secondly, such a catastrophe should have left a far clearer mark in the archaeological record. It is true that in the Mediterranean region we have the sediment layer of the Younger Fill at the correct time. However, this feature is entirely absent in temperate Europe, which also seems to have experienced complete abandonment and population implosion. Here, there exist numerous settlements spanning the late Roman period through to the High Middle Ages. In all of these, there seems to be continued and unbroken occupation in all ages – with the

---

7 Claudio Vita-Finzi, op cit.

8 Mike Baillie, *Exodus to Arthur: Catastrophic Encounters with Comets* (Batsford, 1999)

exception of the seventh to tenth centuries. Yet between these two epochs there is no layer of sediment of destruction. On the contrary, the early seventh century material appears to lie directly underneath that of the mid-tenth century, and to be culturally closely related to the latter.

Another and perhaps even more radical solution to this problem has recently been suggested by Heribert Illig, whose ideas about the early expansion of Islam we have briefly alluded to. According to him, the three centuries stretching from 614 to 911 never existed at all; they were phantom years inserted into the calendar by the Emperor Otto III around 1000. Thus for Illig all history after the tenth/eleventh century needs to be backdated by almost three centuries. The Norman Conquest of England therefore would have occurred in 769 rather than 1066, and the First Crusade would have been launched in 798 rather than 1095. (In the same way, the year of publication of the present book would be 1715 rather than 2012).

It is undeniable that Illig's proposal would make sense of many hitherto puzzling facts. Thus settlements like Helgö, and many others throughout Europe, which were apparently occupied continuously from the fifth and sixth centuries through to the High Middle Ages, but which lack any material from the mid-seventh to mid-tenth centuries, would no longer cause a problem for historians. And the occurrence of Islamic coins and Viking trading stations in Russia dating from the seventh century would make perfect sense, with the Viking raids, which are in any case recognized as being elicited by the Islamic demand for European slaves, commencing in the seventh century rather than the ninth.

It should be noted too that Illig's proposals would dramatically alter the narrative of European-Islamic interaction. For one thing, the Crusades would then have been launched in the late eighth century, rather than the eleventh, and would be a natural European response to ongoing Islamic aggression; whilst the Islamic Golden Age, which is said to have endured between the seventh and eleventh centuries, but which archaeology can find no trace of before the late tenth century, would therefore rightly have commenced in the second half of the seventh century and have come to an end by the late eighth century. Thus the period during which the Islamic world was ahead of the West is dramatically reduced; and indeed the much-vaunted Islamic Golden Age would be revealed (just as Islam's critics have long suggested) as little more than the final afterglow of the splendors of the late Sassanid and Byzantine civilizations; an afterglow quickly crushed under the dead weight of Islamic theocracy.

It is of course impossible to do justice to a concept so radical and so revolutionary in a few paragraphs. A thousand objections immediately spring to mind, and mainstream academics, both in Germany and elsewhere, have thus far – on the whole – come out against it. And it should be remarked that the two alternative theories, the "Climate Catastrophe" and the "Phantom Time," are mutually incompatible and contradictory. One would accept the existence of the Dark Age, both in Europe and the Middle East; the other would deny its existence in both areas.

Both alternative theories take a leap of the imagination even to allow the possibility that they may be right. Yet we should remember that all revolutionary ideas initially seem absurd. Later, when we have become used to thinking in such terms, they appear self-evident. I would not be surprised if one of the above theses were to go through a similar process.

* * *

If we leave aside the, as yet, insoluble questions raised by the Climate Catastrophe and the Phantom Time theorists, we may nonetheless conclude by stating that archaeological investigation over the past half century has revealed the following:

(a) Classical civilization showed a marked decline from the beginning of the third century onwards. From then through to the first half of the fifth, there is evidence of a fairly dramatic drop in the population of the Roman Empire, particularly in the western provinces. By the late-fifth century, this decline was halted and even reversed. Archaeology shows the greatest revival of trade, expansion of population, and recommencement of high-quality architecture in North Africa and Spain, two regions which now experienced something of a golden age. But by the mid-sixth century Latin civilization was also expanding in Gaul, central Europe and even Britain. Indeed, it now began to spread into regions never reached by the Roman Legions, such as eastern Germany, Ireland and northern Britain. Only Italy, particularly central Italy, showed signs of decay; but this was not primarily the result of the Barbarian

Invasions of the fifth century, and is adequately explained by the decline of Rome's political importance.

(b) The same pattern is observed in the East, where numerous cities with very large populations were sustained by a thriving economy and agriculture. That the great plague of 542, which swept the Mediterranean world, did not inflict terminal damage, is proved beyond question by the discovery of thriving and prosperous cities of the late sixth and early seventh centuries throughout the Levantine region. Indeed, by the second half of the sixth century these regions now began to experience an epoch of unparalleled prosperity and opulence. Cities expanded and trade increased well into the second decade of the seventh century.

(c) By the third or perhaps fourth decade of the seventh century classical civilization began rapidly to disappear. The cities of the East were either destroyed or abandoned – or both. This destruction was without question the work of first the Persians and then the Arabs. With the disappearance of the cities came the decline of the classical system of agriculture. Enormous areas of previously cultivated and fertile land quickly became barren and overgrown, a phenomenon almost certainly explained by the Arab custom of allowing their herds to graze on cultivated fields; which behavior was prompted by the Islamic doctrine that "the faithful" had a right to live off the labour of "the infidel." In Mediterranean Europe at the same time, the classical system of agriculture also disappears. Furthermore, the scattered lowland settlements of classical times are abandoned and replaced by defended hilltop settlements. If these developments were not caused by Arab piracy and slave-raiding, then no explanation for them is forthcoming.

(d) From about the third decade of the seventh century the great majority of urban settlements in Europe and throughout the Near East were abandoned. Indeed, almost all settlement of any kind seems to disappear. Little or no archaeology from the mid-seventh to mid-tenth centuries has been discovered in a wide arc stretching from Scotland and Ireland in the north-west to the eastern borders of Persia in the south-east. Then, around the third or fourth decade of the tenth century, new urban centers appear. These are not – in the East at least – nearly as large as those of the early seventh century, and they are distinctly medieval, rather than classical, in character. Nonetheless, the material culture of these settlements, in terms of art and artifacts, often bears striking comparison with the material culture of the early seventh century.

These then are the fact revealed by archaeology. The reader may make of them what he chooses.

EPILOGUE

We have seen that, irrespective of what happened in Europe, Graeco-Roman civilization was terminated very abruptly in the seventh century in its heartlands, in the Near and Middle East, and in North Africa. In these vast territories a new civilization, quite unlike that which had gone before, appeared with surprising rapidity. This new Islamic culture inherited the resources, wealth, and learning of the old one, and was, from the very beginning, at an enormous advantage over the remnant "Roman" lands which yet survived in Europe. The latter continent was still largely rural and, for the most part, "pagan" and tribal. Nonetheless, as we have demonstrated in great detail in the foregoing pages, it was home to a large and growing population, which, in the territories of the former Roman Empire, in Gaul, central Europe, and Spain, was still heavily under the influence of Rome and, more especially, of Byzantium. The loss of the Middle East and North Africa to Islam did, as Pirenne argued, terminate most of the commercial and cultural contacts which had previously existed between those territories and Europe. But it did not impoverish Europe. The latter continent was, by the late sixth century, largely self-sufficient economically. Trade in luxuries such as wines and spices certainly came to an end, as did the cultural and political influence of Byzantine. The great basilicas of the Visigoths and the Merovingians, with their marble columns and brightly-colored mosaics, were replaced – after a somewhat lengthy period of non-construction – by the more somber and smaller structures of the tenth-century Romanesque. Yet on the whole the loss of contact with the East had no terrible economic consequences for the majority of Europe's peoples. On the contrary, Europe was thrown back on its own resources, and it may well be that the great western tradition of inventiveness and innovation was stimulated into life at this time. There was, however, one product whose loss could not be easily made good, and whose absence had a profound impact on the west – papyrus.

The termination of the papyrus supply to Europe, as a cultural event, cannot be overestimated. Indeed, it has hitherto been radically underestimated. Papyrus, a relatively cheap writing material, had a thousand uses in an urban and mercantile culture. And, as we saw in Chapter 15, it was the material upon which was preserved the vast majority of the learning and thinking of the ancients. The loss of papyrus led inexorably to the loss of the bulk of classical literature – irrespective of the efforts of churchmen to preserve it on parchment. Thus from the mid-seventh century Europe became a largely illiterate society, and the educated and articulate town-dwellers, so typical of classical antiquity, disappeared. From then on, few people other than churchmen (and not all of these) could read and write.

The impact of Islam then, on Europe, was primarily cultural rather than, as Pirenne thought, economic. And, having cut Europe off from the sources of classical learning, Islam now began to exert its on influence on the continent. Here again we need to emphasize something that has hitherto received insufficient attention: namely the fact that Islam's influence upon medieval Europe was immense. In the years before the arrival of Islam, the predominant cultural influence had been from the East, from Byzantium and the Levant. In the years after, it continued to be from the East; but the East now meant Islam. And the ideas which then began to cross the Mediterranean, from the Middle East and North Africa, were anything but enlightened.

It is of course widely accepted that Islam had a significant cultural and ideological impact upon Europe in the early Middle Ages. Historians, as we saw, tend to focus on science and philosophy. It is well-known, for example, that Muslim scholars, beginning with the Persian Avicenna (Ibn Sina) in the late tenth and early eleventh century, had made extensive commentaries upon the works of Aristotle, which they attempted to integrate, with a very limited degree of success it must be noted, into Islamic thought. In the second half of the twelfth century Avicenna's work was taken up by the Spanish Muslim Averroes (Ibn Rushd), who made his own commentaries and writings on the Greek philosopher. By that time European scholars were very much aware of Arab learning, and men like John of Salisbury even had agents in Spain procuring Arabic manuscripts, which were then translated into Latin. "Soon the commentaries of Averroes were so well known in Europe," says one historian, "that he was called 'the Commentator,' as Aristotle was called 'the Philosopher.'"[1] At a slightly earlier stage, Christian Europeans had found their way into Muslim-controlled regions such as Sicily, often in disguise, in order to avail themselves of the scientific and alchemical knowledge of the Saracens. No less a person than Gerbert of Aurillac, the genius of the tenth

---

1 Painter, op cit., p. 303

century, on whom the figure of Faust was based, journeyed into the Muslim territories for this very purpose.

The profound influence exerted by Islam upon the philosophical and theological thinking of Europeans was stressed by Briffault, who noted how, "The exact parallelism between Muslim and Christian theological controversy is too close to be accounted for by the similarity of situation, and the coincidences are too fundamental and numerous to be accepted as no more than coincidence. ... The same questions, the same issues which occupied the theological schools of Damascus, were after an interval of a century repeated in identical terms in those of Paris."[2] Again, "The whole logomacy [of Arab theological debate] passed bodily into Christendom. The catchwords, disputes, vexed questions, methods, systems, conceptions, heresies, apologetics and irenics, were transferred from the mosques to the Sorbonne"[3]

Europeans could not, of course, fail to be impressed by what they found in Islamic Spain and southern Italy. They themselves lived in a relatively backward environment. Crucial technologies began to creep into Europe at this time, often via Jewish traders and scholars, who were, for a while, the only class of people able to safely cross the Christian-Islamic frontiers. To these Jewish travelers, some of whom were physicians, alchemists and mathematicians, Europe almost certainly owes the acquisition of such things as the "Arabic" numeral system, knowledge of alcohol distillation, and probably algebra and a host of other information. "Muhammedan philosophy and theology had, we know, been carried to the Benedictine monasteries through the Jews, and the metropolitan house of Monte Cassino."[4] The Spanish Jews in particular "supplied Arabic versions of Greek writers to Christendom."[5] Indeed, so important was the influence of these Jewish traders and scholars that we might even say that, at a crucial moment, the Jews delivered to Europe the knowledge that helped her survive the Muslim onslaught. And we know how Europe later thanked them!

All of the above is well known and denied by no one. Yet, as we saw, Europeans were by no means devoid of their own Greek and Latin texts; and virtually all the classical literature that has survived into modern times did so through the good offices of Christian monks, not Arab philosophers. And, as I will now argue, the real ideological im-

2 Briffault, op cit., p. 217

3 Ibid. p. 219

4 Ibid. p. 217

5 Trevor-Roper, op cit., p. 143

pression of Islam was not the enlightened thinking of Avicenna and Averroes, who were in any case rejected and expelled from the Muslim canon, but the darker thinking found in the Koran and the Haditha: the doctrines of perpetual war against non-believers; of holy deception (taqiyya); of death for apostates and heretics; of judicial torture; of slave and concubine-taking as a legitimate occupation. These were the teachings, and not those of the philosophers, which left an indelible imprint on medieval Europe. And this began right at the beginning.

* * *

The first Islamic (or Koranic) idea to find followers in Europe, and the one most obvious and recognized, was the impulse to iconoclasm, to the destruction of religious imagery and art. Iconoclasm began sometime between 726 and 730 when the Byzantine Emperor Leo III ordered the removal and destruction of all sacred statues and images throughout the Empire. His justification for doing so came from the Old Testament denunciation of idol-worship, yet it is evident that the real inspiration came from Islam.

The question of the Iconoclast episode is one of primary importance. Above all, it has been asked: What could have prompted Byzantine Emperors to go against one of the most fundamental tenets of their faith (the honoring of sacred images) and start destroying these in a manner reminiscent of Oliver Cromwell? Such action can only have been prompted by a crisis of the most profound kind. We have seen that in the early years the advance of Islam seemed unstoppable. The Empire suffered defeat after defeat. Within little more than a decade she had lost all her Middle Eastern possessions outside Anatolia. These included the most prosperous and populous provinces, Egypt and Syria; core areas of the Empire, and part of Imperial territory for seven hundred years. The Empire was experiencing its darkest days; and the fall of Constantinople must surely have seemed imminent. It is precisely crises of such type – those which threaten our very existence – that lead human beings to question fundamentals, to think the previously unthinkable. The Byzantines would have seen their reverses as a sign of divine anger, and a sure indication that they were doing something wrong – something perhaps that their Muslim foes were doing right! A central tenet of Islam is the rejection of images, which are regarded as idols and their honoring condemned as idolatry. No doubt some in Byzantium began to see this as the key.

If this was the psychology behind Byzantine Iconoclasm, then it is clear that Constantinople did not willingly and enthusiastically adopt Islamic thinking. Rather, the success of the new faith from Arabia was such that the Byzantines began to believe that it might enjoy God's favor. Islamic ideas were therefore considered as a way of resolving a profound crisis. Yet, it is important to remember that, for whatever reason, Islamic ideas were copied. The whole of Christendom, East and West, was threatened by Islam; and, one way or another, ideas derived from Islam itself began to be considered by Christians as an answer to that very crisis.

Iconoclasm caused great divisions within the Empire, and was firmly rejected by the West – creating, it seems, some of the conditions leading to the final break between the Pope and Constantinople. Yet the very fact that a Roman Emperor could introduce a policy so obviously inspired by the beliefs of the Arabs tells us eloquently the extent to which the influence of Islamic ideology now began to make itself felt throughout Europe.

* * *

One of the most outstanding characteristics of the Middle Ages, and one that above all others perhaps differentiates it from classical antiquity, was its theocracy. The Middle Ages were, par excellence, the age of priestly power. In the West, the influence of the Church was immense, reaching much further than it ever had under the Christian Roman Emperors or the Germanic kings of the fifth and sixth centuries. The Papacy now stood in judgment of kings and Emperors, and had the power to choose and depose them. "By me kings reign" was the proud boast of the medieval papacy.[6]

How did this come about? The refounding of the Western Empire under Charlemagne, according to Pirenne, was intimately connected with the rise of Islam and the destruction of Byzantine power. It was also, very consciously, seen as a method of strengthening Western Christendom against the advance of Islam. In years to come, the new Western Empire would be renamed the Holy Roman Empire – a singularly appropriate title, for the Empire represented a symbiotic union, at the heart of Europe, of spiritual and temporal authority. The crowning of the Emperor – for which the inauguration of Charlemagne became the model – was an event loaded with religious sig-

6 Ibid., p. 133

nificance. These men ruled *Dei gratis*, and made the Church the main instrument of royal government. The authority of the Western Emperor would henceforth not simply be derived from his own military and economic strength, as it had been under the Caesars and Germanic kings of the fifth and sixth centuries, but ultimately upon the sanction and approval of the Church.

There were several factors in this crucial development. Pirenne, as we saw, noted that with the decline in literacy in the seventh century – following the closing of the Mediterranean – kings were forced to look to the Church to supply the educated functionaries needed to run the apparatus of the state. Again, the loss of tax revenue after the termination of the Mediterranean trade meant that the position of the monarch was weakened *vis a vis* the barons and minor aristocrats. These now gained in power and independence. The kings desperately needed a counterbalance to this, and the support of the Church carried great weight indeed. With the Church on their side the kings could – just about – keep the barons under control. But there was necessarily a trade-off. The Church might keep the king on his throne, but it gained in return an unheard-of influence and authority. Eventually the kings of Europe became, quite literally, subordinate to the Pope, who could even, in extreme cases, dethrone them. Everything a medieval ruler did, or proposed to do, he had to do with the sanction of the Church. Even powerful and independent warriors, such as William of Normandy, could only proceed with a project like the invasion of England after gaining papal approval.

The Carolingian and Ottonian Emperors thus laid the foundations of the medieval theocracy; yet in their time (ninth/tenth century), the papacy was still relatively weak. It was to elicit the support of Otto I against his Italian opponents that Pope John XII revived the dignity of Emperor in the West, after it had lapsed again following the death of Charlemagne. Here we see that in the tenth century, supposedly at the end of a 300-year-long Dark Age, there existed conditions remarkably similar to those pertaining in the sixth and early seventh centuries: Germanic kingdoms that were essentially secular in character, where Popes and prelates were subordinate to the monarchs. Yet conditions were changing. Otto I and his successors staffed their administrations with churchmen, who by then clearly had a monopoly on learning and even literacy. The old, Roman world, was very definitely a thing of the past. From this point on, the power of the Church would grow and grow.

Yet even now the Church had to fight for supremacy, a struggle which commenced in the tenth century, with the aid of the Ottonians, and which ended in the eleventh, with papal victory. "They [Church reformers] fought to secure ultimate control of a self-contained, independent, dominant, monarchical Church. Such a contest was a frontal challenge to the old system of the Roman Empire. It was a frontal attack on the kings who presumed that they had inherited the rights of the Roman emperors. It was an indirect attack on the emperor of Constantinople who, in the East, continued to maintain the old system [of secular supremacy] and was now called schismatic for his pains."[7]

The very peak of the medieval Church's power came a century later in the age and in the person of Innocent III (1198 – 1216). This man judged between rival Emperors in Germany and had Otto IV deposed. He laid England under an interdict and excommunicated King John for refusing to recognize Stephen Langdon as Archbishop of Canterbury. His two most memorable actions however were the establishment of the Inquisition and the launching of the notorious Albigensian Crusade, which led to the elimination of the Cathar movement. Innocent III then, the most powerful of medieval theocrats, was a proponent of Holy War, and an enforcer of absolute doctrinal conformity. Apostasy under Innocent III became a capital offence. During his time too the other Crusades, against Islam in Spain and in the Middle East, continued to rage.

Ironically, Innocent's attitude to apostasy and doctrinal conformity – as well as to "Holy War" – is completely in accord with Islamic notions, and we must consider to what extent these extreme positions of the European theocracy derived ultimately from the Islamic one.

Islam itself was, of course, from the very beginning, theocratic in nature. In it, there was no "render unto Caesar the things that are Caesar's, and unto God the things that are God's". Right from the start, in the person of Muhammad, spiritual and temporal power was united. After Muhammad, under the Caliphs, the same situation pertained. Every Caliph was, first and foremost, a "commander of the faithful". For all that, we cannot judge that the founding of theocracy in Europe was a result of deliberate imitation of Islamic notions, as was iconoclasm and Holy War. Islam's contribution to the European theocracy was real enough, but rather more accidental, or rather, inferential As we saw, the impoverishment of Europe and her monarchs caused by Islam's blockade of the Mediterranean, left them little option but to

---

7 Ibid., p. 137

turn to the Church for support. Also, the fight for the defense of Europe, because of the very nature of the enemy, took on a religious dimension (all faiths gain in strength when faced with opposition), and this too would have increased the power and prestige of the Church.

So, whilst the medieval European theocracy was not the result of direct imitation of Islamic ideas, Islam was still instrumental in giving birth to it. Furthermore, the type of theocracy which took shape in Europe, and some of the underlying ideas associated with it, very definitely derived from Islam.

* * *

From its inception, Islam regarded apostasy and heresy as capital offences,[8] and almost immediately after the death of Muhammad there erupted serious and extremely violent disputes over conflicting claims to the leadership of the movement. Assassination and murder was the order of the day. Even those with no leadership pretensions, but with heterodox views, were subject to violent suppression. The most notorious early example is found in the fate of Mansur Al-Hallaj (858 – 922), the Persian mystic, whose death mimicked that of Christ – though before being crucified Al-Hallaj was first, it is said, blinded and otherwise tortured. And the killing of political and religious opponents, or those who deviated in any way from orthodox Islam, occurred at the very start and was continuous throughout Muslim history. So it was with infidels such as Christians and Jews who, though theoretically dhimmi, or "protected," were in fact always the subject of violent attack. We know, for example, that in 704 or 705 the caliph Walid (705-715) "assembled the nobles of Armenia in the church of St Gregory in Naxcawan and the church of Xrain on the Araxis, and burned them to death. Others were crucified and decapitated and their wives and children taken into captivity. A violent persecution of Christians in Armenia is recorded from 852 to 855."[9] There even existed, in Spain and North Africa, at least from the time of the Almohads (early twelfth century), a commission of enquiry, a veritable "inquisition", for rooting out apostates. We are told that the Jews, who had at this time been forced to accept Islam, formed a mass of "new converts" who nevertheless continued to practice their own religion

---

8 Muhammad said, "If anyone changes his religion, kill him." (Bukhari, Vol. 9, book 84, no. 57).

9 Bat Ye'or, op cit., pp. 60-1

in secret. But the "Almohad inquisitors, doubting their sincerity, took away their children and raised them as Muslims."[10]

Medieval Christianity, beginning in the late twelfth/early thirteenth century, adopted the same attitude. Christians now had their own Inquisition for exposing heretics, and the death penalty was now prescribed for such miscreants. The judicial use of torture too, "a novelty in Europe" at the time, became accepted practice.[11] All of these practices were in fact novel in Europe of the eleventh or twelfth century: The barbarous treatment of criminals and dissidents which had been customary in Imperial Rome was phased out during the early Christian centuries. Constantine abolished crucifixion as a form of execution, and attempted to do away with gladiatorial displays. These were finally abolished in the time of Honorius (early fifth century). The condition of slaves was dramatically improved by the Christianization of the Empire, and the Church worked to end the institution entirely – a goal finally accomplished by the eighth or perhaps ninth century. Torture of prisoners, routine in Imperial Rome, was gradually done away with around the same time. Nor is there any evidence, in the early Christian centuries, of the lethal intolerance which characterized the Inquisition. It is true that in the early centuries, the Church was involved in a series of prolonged and bitter disputes over the correct interpretation of Christ's life and mission. Those who disagreed with the mainstream dogmas, as laid down by various Councils, were decreed to be heretics, and fairly severe condemnation of these people and groups was common: indeed, it was almost endemic. Yet, intemperate as was the language used in these disputes, they rarely turned violent; and even when they did, the violence was on a very small scale and invariably perpetrated by those with no official sanction or approval. And the use of force to enforce orthodoxy was condemned by all the Church Fathers. Thus Lactantius declared that "religion cannot be imposed by force; the matter must be carried on by words rather than by blows, that the will may be affected." He wrote,

> Oh with what an honorable inclination the wretched men go astray! For they are aware that there is nothing among men more excellent than religion, and that this ought to be defended with the whole of our power; but as they are deceived in the matter of religion itself, so also are they in the manner of its

10 Ibid., p. 61

11 Trevor-Roper, op cit., p. 159

defense. For religion is to be defended, not by putting to death, but by dying; not by cruelty, but by patient endurance; not by guilt, but by good faith. ... For if you wish to defend religion by bloodshed, and by tortures, and by guilt, it will no longer be defended, but will be polluted and profaned. For nothing is so much a matter of free will as religion; in which, if the mind of the worshipper is disinclined to it, religion is at once taken away, and ceases to exist.[12]

Later, St. John Chrysostom wrote that "it is not right to put a heretic to death, since an implacable war would be brought into the world."[13] Likewise, St. Augustine was to write of heretics that "it is not their death, but their deliverance from error, that we seek."[14] In spite of these and many other such admonitions, incidents of violence against heretics did occur; but they were isolated and never approved by Church authorities. Such, for example, was the case with the suppression of the so-called Priscillian Heresy in Spain in the latter years of the fourth and early years of the fifth century. Several followers of Priscillian were put to death, and the sect was persecuted in other ways. Yet the killing of Priscillian and his immediate associates (seven in all) was thoroughly condemned by the ecclesiastical authorities.

The same was true of another, and more famous, case – the murder of Hypatia. This incident, in the early fifth century, has achieved, in some quarters, almost legendary status, and is seen as the example par excellence of Christian bigotry and obscurantism. But from what little we know of it, it is clear that the murder was carried out by a group of lawless fanatics and not by the Church. We should note too that the murder occurred in Egypt, a land with a long tradition of religious fanaticism. During the time of Julius Caesar an Egyptian mob lynched a Roman centurion (an act which could have brought upon them a terrible retribution) for having the temerity to kill a cat. Such isolated acts of fanaticism have occurred in all faiths at all periods of history. Even that most pacifist and tolerant of religious ideologies,

---

12 Lactantius, "The Divine Institutes," in "Fathers of the Third and Fourth Centuries," in *The Ante-Nicene Fathers*, 156-7.

13 John Chrysostom, Homily XLVI, in George Prevost, trans. "The Homilies of St. John Chrysostom" in Philip Schaff, ed. *A Select Library of the Nicene and Post-Nicene Fathers of the Christian Church*, Vol. X (Eedermans, Grand Rapids, MI, 1986), p. 288

14 St Augustine, Letter C, in "Letters of St. Augustine," in J. G. Cunningham, trans. in *A Select Library of the Nicene* (etc as above)

Buddhism, is not entirely free of it. So, in itself, the murder of Hypatia cannot tell us much. The Christian writer Socrates Scholasticus, in the fifth century, regarded it as a deplorable act of bigotry, whilst just three centuries later his fellow-countryman John of Nikiu fully approved of the killing. He described Hypatia as "a pagan" who was "devoted to magic" and who had "beguiled many people through Satanic wiles." What could have produced such a change?

The world we call "medieval" was one in which the reason and humanism of the classical world had to some degree disappeared. Dark fantasies and superstitions became more prominent. Belief in the power of magicians and sorcerers, a belief associated with the most primitive type of mind-set, made a comeback. In the most backward of modern societies we still find perfectly innocent people accused of "witchcraft" and brutally put to death for a crime which they never committed and which does not even exist. By the end of the Middle Ages this mentality had returned to Europe; and in 1487 a papal Bull named *malleus maleficarum* ("hammer of the witches") pronounced the death of witches and Satanists. Even in Innocent III's time the "heretics" of the age, the Cathars and Waldensians, were believed to be under the inspiration of Satan.

Yet Europe, as she emerged from the so-called Dark Age in the tenth century, still bathed in the light of reason and humanitarianism. Thus a tenth century canon of Church Law criticized and condemned the belief among country folk that "certain women" were in the habit of riding out on beasts in the dead of night and crossing great distances before daybreak. According to the canon, anyone who believed this was "beyond doubt an infidel and a pagan." Somewhat earlier, Saint Agobard, Bishop of Lyons, declared it was not true that witches could call up storms and destroy harvests. Nor could they devour people from within nor kill them with the "evil eye".[15] "Only a few generations later," note Colin Wilson and Christopher Evans, "any person who did not believe in night flying and witches as the Church defined them was in danger of being burned as a heretic."[16] What, ask these two authors, had happened in the intervening years to change the Church's attitude?

In answer to that question, let us recall how, in the eleventh and twelfth centuries inquisitive young men from northern Europe flocked

---

15 Colin Wilson and Christopher Evans, (eds.) *Strange but True* (Parragon Books, 1995), p. 285

16 Ibid. p. 285

to Islamic Spain to study the knowledge and learning to be found there. But, as Louis Bertrand remarked, it was not so much the "science" of the Moors that attracted them as the pseudo-science: the alchemy, the astrology and the sorcery.[17] What the Moors taught was a far cry from the learning now so widely praised in the politically-correct textbooks that fill our libraries and bookshops.

Sorcery and alchemy were not the only things learned by the Europeans from the Muslims: they took also ideas directly from the Koran and the Haditha; ideas about how heretics, apostates and sorcerers should be treated. And it is scarcely to be doubted that in establishing his own Inquisition Innocent III was directly imitating the example of the Almohads in Spain, who had set up their own commission for investigating heretics and apostates fifty years earlier.

Innocent III is viewed by the enemies of Christianity as the *bête noir*, the living embodiment of everything that was and is wrong with Christianity. Yet the fact that his attitudes had Islamic – but not Christian – precedents is never mentioned. And there is another point to consider: Whilst we do not seek to minimize the enormity of Innocent's actions, we must never forget that in the 12th and 13th centuries the Muslim threat had by no means receded: it remained as potent and dangerous as ever. In such circumstances – indeed, in any war situation – internal dissent (such as the Cathars represented) is liable to be viewed as representing a fifth column working for the enemy. And it is well-known that all wartime dissent is suppressed with a thoroughness and ruthlessness much more severe than would normally be the case. The later Spanish Inquisition, which implemented draconian measures against dissenters in the Iberian Peninsula, must be seen in the same light. The threat of Islam was ever present, and we can be reasonably certain that the severe repression of Muslims at this time was directly attributable to the fear of a renewed Muslim invasion of the Peninsula (by the Ottomans) and the possibility that the native Muslims would form a fifth column in support of the invaders.

* * *

We have found that in the years after 600 classical civilization, which was by then synonymous with Christendom, came into contact with a new force, one that extolled war as a sacred duty, sanctioned the enslavement and killing of non-believers as a religious obligation,

17 Bertrand, op cit., p. 76

sanctioned the judicial use of torture, and provided for the execution of apostates and heretics. All of these attitudes, which, taken together, are surely unique in the religious traditions of mankind, can be traced to the very beginnings of that faith. Far from being manifestations of a degenerate phase of Islam, all of them go back to the founder of the faith himself. Yet, astonishingly enough, this is a religion and an ideology which is still extolled by academics and artists as enlightened and tolerant. Indeed, to this day, there exists a large body of opinion, throughout the Western World, which sees Islam as in every way superior to, and more enlightened than, Christianity.

By around 650 almost half the Christian world was lost to this new and "enlightened" faith; and by 715 the remainder was in serious danger. These events had an enormous impact. The closure of the Mediterranean meant the impoverishment of Western Europe, which was then compelled to improvise as best it could. The lack of papyrus forced the use of the immensely expensive parchment, leading naturally to a serious decline in literacy. The Viking Wars, which the Islamic Invasions elicited, brought enormous disruption also to the northern part of the continent. Desperate for a unifying force that could bring together all the Germanic kingdoms of the West for the defense of Christendom, the Western Empire was re-established, and Constantinople, fighting for her very survival, could do little about it.

Western culture changed radically. For the first time, Christians began to think in terms of Holy War, and the whole theology of the faith went into a sate of flux. This great transformation began in the years after 650, and the phenomenon we call "Crusading" began, properly speaking, in southern Italy and more especially Spain, during the seventh and eighth centuries, as Christians fought a desperate rearguard action to save what they could from the advancing Saracens. This action was to develop into a protracted struggle that was to last for centuries, and was to have a profound and devastating effect upon European civilization. Above all, it meant, by sheer impact of force and time, the gradual adoption by the Christians of many of the characteristics of their Muslim foes. Thus by the eleventh and twelfth centuries Christian kings in Spain and southern Italy reigned over arabized courts and had adopted typically Muslim (and utterly non-Christian) customs, such as polygamy. The most famous, or infamous, example of this was the Emperor Frederick II, "the baptized sultan of Sicily," who kept an expensive harem guarded by eunuchs.[18]

---

18 Trevor-Roper, op cit., p. 147

As well as this direct influence, there was the barbarizing effect of the continual war into which the whole Mediterranean littoral was now plunged. The arrival of Islam brought to a definitive end the peace of the Mediterranean, the *pax Romana* that had even survived the fall of Rome. With the appearance of Islam, the Mediterranean was no longer a highway, but a frontier, and a frontier of the most dangerous kind. Piracy, rapine, and slaughter became the norm – for a thousand years! And this is something that has been almost completely overlooked by historians, especially those of northern European extraction. For the latter in particular, the Mediterranean is viewed in the light of classical history. So bewitched have educated Europeans been by the civilizations of Greece and Rome, that they have treated the more recent part of Mediterranean history – over a thousand years of it – as if it never existed. The visitor to Mediterranean lands, perhaps on the Grand Tour, was shown the monuments of the classical world; here Caesar fought a battle, there Anthony brought his fleet, etc.

This distorted and romanticized view of the Mediterranean and its past, which ignored the savagery and fear of the past millennium, was particularly characteristic of those of Anglo-Saxon origin, with whom there was the added problem of religious antagonism. With the reign of Elizabeth I, England became the mortal enemy of Catholic Europe; and the Catholic power of the time was of course Spain. From this point on, English-speaking historians tended to be heavily biased against Catholic Spain and, unsurprisingly, extremely favorable towards Spain's Muslim enemies, who were romanticized and portrayed as cultured and urbane. It was then that the myth of the "golden age" of the Spanish Caliphate was born – a myth which, as we have seen, still has a very wide circulation.

Yet the reality was quite different: With the Muslim conquest of North Africa and Spain, a reign of terror was to commence that was to last for centuries. The war in Spain dragged on until the fifteenth century. By then, a new front was opened in Italy, as the rising power of the Ottoman Turks, having already engulfed Greece and the Balkans, threatened to penetrate Italy. This danger remained active and alive for the next three centuries, until the Turks were finally beaten back at the gates of Vienna in 1683. In the interim, the Pope was ready to flee from Rome on more than one occasion, as Ottoman fleets scoured the Adriatic and Ionian Seas. After the fall of Constantinople in 1453, it seemed that all of central Europe, including Hungary and Austria, was about to be overwhelmed; and though the imminent danger was averted by the victory of John Hunyadi at Belgrade (1456), it was renewed again in the sixteenth century, when an enormous Turkish invasion force was stopped by the Holy League at the naval battle of Lepanto (1571). And it is worth noting here that the Turkish losses at Lepanto, comprising 30,000 men and 200 out of 230 warships, did not prevent them returning the following year with another enormous fleet: Which speaks volumes for their persistence and the perennial nature of the threat they posed. A short time before this, in the 1530s, the Turks had extended their rule westwards along the North African coast as far as Morocco, where they encouraged an intensification of slaving raids against Christian communities in southern Europe. Fleets of Muslim pirates brought devastation to the coastal regions of Italy, Spain, southern France, and Greece. The Christians of the islands, in particular, Sicily, Sardinia, Corsica and the Balearics, had to get used to savage pirate raids, bent on rape and pillage.

Hugh Trevor-Roper was at pains to emphasize that the epoch we now call the Renaissance, which we view as an age of artistic and intellectual achievement, as well as exuberant optimism, seemed very different to the inhabitants of Europe at the time. Even as Cortes and Pizarro conquered the vastly wealthy lands of Mexico and Peru in his name, the Emperor Charles V gloomily awaited the dissolution of Christendom. "We set out to conquer worthless new empires beyond the seas," lamented Busbequius, the Belgian whom the King of the Romans sent as ambassador to the Sultan of Turkey, "and we are losing the heart of Europe."[19] Christendom, he wrote, subsided precariously by the good will of the king of Persia, whose ambitions in the east continually called the Sultan of Turkey back from his European conquests.[20]

These events had a profound effect on the character of the Christian peoples of the Balkans and of the Mediterranean, a fact which has never been fully appreciated by northern Europeans. From the vantage-point of London or Paris, the Ottomans and the Barbary Pirates do not loom large. From Rome however things looked quite different. Rome, the very seat of the Catholic faith, was on the front line of this never-ending war. Viewed from central Italy, the paranoia of medieval Popes about heresies and internal enemies becomes somewhat more understandable.

And the people of Spain, who held the front line of the bloody

19 Ibid., p. 17
20 Ibid.

boundary for centuries, were transformed. The war against Islam became the *raison d'être* for many, even most, Spanish kings. It was a perennial project; not an obsession, more like a normal part of life. It was taken for granted that there could never be peace with the Islamic world. How could it be otherwise, when making war against the infidel was a religious duty for every Muslim? Christians had understood this centuries earlier, and it was reiterated in the fourteenth century by the Islamic historian Ibn Khaldun:

> In the Muslim community, the holy war is a religious duty, because of the universalism of the [Muslim] mission and [the obligation to] convert everybody to Islam either by persuasion or by force. Therefore, caliphate and royal authority are united [in Islam], so that the person in charge can devote the available strength to both of them [religion and politics] at the same time.
>
> The other groups did not have a universal mission, and the holy war was not a religious duty to them, save only for purposes of defense. It has thus come about that the person in charge of religious affairs [in other religious groups] is not concerned with power politics at all. [Among them] royal authority comes to those who have it, by accident and in some way that has nothing to do with religion. It comes to them as a necessary result of group feeling, which by its very nature seeks to obtain royal authority, as we have mentioned before, and not because they are under obligation to gain power over other nations, as is the case with Islam. They are merely required to establish their religion among their own [people].
>
> This is why the Israelites after Moses and Joshua remained unconcerned with royal authority for about four hundred years. Their only concern was to establish their religion (1: 473).
>
> Thereafter, there was dissension among the Christians with regard to their religion and to Christology. They split into groups and sects, which secured the support of various Christian rulers against each other. At different times there appeared different sects. Finally, these sects crystallized into three groups, which constitute the [Christian] sects. Others

have no significance. These are the Melchites, the Jacobites, and the Nestorians. We do not think that we should blacken the pages of this book with discussion of their dogmas of unbelief. In general, they are well known. All of them are unbelief. This is clearly stated in the noble Qur'an. [To] discuss or argue those things with them is not up to us. It is [for them to choose between] conversion to Islam, payment of the poll tax, or death.[21]

Ibn Khaldun was a native of Andalusia, but what he wrote about jihad would have been understood by every monarch of Spain, Christian and Moor. Thus for the kings of Castile the survival in the Iberian Peninsula of any region from which Islam could launch attacks was seen as a real and ever present threat, and the reduction of Islamic Spain to the southern strongholds of Andalusia did not make Christians feel any more secure. Now the threat was not from North Africa but from Turkey. The existence of Granada threatened the existence of Christian Spain, for the Ottomans could at any moment use it as a beach-head for a second conquest of the Peninsula. Thus Granada had to be reduced, no matter what the cost. And even after that, the Spaniards did not feel secure. The war against Islam would continue, as it always had. The Ottomans were now threatening Italy and the entire western Mediterranean, Spain herself could be next. Even the voyages of discovery were undertaken with the struggle against Islam in mind. Columbus' first voyage, for example, had as its object the discovery of a direct route to the East Indies, bypassing Muslim territory, "so as to take Islam in the rear," says Louis Bertrand, "and to effect an alliance with the Great Khan – a mythical personage who was believed to be the sovereign of all that region, and favourable to the Christian religion ..."[22] Bertrand was very insistent on this point, which he emphasized in half a dozen pages. The voyage of discovery was to begin a new phase, he says, in "the Crusade against the Moors which was to be continued by a new and surer route. It was by way of the Indies that Islam was to be dealt a mortal blow."[23]

So certain was Bertrand of the connection between the exploits

21 Ibn Khaldun, *The Muqaddimah: An Introduction to History* Vol. 1 (Trans. Franz Rosenthal, Bollingen Series 43: Princeton University Press, 1958), p. 480. Cited from Bat Ye'or, *The Dhimmi*, p. 162

22 Bertrand, op cit., p. 163

23 Ibid.

of the Conquistadores in the Americas and the war against Islam that he actually describes the conquest of America as the "last Crusade."

The record of the Conquistadores in the New World needs no repetition here: It is one of cruelty and greed on a truly monumental scale. Yet the habits of the Spaniards here, habits which gave rise to the "Black Legend," were learned at the school of the Caliphs. In Bertrand's words: "Lust for gold, bloodthirsty rapacity, the feverish pursuit of hidden treasure, application of torture to the vanquished to wrest the secret of their hiding-places from them – all these barbarous proceedings and all these vices, which the conquistadores were to take to America, they learnt at the school of the caliphs, the emirs, and the Moorish kings."[24]

Indeed all of the traits associated with the Spaniards, for which they have been roundly criticized by English-speaking historians, can be traced to the contact with Islam.

"The worst characteristic which the Spaniards acquired was the parasitism of the Arabs and the nomad Africans: the custom of living off one's neighbour's territory, the raid raised to the level of an institution, marauding and brigandage recognized as the sole means of existence for the man-at-arms. In the same way they went to win their bread in Moorish territory, so the Spaniards later went to win gold and territory in Mexico and Peru.

> They were to introduce there, too, the barbarous, summary practices of the Arabs: putting everything to fire and sword, cutting down fruit-trees, razing crops, devastating whole districts to starve out the enemy and bring them to terms; making slaves everywhere, condemning the population of the conquered countries to forced labour. All these detestable ways the conquistadores learnt from the Arabs.

> For several centuries slavery maintained itself in Christian Spain, as in the Islamic lands. Very certainly, also, it was to the Arabs that the Spaniards owed the intransigence of their fanaticism, the pretension to be, if not the chosen of God, at least the most Catholic nation of Christendom. Philip II, like Abd er Rahman or El Mansour, was Defender of the Faith.

> Finally, it was not without contagion that the Spaniards lived

---

24 Ibid., p. 159

for centuries in contact with a race of men who crucified their enemies and gloried in piling up thousands of severed heads by way of trophies. The cruelty of the Arabs and the Berbers also founded a school in the Peninsula. The ferocity of the emirs and the caliphs who killed their brothers or their sons with their own hands was to be handed on to Pedro the Cruel and Henry of Trastamare, those stranglers under canvas, no better than common assassins.[25]

One of the most deplored characteristics of medieval Europe was its virulent and frequently violent anti-Semitism. Yet the extreme form of anti-Semitism encountered in Europe during the Middle Ages did not predate the eleventh century. Indeed, the first massacres of Jews in Europe were carried out in Spain by Muslim mobs early in the eleventh century; in 1011 (in Cordoba) and 1066 (in Granada). It is true of course that Christians had a long history of antagonism towards the Jews, one that preceded the appearance of Islam. The antagonism was mutual, and Jewish leaders were in the early centuries as vociferous in their condemnation of Christianity as Christians were of Judaism. Serious violence between the two groups was however uncommon; and the first real pogrom launched by Christians against the Jews in Europe did not happen until the beginning of the First Crusade, in 1096, that is, thirty years after the massacre in Granada. And it seems a virtual certainty that the German mobs who carried out the 1096 massacres learned their hatred in Spain.

From Roman and perhaps even pre-Roman times Spain was home to a very large Jewish community. Following the Islamic conquest of that land in 711, the Jews came under the domination of a faith that was from its inception virulently and violently anti-Jewish. For Muslims the lead was given by none other than their founder, the Prophet Muhammad. It would be superfluous to enumerate the anti-Jewish pronouncements in the Koran and the Haditha, where the Hebrews are portrayed as the craftiest, most persistent and most implacable enemies of Allah. In the Koran (2: 63-66) Allah transforms some Jews who profaned the Sabbath into apes: "Be as apes despicable!" In Koran 5: 59-60, He directs Muhammad to remind the "People of the Book" about "those who incurred the curse of Allah and His wrath, those whom some He transformed into apes and swine, those who worshipped evil." Again, in 7: 166, we hear of the Sabbath-breaking Jews

25 Ibid., p. 160

that "when in their insolence they transgressed (all) prohibitions," Allah said to them, "Be ye apes, despised and rejected."

From the same sources we know that Muhammad's first violent action against the Jews involved the Qaynuqa tribe, who dwelt at Medina, under the protection of the city. Muhammad "seized the occasion of an accidental tumult," and ordered the Qaynuqa (or Kainoka) to embrace his religion or fight. In the words of Gibbon, "The unequal conflict was terminated in fifteen days; and it was with extreme reluctance that Mahomet yielded to the importunity of his allies and consented to spare the lives of the captives." (*Decline and Fall*, Chapter 50) In later attacks on the Jews, the Hebrew captives were not so fortunate.

The most notorious of all Muhammad's attacks against the Jews was directed at the Banu Quraiza tribe. This community, which dwelt near Medina, was attacked without warning by the Prophet and his men, and, after its defeat, all the males over the age of puberty were beheaded. Some Islamic authorities claim that Muhammad personally participated in the executions. The doomed men and boys, whose numbers are estimated at anything between 500 and 900, were ordered to dig the trench which was to be their communal grave. All of the women and children were enslaved. These deeds are mentioned in the Koran as acts carried out by Allah himself and fully sanctioned by divine approval.

The Massacre of Banu Quraiza was followed soon after by the attack on the Khaybar tribe. On this occasion, the Prophet ordered the torture of a Jewish chieftain to extract information about where he had hidden his treasures. When the treasure was uncovered, the chieftain was beheaded.

What caused Muhammad's seemingly implacable animosity towards the Jews? According to Gibbon, it was their refusal to recognize him as their long-awaited Messiah that "converted his friendship into an implacable hatred, with which he pursued that unfortunate people to the last moment of his life; and, in the double character of apostle and conqueror, his persecution was extended into both worlds." (*Decline and Fall*, Ch. 50)

It is a widely-held fiction that, aside from the Prophet's persecution of the Jews of Arabia, Muslims in general and Islam as a rule was historically tolerant to this People of the Book, who were generally granted dhimmi ("protected") status in the Islamic Umma, or community. But dhimmi status, also accorded to Christians, did not, as Bat Ye'or has demonstrated at great length, imply equal rights with Mus-

Epilogue

lims. On the contrary, dhimmis were subject, even at the best of times, to a whole series of discriminatory and humiliating laws and to relentless exploitation. At the worst of times, they could be murdered in the streets without any hope of legal redress. One of the most noxious measures directed against them was the requirement to wear an item or color of clothing by which they could be easily identified: identified for easy exploitation and abuse. Bat Ye'or has shown that this law was enforced in Islam right from the beginning. The violence was not continuous, but the exploitation was, and the pattern of abuse initiated by Muhammad in Arabia in the seventh century was to be repeated throughout history. The first massacres of Jews in Europe, carried out by Muslim mobs in Spain, were preceded by other massacres carried out in North Africa, and clearly formed a continuum with Muhammad's massacres of that people in Arabia.

There was, however, at times, a semblance of tolerance for both Jews and Christians. It could not have been otherwise. When the Arabs conquered the vast territories of Mesopotamia, Syria, and North Africa during the seventh century, they found themselves a small minority ruling over enormous populations comprising mainly Christians and, to a lesser degree, Jews. As such, they needed to proceed with caution. Like all conquerors, the Arabs were quick to exploit any internal conflicts; and it was in their interests, above all, to divide the Christians from the Jews. This was particularly the case in Spain, where the Jewish population was very large. A united Jewish and Christian front could have proved extremely dangerous, and it was entirely in the interest of the conquerors to sow mistrust and suspicion between these communities. In the words of Bat Ye'or, "The [Arab] invaders knew how to take advantage of the dissensions between local groups in order to impose their own authority, favoring first one and then another, with the intention of weakening and ruining them all through a policy of 'divide and rule.'"[26]

Jewish communities, both in Spain and elsewhere, tended to be both educated and prosperous. Jewish doctors, scientists and merchants could be usefully employed by any ruling group. And employed they were by the Arabs. Some, such as Ibn Naghrela, rose to positions of great prominence. The international connections of the Jews and their mastery of languages proved invaluable to the new rulers. The Jews frequently found themselves in the role of intermediaries between Muslims and Christians. Yet such favors as they enjoyed was

26 Bat Ye'or, op cit., p. 87

transitory and uncertain. There was never any real security, as the massacres of 1011 and 1066 illustrate only too well. On the other hand, it was entirely in the interests of the Muslims that the Christians believed the Jews were favored. And part of that myth was the notion that "the Jews" had actually assisted the Muslims in their conquest of the country.

The likelihood that this story was true is vanishingly small, especially when we consider the massacres of Jews carried out in Arabia by Muhammad himself just a few decades earlier. No people had better international links than the Jews, a nation of merchants par excellence, and those of Spain would have been very much aware of Muhammad's behavior long before the first Muslim armies landed on Spanish soil. Nonetheless, the story got out that the Jews had helped the Muslims, and there can be little doubt that this story was fostered by the Muslim invaders themselves, as part of the policy of divide and conquer.

All during the tenth and eleventh centuries, the war for possession of the Iberian Peninsula raged between Christians and Muslims. This conflict was to grow into a real clash of civilizations, as both groups called in the assistance of co-religionists from far and wide. The Shrine of Santiago de Compostela became a rallying symbol for the Christians of the north and for those of France and Germany, who crossed the Pyrenees to join the struggle against Islam. Their Christian allies in Spain already had the conviction that the Jews were secret allies of the Muslims. They were convinced that the Jews had assisted the Muslims in their conquest of the country; and they came into contact with Muslim antisemitic attitudes – attitudes which the Christians began to imbibe. It is an acknowledged fact that it was in Spain that the warriors who later joined the First Crusade learnt their antisemitism. In the words of Steven Runciman, "Already in the Spanish wars there had been some inclination on the part of Christian armies to maltreat the Jews."[27] Runciman notes that at the time of the expedition to Barbastro, in the mid-eleventh century, Pope Alexander II had written to the bishops of Spain to remind them that there was all the difference in the world between Muslims and Jews. The former were irreconcilable enemies of the Christians, but the latter were ready to work for them. However, in Spain "the Jews had enjoyed such favour from the hands of the Moslems that the Christian conquerors could not bring themselves to trust them."[28] This lack of trust is confirmed by more than

---

27 Steven Runciman, *The History of the Crusades*, Vol. 1 (London, 1951), p. 135
28 Ibid.

one document of the period, several of which are listed by Runciman.

Just over a decade after the Christian knights of France and Germany had helped their co-religionists in Spain to retake the city of Toledo from the Muslims, some of them prepared to set out on the First (official) Crusade. Before they did so, a few of them took part in the mass murder of several thousand Jews in Germany and Bohemia – an atrocity unprecedented in European history.

In view of the fact that these pogroms were committed by warriors some of whom had learned their trade in Spain, and in view of the fact that such atrocities were hitherto unknown in Europe, we may state that there is strong circumstantial evidence to suggest that the Christians had been influenced by Islamic ideas.

To conclude, I am not trying to argue that antisemitism did not exist among Christians before the rise of Islam. Obviously it did. Yet the influence of Islam, and the terrible struggle between the two intolerant ideologies of Christianity and Islam which began in the seventh century, had a profoundly detrimental effect upon the Jews; and it was then, and only then, that the virulent and murderous antisemitism so characteristic of the Middle Ages entered European life.

* * *

The undoubted negative influence of Islam upon the character and culture of Spain and the other Mediterranean lands should not blind us to the fact that the Christian message was never completely lost nor the church as an institution completely corrupted. Following the rise of the Germanic kingdoms in the fifth century, the church worked hard to uphold the rights of slaves and the peasants against the cupidity and passions of the fierce warrior-class which now ruled Spain, Gaul and Italy. This continued during the period of the Muslim and Viking invasions and afterwards. "The tenth and eleventh centuries saw a struggle between the lords and the church over the rights of these people [the peasants]. The lords wanted to deprive the serfs of all the rights of human beings, to say that they had no souls and to refuse to call their unions marriages."[29] The church, notes the above writer, won this battle, but not without fierce resistance on the part of the nobles. This struggle on behalf of the poor continued right throughout the Middle Ages and beyond, and we have already noted how the monasteries, for example, provided free medical care, as well

29 Painter, op cit., p. 100

as alms and shelter, to the poor and destitute all throughout this epoch. And the church further protected the poor by ensuring the enactment of laws against speculation, such as the fixed price of bread and grain, and the various rules which governed the business of the guilds. Even war was regulated by the church, and medieval conflicts, at least within Europe, were not nearly as violent as many imagine. As Sidney Painter notes; "Even when kings and feudal princes fought supposedly serious wars in the early Middle Ages, they were not bloody. At the great and decisive battle of Lincoln in 1217, where some 600 knights on one side fought 800 on the other, only one knight was killed, and everyone was horrified at the unfortunate accident."[30]

There is no question that the medieval custom of ransoming important hostages provided an economic motive for this remarkable unwillingness to use lethal force; but it is equally clear that the idea of chivalry, with its strongly Christian overtones, exerted a powerful moderating influence.

Nor should we forget that during the centuries which followed the First Crusade, when we might imagine Christians in Europe to have become thoroughly accustomed to the idea of fighting and killing for Christ, there is much evidence to show that this did not happen. The idea of violence in the name of Christ was, in the words of Jonathan Riley-Smith, "without precedent" when it was first promoted in the eleventh century.[31] "So radical was the notion of devotional war," says Riley-Smith, that it is surprising that there seem to have been no protests from senior churchmen"[32] Be that as it may, Christians could never be fully at ease with the idea, and enthusiasm for crusading soon waned. Riley-Smith notes that, following the success of the First Crusade, the supply of new recruits immediately dried up, even among those groups and families who had been its strongest supporters. These reverted, instead, to the traditional non-military pilgrimage to the Holy Land.[33] We should note too individual statements like that of the English Franciscan Roger Bacon in the 1260s, who criticized the very idea of Crusading, arguing that such military activities impeded efforts to peacefully convert Muslims.[34] Contrast this with the attitude

---

30 Ibid., p. 119

31 Jonathan Riley-Smith, "The State of Mind of Crusaders to the East: 1095-1300," in Jonathan Riley-Smith (ed.) *Oxford History of the Crusades*, p. 79

32 Ibid., p. 78

33 Ibid., pp. 80-2

34 Alan Forey, "The Military Orders, 1120-1312," in Jonathan Riley-Smith (ed.)

in Islam, where all warriors who died in the Jihad were "martyrs" and guaranteed an immediate reward of 72 virgins in Paradise. And the contrast is seen very clearly in the words of Gregory Palamas, an Orthodox metropolitan, who was a captive of the Turks in 1354: " ... these infamous people, hated by God and infamous, boast of having got the better of the Romans [Byzantines] by their love of God. ... They live by the bow, the sword, and debauchery, finding pleasure in taking slaves, devoting themselves to murder, pillage, spoil ... and not only do they commit these crimes, but even – what an aberration – they believe that God approves of them."[35]

And when the Spaniards began the conquest of the New World, one should not forget that the great majority of the excesses carried out were by individual and unregulated adventurers, over whom the royal and church authorities had little control. Nor should we neglect to mention that it was owing to the enormous and sustained pressure of many humane and courageous churchmen that the custom of enslaving the native inhabitants of the New World was finally abandoned.

Thus it would be a mistake to imagine, amidst the Crusades, the Inquisition, and the colonization of the Americas, that the original spirit and teaching of the Carpenter of Galilee was irretrievably lost. Nonetheless, the violent world in which the church found itself put many strains upon it; and the message of Christ was undeniably diluted.

* * *

The removal of Roman power in the fifth century and the flooding of the western provinces by barbarian armies produced in Europe a revival of the military and warrior spirit which had characterized Rome herself in her earlier days. But the barbarians themselves became "softened" by the settled lives they began to lead in the western provinces and by the influence of the Christian faith. Even newly-arrived hordes, like the Franks and Langobards in the late fifth and sixth centuries, fell under the civilizing spell of Rome and of Christianity; and the fierce customs of the men who, just a generation earlier had dwelt in the forests and wildernesses of Germany, soon began to be

Oxford History of the Crusades, p. 205

35 Robert Irwin, "Islam and the Crusades: 1096-1699," in Jonathan Riley-Smith (ed.) *Oxford History of the Crusades*, p. 251

softened in the vineyards of Gaul and the olive-groves of Spain. Then, however, early in the seventh century, when the West was about to be re-Romanized, there appeared a new enemy: one that could not be placated and could not be Christianized. To the normal horrors of war the Muslim invaders added a new and dangerous element: religious fanaticism. Here were conquerors intent not only on plunder and enslavement, but also on the extinction or at the very least subjugation of the Christian faith. Against the barbarians of Germany and Scythia, the Christians of the west might fight for the possession of their homes and their lands, but such enemies were not intent on the destruction of the Christian religion. Christians were free to worship as they wished; and indeed many of the barbarians showed, from the very start, that they could be influenced by and even converted to the Christian faith.

With the Muslims, this was never an option. These were the "unconvertibles", men who were driven by their own religious zeal, and who waged war specifically to spread that faith. And this was an enmity that time did not ameliorate: for centuries after the invasions of southern Italy, Spain and the islands of Sicily, Sardinia and Corsica, Muslim freebooters scoured the Mediterranean and the coastlands of southern France and Italy, robbing, killing and enslaving. With the arrival of Islam, Mediterranean Europe was never again at peace – not until the early part of the nineteenth century, anyway. Muslim privateers based in North Africa, the Barbary Pirates, terrorized the Mediterranean until after the end of the Napoleonic Wars. In the centuries preceding that, Muslim armies, first in the form of the Almoravids and later the Ottomans, launched periodic large-scale invasions of territories in southern Europe; and even when they were not doing so, Muslim pirates and slave-traders were involved in incessant raids against coastal settlements in Spain, southern France, Italy, Dalmatia, Albania, Greece, and all the Mediterranean islands. This activity continued unabated for centuries, and the only analogy that springs to mind is to imagine, in northern Europe, what it would have been like if the Viking raids had lasted a thousand years.

It has been estimated that between the sixteenth and nineteenth centuries Muslim pirates based in North Africa captured and enslaved between a million and a million-and-a-quarter Europeans.[36] Although their attacks ranged as far north as Iceland and Norway, the impact was most severe along the Mediterranean coasts of Spain, France and

36 http//:en.wikipedia.org/wiki/Barbary_pirates

Italy, with large areas of coastline eventually being made uninhabitable by the threat.

The impact of this incessant violence has never, I feel, been either thoroughly studied or fully understood. The Mediterranean
coastlands must learn to live in a state of constant alert, with fear
never far removed. Populations needed to be ready, at a moment's notice, with a military response. Fortifications must be built and young
men trained in the use of arms. There was the development of a semi-
paranoid culture in which killing and being killed was the norm, or at
least not unusual. Small wonder that some of these territories, particularly Southern Italy, Sicily, Spain, Corsica, parts of Greece and Albania, would in time develop their own violent and relentless cultures;
and that it would be above all in Spain that the Inquisition would find
its spiritual home. Small wonder too that it would be from this same
land that Holy Warriors would set out, in the fifteenth and sixteenth
centuries, to conquer the peoples of the New World for Christ.[37]

It is not true, of course, that Christendom and the Christian
Church can be entirely absolved of the guilt for what happened in
the decades and centuries that followed the First Crusade. There can
be little doubt that some Christian doctrines made their own contribution. The narrow teaching which confined truth and salvation to
the Christian community alone cannot have but produced a intolerant
and irrational attitude to those of other faiths. In the end, however, it
seems that without the continued and incessant violence directed at
Christendom by Islam over a period of many centuries, Europe would
have developed in a very different way: And it seems certain that the
rapacious militarism which characterized Europe from the beginning
of the Age of the Crusades would never have appeared.

How then, without Islam, would events have unfolded? It is of
course impossible to say with certainty, but it seems fairly obvious that
the "medieval" world as we now know it would never have appeared.
Certainly, the period we now call the Middle Ages would have been a
lot less "medieval" and a lot more Roman. It is likely that Byzantium
would have continued the process, already well under way in the late
sixth century, of raising the cultural level of the West. The break
between Rome and Byzantium might not have occurred, or been so
acrimonious, and there seems little doubt that Western Europe would

---

37 We should not forget of course that the Conquistadors usually acted without official sanction, and that the Church, often in co-operation with the Spanish Government, worked very hard to control their excesses.

have experienced its "Renaissance", or re-flowering of classical civilization, much earlier; perhaps half a millennium earlier. Indeed, it is likely that by the late seventh century the whole of western Europe would have come to resemble contemporary Byzantium, with expanding cities and a thriving cultural and intellectual life. The Viking raids would not have occurred, or at least would not have been as destructive as they were. There would certainly have been no Crusades, there being no Islam to launch them against. And the lack of Viking and Islamic influence would almost certainly have induced the development in Europe of a more pacific culture. Without Islamic influence it is doubtful if the particularly virulent form of antisemitism that characterized Europe from the eleventh century would have arisen. The lack of an external and dangerous enemy like Islam would have hindered the development of the paranoia that gripped Europe over the issue of heretics and "witchcraft". There would probably have been no Inquisition. And without the Islamic example of slavery, the contact with the natives of the New World, when it came, would have been very different, as would Europe's relations with the peoples of sub-Saharan Africa.

So much for a world without Islam. But what if Islam had been triumphant? What if Europe had become Muslim in the seventh and eighth centuries? No less a person than Gibbon mused on the likely outcome of an Islamic conquest of France, when he noted that, had such an event transpired, then the whole of western Europe must inevitably have fallen, and the Dean of Oxford would likely then have been expounding the truths of the Koran to a circumcised congregation. Against such "calamities," noted Gibbon, was Christendom rescued by the victory of Charles Martel at Tours in 732. But an Islamic conquest of Europe would have had far more serious consequences than that. From what we have seen of Islam's record elsewhere, it is likely that the continent would have entered a Dark Age from which it would never have emerged. If we seek the model for Europe as a whole we might look to Albania or the Caucasus of the nineteenth century. These regions, inhabited by semi-Islamicized tribes, were the theatres of perpetual feuding. A Europe under Islam would have been no different: A backward and greatly under-populated wasteland fought over by Muslim tribal chiefs, conditions which would have persisted right into the present century. There would perchance have remained a few, largely decaying and very small, urban centers, in places like Italy, France and Spain; and these territories would have housed an impoverished and sorely oppressed remnant population of Christians. In Rome the Pope would preside over a miserable and decaying Vatican, whose main monuments, such as the original Saint Peter's, founded by Constantine, would long ago have been transformed into mosques. In such a Europe the entire heritage of classical civilization would have been forgotten. Of Caesar and his conquests, of Greece with her warriors and philosophers, the modern world would know nothing. The very names would have been lost. No child now would know of Troy or Mycenae, of Marathon or Thermopylae. The history of Egypt too, and all the great civilizations of the Near East, would lie buried in the drifting sands of those lands, forever lost and forgotten.

There would have been no High Middle Ages, with their Gothic cathedrals, no Renaissance, no Enlightenment, and no Age of Science.

The fall of Europe would have had consequences far beyond its shores; and the twenty-first century may have dawned with an Islamic (and underpopulated and impoverished) India threatening the existence of China, which would then likely be the last significant non-Muslim civilization. The wars waged between the two would be premodern, and though the two sides might employ primitive firearms and cannons, the sword and the bow would remain the most important weaponry, and rules of engagement would be savage.

But these are all what-ifs. History happened, and what happened cannot be changed. Yet if we are not to repeat the mistakes of the past, it is important that we understand exactly what did happen, and why.

BIBLIOGRAPHY

BOOKS:

Albertini, Eugène. "Ostrakon byzantin de Négrine (Numidie)," in *Cinquantenaire de la Faculte des Letteres d'Alger*, (1932)

Andrew Beattie, Andrew. *Cairo: A Cultural History* (Oxford University Press, 2005)

Atroshenko, V. I. and Judith Collins. *The Origins of the Romanesque* (Lund Humphries, London, 1985)

Baillie, Mike. *Exodus to Arthur: Catastrophic Encounters with Comets* (Batsford, 1999)

Balbas, Leopoldo Torres. *Ciudades hispano-musulmanas* 2 Vols. (Ministerio de Asuntos Exteriores, n.d., Madrid)

Bat Ye'or, *The Dhimmi: Jews and Christians Under Islam* (Fairleigh Dickinson University Press, 1985)

Bertrand, Louis and Sir Charles Petrie. *The History of Spain* (2nd ed., London, 1945)

Boyer, Carl B. *A History of Mathematics*, Second Edition (Wiley, 1991)

Briffault, Robert, *The Making of Humanity* (London, 1919)

Brunner, H. *Deutsche Rechtsgeschichte*, 2 Vols. (2nd ed., Leipzig, 1906)

Buchner, R. *Die Provence in Merowingischer Zeit* (Stuttgart, 1933)

Butler, Alfred. *The Arab Conquest of Egypt* (London, 1902)

Charles Montalembert, Charles. *The Monks of the West: From St. Benedict to St. Bernard*, 5 Vols. (London, 1896)

Clark, Kenneth. *Civilisation* (BBC publication, London, 1969)

Clarke, H. and B. Ambrosiani. *Towns in the Viking Age* (St. Martin's Press, New York, 1995)

Collins, Roger. *Early Medieval Spain: Unity in Diversity, 400 – 1000*, (2nd ed. Macmillan, 1995)

Collins, Roger. *Spain: An Oxford Archaeological Guide to Spain* (Oxford University Press, 1998)

Cottrell, L. *The Mountains of Pharaoh* (London, 1956)

Creswell, K. A. C. *Early Muslim Architecture*, 2 Vols. (2nd ed. London, 1968)

Dark, Ken. *Britain and the End of the Roman Empire* (Stroud, 2001)

Deanesley, Margaret. *A History of Early Medieval Europe*, 476 to 911 (Methuen, London, 1965)

Demolon, P. *Le village mérovingian de Brebières, Vie-VIIe siècles* (Commission départementale des monuments historiques du Pas-De-Calais, Arras, 1972)

Dopsch, Alfons. *Wirtschaftliche und soziale Grundlagen der europäischen Kulturentwicklung* (Vienna, 1918-20).

Dozy, R. *Histoire des Musulmans d'Espagne : jusqu'à la Conquête de l'Andalousie par les Almoravides (711-1110)*, 4 Vols (Paris, 1861)

Dunand, M. *Fouilles de Byblos*, 2 Vols. (Paul Geuthner, Paris, 1939)

Edwards, Nancy. T*he Archaeology of Early Medieval Ireland* (B. T. Batsford Ltd., London, 1996)

Engel, Arthur and Raymond Serrure. *Traité de numismatique du Moyen Age*, 2 Vols. (Paris, 1891)

Fleming, Robin. *Britain after Rome: The Fall and Rise, 400-1070* (Allen Lane, 2010)

Flick, Alexander Clarence. *The Rise of the Medieval Church* (New York, 1909)

Folz, Robert. *The Coronation of Charlemagne* (English trans., 1974)

Geary, Patrick J. *Before France and Germany: The Creation and Transformation of the Merovingian World* (Oxford University Press, 1988)

Gibbon, Edward. *Decline and Fall of the Roman Empire* (London,)

Grant, Edward. *God and Reason in the Middle Ages* (Cambridge, 2001)

Grégoire, Réginald. Léo Moulin and Raymond Oursel. *The Monastic Realm* (Rizzoli, New York, 1985)

Hårdh, B. and L. Larsson. (eds.), *Central Places in the Migration and Merovingian Periods* (Department of Archaeology and Ancient History, Lund, 2002)

Hartmann, L. *Das Italienische Königreich*, 4 Vols. (Leipzig, 1897-1911) (in Geschichte Italiens in Mittelalter, Vol. 1)

Hay, Denys. *Annalists and Historians* (London, 1977)

Herzfeld, Ernst. *Ausgrabungen von Samarra VI. Geschichte der Stadt Samarra* (Berlin, 1948).

Hodges, Richard and David Whitehouse. *Mohammed, Charlemagne and the Origins of Europe*, (London, 1982)

Hubert, Jean. *L'Art Préroman* (Paris, 1938)

Huff, Toby E. *The Rise of Early Modern Science: Islam, China and the West* (Cambridge University Press, 1993)

Illig, Heribert. *Das erfundene Mittelalter* (Econ Verlag, 1996)

Illig, Heribert. *Wer hat and er Uhr gedreht?* (Econ Taschenbuch Verlag, 2000)

Jaki, Stanley L. *The Savior of Science* (William B. Eerdmans, 2000)

James, Edward, *The Franks* (Basil Blackwell, Oxford, 1988)

Leblant, Edmond. *Inscriptions chrétiennes de la Gaule antérieures au VIIIe siecle*, 3 Vols. (Paris, 1856-1892)

Lewis, Bernard. *What Went Wrong? The Clash Between Islam and Modernity in the Middle East* (New York, 2002)

Lewis, David Levering. *God's Crucible: Islam and the Making of Europe, 570-1215* (W. W. Norton and Company, New York, 2008)

Lot, Ferdinand. *Christian Pfister and Francois L. Ganshof, Histoire du Moyen Age*, 2 Vols. (Paris, 1929)

Lüling, Günter. *Die Wiederentdeckung des Propheten Muhammad. Eine Kritik am "christlichen" Abendland* (Erlangen, 1981)

Mango, Cyril. *Byzantium: the Empire of New Rome* (London, 1980)

McCormick, Michael. *Origins of the European Economy: Communications and Commerce, AD 300 – 900* (Cambridge, 2002)

Mickwitz, Gunnar. *Geld und Wirtschaft im Romischen Reich des IV. Jahrhunderts nach Christi* (Helsingfors, 1932)

Montalembert, Charles. *The Monks of the West: From St. Benedict to St. Bernard*. 5 Vols. (London, 1896)

Moss, H. St. L. B. *The Birth of the Middle Ages; 395-814* (Oxford University Press, 1935)

Newhall, R. A. *The Crusades* (London, 1927)

Norwich, John Julius. *The Middle Sea: A History of the Mediterranean* (London and New York, 2006)

Painter, Sidney. *A History of the Middle Ages, 284-1500* (Macmillan, 1953)

Pirenne, Henri. *Mohammed and Charlemagne* (English ed. 1939)

Prou, Maurice. *Catalogue des monnaies mérovingiennes d'Autun*, (Paris, 1888)

Riegl, Alois. *Die spätrömische Kunstindustrie nach den Funden in Österreich-Ungarn* (Vienna, 1901)

Riley-Smith, Jonathan. (ed.) *Oxford History of the Crusades* (Oxford University Press, 1999)

Risse, Günter B. *Mending Bodies, Saving Souls: A History of Hospitals* (Oxford University Press, 1999)

Runciman, Steven. *The History of the Crusades*, 3 Vols. (London, 1951-1954)

Russell, Jeffrey Burton. *Inventing the Flat Earth: Columbus and Modern Historians* (Praeger Paperback, 1991)

Sambursky, Samuel. *The Physical World of Late Antiquity* (Routledge and Kegan Paul, 1962)
Simmonds, Charles. (1919). *Alcohol: With Chapters on Methyl Alcohol, Fusel Oil, and Spirituous Beverages* (Macmillan, 1919)
Stark, Rodney. *The Rise of Christianity: A Sociologist Reconsiders History* (Harper Collins, 1996)
Stenton, Frank. *Anglo-Saxon England* (3rd ed., Oxford, 1973)
Stephenson, Carl. *Medieval History: Europe from the Second to the Sixteenth Century* (Harper and Row, New York, 1962)
Tchalenko, G. *Villages antiques de la Syrie du nord ??* Vols. (Paris, 1953)
Thompson, James W. and Edgar N. Johnson. *An Introduction to Medieval Europe, 300-1500* (New York, 1937)
Trevor-Roper, Hugh. *The Rise of Christian Europe* (2nd. ed., London, 1966)
Twain, Mark. *The Innocents Abroad* (New York, 1869)
Vita-Finzi, Claudio. *The Mediterranean Valleys* (Cambridge, 1969)
Volney, C. F. *Travels through Syria and Egypt* 2 Vols. (London, 1787)
Wells, Peter S. *Barbarians to Angels* (New York, 2008)
Whitehouse, D. Siraf III. *The Congregational Mosque* (London, British Institute of Persian Studies, 1980);
Wickham, Chris. *The Inheritance of Rome: Illuminating the Dark Ages 400 – 1000* (2009)

ARTICLES:

Bolin, Sture. "Mohammed, Charlemagne and Ruric," *Scandinavian History Review* 1, (1952)
Bowerstock, Glen W. "The Vanishing Paradigm of the Fall of Rome," *Bulletin of the American Academy of Arts and Sciences*, Vol. 49, No.8 (May, 1996)
Daim, F. and M. Mehofer, "Poysdorf," in *Reallexikon der germanischen Alterumskunde*, 23 (2003)
Dennett, Daniel C. "Pirenne and Muhammad," *Speculum: Journal of Mediaeval Studies*, Vol. XXIII, (April 1948), No. 2.
Doppelfled, O. "Das fränkische Frauengrab unter dem Chor des Kölner Doms," *Germania*, 38 (1960)

Forey, Alan. "The Military Orders, 1120-1312," in Jonathan Riley-Smith (ed.) *Oxford History of the Crusades* (Oxford University Press, 1999)

Fulford, M. J. "Carthage: overseas trade and the political economy, c. AD. 400-700," *Reading Medieval Studies* 6, (1980), 68-80

Grierson, Philip. "Commerce in the Dark Ages: a critique of the evidence," *Transactions of the Royal Historical Society* (5th series) 9, (1959), 123-40.

Halsall, G. "Childeric's Grave, Clovis' Succession, and the Origins of the Merovingian Kingdom," in R. W. Mathisen and D. Shanzer, (eds.), *Society and Culture in Late Antique Gaul* (Aldershot: Ashgate, 2001)

Harris, William V. "Child Exposure in the Roman Empire," *The Journal of Roman Studies*, Vol. 84 (1994)

Hendy, M. F. "Byzantium, 1081-1204: an economic reappraisal," *Transactions of the Royal Historical Society*, 5th series, 20 (1970)

Huntington, Samuel P. "The Clash of Civilizations?" *Foreign Affairs*, (Summer, 1993)

Hurst, Henry. "Excavations at Carthage 1977-8. Fourth interim report," *Antiquaries Journal* 59, (1979)

Irwin, Robert. "Islam and the Crusades: 1096-1699," in Jonathan Riley-Smith (ed.) *Oxford History of the Crusades* (Oxford University Press, 1999)

Irwin, Robert. "Islam and the Crusades: 1096-1699," in Jonathan Riley-Smith (ed.) *The Oxford History of the Crusades* (Oxford, 1995)

Jaki, Stanley L. "Medieval Creativity in Science and Technology," in *Patterns and Principles and Other Essays* (Intercollegiate Studies Institute: Bryn Mawr, Pennsylvania, 1995)

Korpås, Ola., Per Wideström and Jonas Ström, "The recently found hoards from Spillings farm on Gotland, Sweden," *Viking Heritage Magazine*, 4 (2000)

Lombard, Maurice. "L'or musulman du VIIe au XIe siècles. Les bases monetaires d'une suprematie économique," *Annales ESC* 2, (1947), 143-60

Margaritis, Evi. and Jones, Martin K. "Greek and Roman Agriculture", in Oleson, John, Peter (ed.): *The Oxford Handbook of Engineering and Technology in the Classical World* (Oxford University Press, 2008)

Murphey, Rhoads. "The Decline of North Africa since the Roman Occupation: Climatic or Human?", *ANNALS, Association of American Geographers*, Vol. XLI, no. 2, (June 1951)

Newman, John Henry in Charles Frederick Harrold, (ed.), *Essays and Sketches*, Vol. 3 (New York, 1948)

Riising, Anne. "The fate of Pirenne's thesis on the consequences of Islamic expansion," *Classica et Medievalia* 13, (1952), 87-130

Riley, J. A. "The pottery from the cisterns 1977. 1, 1977.2 and 1977.3," in J. H. Humphrey (ed.), *Excavations at Carthage 1977 Conducted by the University of Michigan*, (Ann Arbor, 1981), pp. 85-124

Riley-Smith, Jonathan. "The State of Mind of Crusaders to the East: 1095-1300," in Jonathan Riley-Smith (ed.) *Oxford History of the Crusades* (Oxford University Press, 1999)

Rogers, J. M. "Samarra: a study in medieval town planning," in A. Hourani and S. M. Stern (eds), *The Islamic City* (Oxford, 1970).

Smith, Catherine Delano, Derek Gadd, Nigel Mills and Bryan Ward-Perkins, "Luni and the 'Ager Lunensis': the Rise and Fall of a Roman Town and its Territory," *Papers of the British School at Rome*, Vol. 54, (1986)

Stewart, H. F. "Thoughts and Ideas of the Period," in *The Cambridge Medieval History: The Chrsitian Empire*, Vol. 1 (2nd ed., 1936)

Thompson, E. A. "The Barbarian Kingdoms in Gaul and Spain," *Nottingham Mediaeval Studies*, 7 (1963)

Volney, C. F. "Agriculture and Trade in the 1970s," in Charles Issawi, (ed.) *The Economic History of the Middle East, 1800-1914* (University of Chicago Press, 1966)

Werner, J. "Der goldene Armring des Frankenkönigs Childerich und die germanischen Handgelenkringe der jüngeren Kaiserzeit," *Frühmittelalterlicke Studien*, 14 (1980)

Werner, J. "Zur Verbreitung frügeschichtlicher Metallarbeiten (Werkstatt-Wanderhandwerk-Handel-Familienverbindung)," *Early Medieval Studies*, I (Antikvarist Arkiv, 38) (1970)

Whitehouse, D. "Siraf: a medieval port on the Persian coast," *World Archaeology* 2 (1970)

Wickham, C. J. "Historical and topographical notes on early medieval South Etruria: part II," *Papers of the British School at Rome* 47, (1979)

INDEX

Bertrand, Louis, 125, 128, 130,
171, 181, 188-9, 240, 245-6
birth-rate(s) 25, 79
Boethius, 30, 135-8, 140
Bowerstock, Glen, 61
Briffault, Robert, 50, 52, 58-9, 61,
65, 205-6, 214, 231
Britain, xiii, 27, 32, 41-2, 45, 60,
61, 63-4, 75, 79, 85, 87, 89, 93, 94
105-119, 126, 143, 146, 148, 154,
195, 208, 222, 226
Brown, Peter, 60
Burgundians, 31-33, 36, 46
Byblos, 178-9
Byzantine(s), xvii, xx, 27, 29, 34,
36, 37, 39, 40, 42, 45, 70-2, 75, 77,
83, 86, 88, 98, 108-10, 115, 138,
150-1, 153-61, 163, 170-2, 174,
176-8, 184, 191, 199, 204, 210,
218, 219, 221, 223, 225, 229, 232,
233, 253
Byzantium, xiv, 27-9, 36-7, 39,
48, 60, 77, 99, 126, 150-1, 153,
158-9, 163, 198, 207, 210, 218,
20, 229, 230, 232, 256

Caesarea Maritima, 173-4
Cairo, 50, 51, 179, 183, 212-4
Campbell, Joseph, xv
Canterbury, 88, 111
Archbishop of, 235
Carolingian(s), 37, 38, 45, 55,
102-3, 143, 234
Carthage, 35, 68, 70, 72, 74, 75-8,
87, 109, 180, 221
Cassiodorus, 30, 40, 135-8, 140
castle-building, 162-4, 183
castles, xv, xix, 162-4
Cathar(s), 235, 239-40
Charlemagne, xii, 28-31, 37-8 54,
55, 58, 68-70, 141, 233, 234
chapel of, 103, 133, 209
Charles Martel, 256
Charles the Great (see also Char-

lemagne), 29
Childebert, 37-9, 100
China, 66, 128, 145, 171, 201,
204-7, 251
Chlothar II, 29, 46, 101, 107,
160, 222
church-building, 82, 99, 102, 111,
153, 222
Cicero, 135, 141-2, 209-10
Clovis, 34-5, 96, 101
coins, coinage, 27-30, 34-5,
39,44-6, 54, 56-7, 63-4, 69-71,
76-7, 88, 90, 96, 101, 105, 109,
123, 149, 154-5, 157-8, 165, 196,
198--203, 219-20, 222-3
Cologne, 93, 96, 101
Columba, saint, 114, 135
Columbus, Christopher, 59, 245
Conquistadores, 246
Constantinople, vii, xiii, 24,
27-31, 33-6, 38-9, 46, 56, 80, 89,
101, 138, 141, 150-1, 157, 166-7,
170, 176, 187, 195, 232-3, 235,
241-2
Coptic Christians, 176
Cordoba, xvii, 129-31, 181-2,
184, 197, 247
corn, 40, 60, 69, 77, 143
Crusades, Crusaders, ix, 49, 66,
178, 186, 225, 235, 245-7, 250-3,
255-6
Cyrene, 176

Dacia, 23, 25, 64
Dagobert I, 38, 101-2
Damascus, 189, 197, 231
Dar al-Harb, 186
Dar al-Islam, 186, 190, 216
demographic(s), 25-6, 59, 61-2,
76, 78-9, 87, 134, 147, 224
Denmark, 94, 101
dhimmi, 66, 186, 190, 236, 245,
249
Diocletian, emperor, 24

CPSIA information can be obtained at www.ICGtesting.com
Printed in the USA
LVOW08s0840080716

495416LV00001B/3/P